PARABLES OF CRISIS

PARABLES
OF CRISIS

By

Edwin McNeill Poteat

HARPER & BROTHERS . NEW YORK

Dedicated to

DORES ROBINSON SHARPE

Contents

Foreword

GRATEFUL acknowledgment is made of the permissions granted by the following publishers for the use of their copyrighted quotations: Abingdon-Cokesbury Press, The Association Press, E. P. Dutton & Co., Harcourt, Brace & Company, Harper & Brothers, and Whittlesey House. The text used is the Revised Standard Version of the New Testament, published in 1946 by Thomas Nelson & Sons and used by permission of the International Council of Religious Education.

Mrs. Betsy Senter Wooden has been cheerful, diligent and competent in converting a manuscript into a typescript. My thanks to her, and also to Professor William H. Poteat of the University of North Carolina for wise counsel and caution.

E. M. P.

Raleigh, N. C.
September, 1949

PARABLES OF CRISIS

"I will incline mine ear to a parable:
I will open my dark saying upon the
harp."

PSALM 49:4

"It is only by means of . . . tension
thus set up that religious energy can be
communicated to our time."

ALBERT SCHWEITZER

Crisis in A.D. 31

THE priority of crisis to tension or vice versa is as debatable as that of egg to hen. Certainly tension creates crisis and crisis creates tension but whatever their cause-sequence, their psychological bond is simple and inescapable. History may not be the lengthened shadow of a man, a point still mooted by historians, but a man is the lengthened shadow of a tension. We are now assured that tension, far from being a matter of merely biting one's fingernails or accelerating the secretion of adrenalin, is the sign of the vital mind and the spring of creative action. It is tension that makes possible the assimilation of conflicting experiences into a creative synthesis. To accept as final either aspect of a conflict, whether it be the aspect of victory or defeat; to "rest on one's laurels" or to "lick one's wounds," is to deactivate one's self. As many have been defeated by accepting victory as by accepting defeat. No conquest is worth winning if it does not invite further struggle; no defeat is final that is sharpened into a goal. By maintaining tension both between interests and within them we preserve that which is, in sober fact, the elixir of life.[1]

[1] In *The Manhood of the Master*, Harry Emerson Fosdick (New York: The Association Press, 1914, p. 158), is quoted the classical statement of Horace Bushnell concerning man's failure to resolve tension creatively: ". . . so the earnest become violent, the fervent fanatical and censorious, the gentle waver, the firm turn bigots, the liberal grow lax, the benevolent ostentatious. Poor human infirmity can hold

There are those who argue that the repose which is the ideal of the civilizations of the Far East has also been the enemy of their progress. It would follow that the activism which dominates Western life is also the secret of its advance, or its adventuresomeness, or its inventive genius, however one—avoiding the use of the now damaged word "progress"—chooses to describe the West. Activism, dictionaries notwithstanding to the contrary, is a synonym of tension. Whether an active individual be described as tense or intense, the meaning is clear. He is certainly not flaccid though he may be relaxed; he is certainly not languid though he may be sedate.

[1]

These generalizations are immensely significant for any understanding of the last forty days of the life of Jesus. He was a very intense person, which is another way of saying he was a creative person, and another way of saying he created tension wherever he appeared. In a very profound sense this can be taken to mean that he was possessed of God whose holy spirit can be not ineptly described as the spirit of intension (observe how close the word is to "intention"; both derive from the same root *intendere,* to stretch), an emphasis which is perhaps easier for common folk to comprehend than the more orthodox use. It was to be expected that as he and his growing fellowship of hangers-on, friends, and intimates moved toward Jerusalem for the great feast, which provided for his people both the stimulus and the release of all sorts of tensions, situations should arise that would be truly critical. As the dominant figure in any situation where he appeared, he inevitably invited strong feelings, both ill-humored and amicable, and within the tensions thus created, anything was likely to happen. This is exactly what was expected;

nothing steady. Where the pivot of righteousness is broken, the scales must needs slide off their balance."

some looked forward to an apocalypse of victory, some feared a cataclysm of defeat. It was necessary for him to resolve these antitheses creatively, something he tried unsuccessfully to do. "The kingdom of God is not coming with signs to be observed; nor will they say, 'Lo, here it is!' or 'There!' for behold, the kingdom of God is in the midst of you" (Luke 17:20-21) is representative of such an effort. What was to happen under these circumstances would be measurably due to the tensions created by him and his followers; his courage and aplomb, their vacillation and disorder, his analysis and risk, their confusion and panic.

This is what made the Forty Days, called Lent in our times, one of the most significant periods in the history of the Western world, an interval that began on the Mount of Transfiguration —an episode of great tenseness—and ended in the Garden of Joseph, where the crisis appeared momentarily to have subsided. The Resurrection experience was the creative synthesis, but a discussion of that point is beyond our present purpose. As the Galilean fellowship moved toward Jerusalem, political and ecclesiastical issues sharpened more and more. Something either had to snap, or both had to yield to a creative experience that would save the straining extremes. Or, to change the metaphor, Jesus and to some extent his friends, were increasingly aware of the vortex toward which, by their actions they were irreversibly drawn, and into which, if they persisted, they would be plunged.

What happened during these days, we are saying, is to be best understood within the context of mounting tensions, or within crises that could not be avoided short of some divine intervention for which, manifestly, many hoped. Furthermore, and to a sharper focus, all Jesus said is to be understood within this dimension. At no time did he speak flippantly or without a sense of grave concern, but as he moved into the area of crisis we miss some of the artlessness and even the humor of his conversation of which the late T. R. Glover wrote so engagingly. One does not face risk to one's person or one's cause, however stoutly one may be convinced of ultimate success, without reflecting the hazard in the things he says. He will talk only about those things concerning which he cannot keep silent. For this reason there was both weight and urgency in what he said.

[2]

These studies deal basically with the parables Jesus told during these fateful days, and are confined to the report of them contained in Luke's record. The evidence of tension is abundant. Consider it under three aspects: the general restlessness of the crowds, including the so-called authorities; the growing anxiety of the disciples; and the intensity of the Master's own words and actions. Note this important observation of the synoptist: "In the meantime, when so many thousands of the multitude had gathered together that they trod upon one another, he began to say . . . " (Luke 12:1). This is not a description of a congregation or a parade; it is a multitude that trod upon one another. In other words it was a mob, a mob against the caprice of which it was necessary for him to warn the disciples. "Beware of the leaven of the Pharisees, which is hypocrisy," he warned, and added ominously that everything now was out in the open. Concealment which once had been expedient was no longer possible. What secrets they had whispered would now be shouted from the housetops. When a mob is manipulated by hypocrites who shout secrets, anything can happen.

This must suffice as an indication of the general unrest. Manifestly it was being agitated by the authorities of one group or another. Of late Pilate had slaughtered some Galileans while they were in the midst of their ritual sacrifices. That sounded like the mad and impulsive action of a man under great strain. Herod was reported (13:31) as planning to kill Jesus, a desperate proposal by a man whose life as we know it was one long harassment. To Jesus it was already obvious, though less so perhaps to his friends, that the pressure from authorities of all sorts was growing more threatening. It was to him a foregone conclusion that all of them would be brought before "the synagogues and the rulers and the authorities" (12:11), and that they would be discomfited by the questions put to them. He encouraged them to be confident, promising them that "the Holy Spirit will teach you in that very hour what you ought to say" (12:12). They were doubtless reassured momentarily, but the combination of synagogue, praetorium, and palace was a formidable one and they would have been strange people indeed had not trepidation returned to plague them after his consoling words. Later they all, we remember, forsook him and fled.

Life itself was no longer secure. Jesus could not guarantee safe-conduct; he could only admonish them against fear of those who could *only* kill the body. If perchance they were to emerge from the impending crisis, they must not be anxious about life—food and raiment. And in it all they must be keenly alert—"loins girded and lamps burning" (12:35).

If there was general uneasiness in the multitudes and ominous activity among the authorities and growing restlessness on the part of his disciples, it is not surprising that he, seeing things with greater clarity, was drawn by greater tensions. "I came to cast fire upon the earth; and would that it were already kindled! I have a baptism to be baptized with; and how I am *constrained* until it is accomplished! Do you think that I have come to give peace on earth? No, I tell you, but rather *division*" (12:49-50). It would be difficult to describe a state of spiritual tension more convincingly; but there is more to be added. He was on his way to Jerusalem and he knew full well the reputation the holy city had for its treatment of God's prophets and emissaries—stoning and death. Worse than death for so sensitive a spirit as his, was the sense of frustration. He had wanted to gather the children of the city under his wings, but they would not. And yet, observe the tension in his mind between imminent defeat and ultimate victory. They would not be gathered unto him but they would some day say of him, "Blessed be he who comes in the name of the Lord" (13:35).

The certainty of his own defeat communicated itself in the sense of dire consequences to his countrymen. He confided (18:32-34) to his friends the dismay he felt concerning his own death but they did not grasp what he said, perhaps because of their natural preoccupation with their own fortunes. It was, we may be sure, scant comfort to Peter to be told, when he reminded the Master, "Lo, we have left our homes and followed you" (18:27), that he would "receive manifold more in this time, and in the age to come eternal life" (18:30). Tension would inevitably have been felt between the manifold in the now and the manifold in the age to come. The splendor of the temple, noble stones and all, was to be reduced to rubble; nations were to rise up against nations; Jerusalem was to be surrounded by armies as the desolation drew near. Portents in sun and moon and stars were to be nature's convulsive response to man's agonies and to the perplexities of nations (21:25). Yet these were not the last despairing words of a defeated man. After nearly every doleful prediction there followed the promise of victory, both concerning himself, his disciples, and his people (cf. 21:28, e.g.). What these words do, however, is to set forth with great clarity the tension of the times. The hearts of men swung between the abyss of doom and the ramparts of heaven; and the fear of one was mitigated but little by hope for the other.

Elsewhere we shall argue in considerable detail that the miscalled Triumphal Entry and the cleansing of the temple were acts of one living under great spiritual strain. They served no practical or permanent end and were to some extent repudiated by what he did in the days that immediately followed. Far from denigrating the reputation of the Master, this fact gives point to the later struggle in Gethsemane where the tension created by his impulse to escape his fate was creatively resolved in complete surrender to the Father's will. When he entered the city he consented to adulation that he had consistently resisted; in the temple he indulged himself in an act of violence that he had avoided earlier in his ministry. That both episodes were rationalized by quotations, one from the regal David and the other from the rebel Jeremiah is little surprising if we sufficiently understand the strain under which he had been placed.

[3]

At this point it is important for us to note that this welter of confusion did at least two highly significant things for him. In the first place it precipitated in his mind certain inescapable and solid facts that had been suspended in solution during the early part of his ministry. Ever singe Hogg [2] wrote to document his conclusions that during the life of our Lord he changed his mind with reference to the intention and pattern of his ministry, interpreters of the synoptic record have brought increasing clarity to our understanding of his words and acts. The tension of the last days was, by his own confession, extreme. Words like "fire" and "baptism" and "division" are not descriptive of serenity or detachment. Important light is also cast on the much debated question of the eschatological element in some of his latter teachings. Tension, we repeat, is creative, but it is none the less tense. Therefore, one of the ever-present elements in a given critical situation is the wish of the participant to escape, coupled with the invocation, in one way or another, of any or all supernatural or extracosmic aid.

But why, specifically, was the situation critical for him? There was the normal accompaniment of a festival mood and the restlessness of a subjugated people incessantly reminded of their national humiliation by their rulers and the possibility of popu-

[2] A. G. Hogg, *Christ's Message of the Kingdom* (New York: Charles Scribner's Sons, 1911).

lar uprisings among holiday makers who are always easily led to violence by extremist leaders. There was also his own sense of destiny which was certainly heightened by the imminence of danger. The likelihood of defeat could not be casually put off, and it could have communicated itself to his disciples who were already quarreling about positions of preferment in an enterprise they thought was to follow the guaranteed victory. And evidences of the disintegrating morale of the group could not but give him constant anxiety.

The question of his thoughts about *eschaton*, the last days, the proximity of the judgment of God that is transcendent and the judgment of history that is immanent, both of which are aspects of one eschatological operation, cannot be omitted from an effort to understand his mind at this time. Did he think the end of history was at hand? Was the "finis" that was to be written to time the overture to a new posthistory experience called variously the days of the Son of man and the Kingdom of God? Or was it an interval of cleansing by violence in order that a new order of history *(saeculum)* could begin? Or was it a denouement in which both history and posthistory were going to be integrated by a new understanding?

Ever since Schweitzer's famous *Quest for the Historical Jesus* undertook to reconstruct his life on the basis of the eschatological factor in the thought of the Hebrews and of Jesus himself, the study of his teachings has been conspicuously affected. Schweitzer sought to show that Jesus regarded the then current Messianic expectation as likely to occur at any time and certainly within his own lifetime, and that from the moment of his baptism he believed himself to be the Messiah though he enjoined the strictest secrecy on those with whom he shared this confidence. Judas betrayed the secret and Jesus was executed because his claim was regarded by Caiaphas as blasphemous. Everything that Jesus said and did was oriented to this deep conviction. His ethic therefore was designed to create in his followers a pitch of spiritual intensity that was commensurate with the dimensions of the coming fulfillment of history. Those to whom the event was fanciful or remote would therefore repudiate his teaching. There were such people who heard him and they dismissed him as an eccentric. Others thought him dangerous enough to suppress or kill.

[4]

It is not our purpose to recall here the arguments that have supported or disputed Schweitzer's monumental thesis since it appeared in 1910. There are however two matters that are pertinent to our study. How far can what is called an interim ethic be normative, even for an interim? In so far as it is interim it is provisional, contingent, or perhaps opportunistic. It would look toward a time when no ethic would be needed, i.e., after history, or a period within a later phase of history when it would be accommodated to other needs. The assumption that after the "last days" a new ethic would be promulgated within new conditions comes close to holding out for a new dispensation in which, shall we say, "original virtue" will obviate the difficulties caused by "original sin." This, we believe, would add to the sense of moral tension that the times themselves created; it is the tension that exists between a universalistic and timeless and an interim or localized ethic. Schweitzer avoided this by repudiating the universalistic quality of the teachings. If Jesus was aware of a universal and transcendent ethic and compromised with it in order to accommodate an interim, even a glorious one, was there not something unethical about it? This will be discussed in greater detail in the chapter "Ends and Means." If a choice must be made between universalistic and interim ethics, we name the former and will proceed to argue during the subsequent studies the universalistic character of the parables' intentions.

It is to the point to observe that Luke, who was the companion of Paul before he wrote his record, knew something of the ethical teachings of the great apostle. After Paul had got over the eschatological myopia exhibited in his earliest letters, he reasserted his ethical concepts in terms that have no hint of contingency. Did Luke, hearing the *Kerygma* that Paul preached—which is what the Gospels are instead of biographies—find something that made Jesus' ethic interim where Paul's had been universal? Was Paul accommodating his ethical teachings to an interval? How, indeed, does Paul's ethic differ from his Lord's? To compare the ethical maxims of Jesus and Paul yields no such conclusions. The twelfth chapter of Romans and even I Thessalonians 5:12-22 contain sententious precepts that are in no respect different in mood from the Sermon on the Mount. And if I Corinthians 13 is not a universal and trancendent summary of the Christian ethic it is nothing more than a prettified lyric. Because the *operation* of love is contingent and often ambiguous within time it does not follow that love itself is contingent or ambiguous. Furthermore the ethics of Jesus and Paul were never a conscious deviation from the moral corpus of the thought of Israel. Was Hebrew ethics *ad interim?* From Moses to the Maccabees there was a continuing refinement of ethical insight in line with the development of metaphysics and in the directions of universalism, but there was no accommodation to *ad interim* expediency even when the Messianic hope was most vigorous.

One other factor needs mention here. *Eschaton* has two meanings; one deals with time, particularly as regards its consummation; the other deals with judgment. Because there is a natural presumption that the end of time will bring the final judgment on all that has taken place in time, it has been easy to assume that judgment on the character of our living is ex post facto rather than immanent in the act itself. In fact, *so far as we know* moral judgment within space-time is definitive, whether it be regarded as transcendent or immanent or both. Beyond space-time it may be anything. We must act therefore in terms of what we know.

It is possible that only God will survive the end of time and God will therefore alone know the meaning of history. The Christian effort to understand the meaning of history must therefore be within space-time with reference to God who stands alone and beyond history. If it is to be morally discerned, it must therefore provide for an immanent judgment that is implicit in each moral act and which is as definitive as the transcendent judgment that God—beyond the *saeculum*—renders.

[5]

It is within these immense perspectives that we must approach the study of these parables of crisis in Luke's record. They were, for the most part, about "good" people. In them we see immanent and transcendent justice in universal terms. Maybe the crisis was to be resolved eventually by some portent in the sky; in the meantime, however, something had to be done about portents on the earth. The behavior of men was, in its way, as significant for Jesus as the possible ultimate behavior of God. To their distorted perspectives he must bring readjustment; to their greed he must offer a corrective lest it destroy them; to their superficial and proud religious rigmarole he must try to bring honesty and practical action; to their adulation of power and their servility to the tyrant-mind he must address the protective wisdom of gentler and more creative moods.

Thus he spoke to the grave needs of his day, and spoke much, we shall be saying, in parables. This is an educative or didactic device momentarily out-of-date, but its value can be reassessed if we study it as he used it. By subtlety where it was needed, the parable sped to its mark; and by indirection where the forthright word was injudicious, the parable carried its message. Rarely long, often sententiously short, the parable was like a lance with a short shank and a large head. It was easy to carry and handy to cast and never was it used with greater dexterity. It is with such an understanding of the need of the parables he told, and of the parables themselves, that we shall make our study. We must be warned, however, against misuse of them. Dr. Samuel Johnson said a figure of speech must not be required to run on all four legs. Similarly a parable must not be made into a system of philosophy or even a syllogism. We must not ask it to do more than it can, or keep it from doing all that it intends. In understanding parables therefore the wise man is he from whom the explicit facts do not conceal the implicit truth. He will no more look for a mole in a mountain than he will make a mountain out of a molehill.

If, as we have said, the intrusion of the eschatological or apocalyptic element is to be expected in crisis situations, it is important to point out that this element in his utterances disappeared entirely after he had creatively resolved the tension. Were we less familiar with the events of the last week, we might normally have expected a rising crescendo of bravado as the clouds gathered. As his support fell sharply and tragically away in the defection and denial of his friends, what would have been more natural than that he should cry for the final revelation, the twelve legions of angels, the invincible arm of the Lord? The reverse is true; he refused apocalyptic help; he stood in his own defense before the insolence and hostility of the authorities he predicted would destroy him; and his last grand word was not the shrill, defiant threat of apocalyptic vengeance, but the quiet commitment of his soul, clothed in serenity such as the world can never forget, into the hands—not of delayed justice—but of Fatherly love.

With these preliminary comments we proceed to an analysis of crisis in A.D. 31. Before we are done we shall see how profoundly it parallels crisis in 1949.

CHAPTER II

Small Barn, Big Fool

THE crowd, so the story goes, was big and jostling, and clearly ill-behaved. It is a symptom of the restlessness of the human spirit that while a man may be diffident about his selfish desires when in the company of one or two of his fellows, he can be raucous about them in a crowd. The reason is that a crowd is often more likely to be a composite of selfishness than of generosity. These "many thousands of the multitude" were stepping on each other for a variety of reasons, no doubt; but what made them heedless of the restraints imposed by limited numbers was that each had his personal interest to exploit. Here in their community a man had appeared, whose advance had been accompanied by fantastic rumors. He was a new king, a thaumaturge, a prophet, an avatar, a teacher, a judge. "One of the multitude said to him, 'Teacher, bid my brother divide the inheritance with me.' But he said to him, 'Man, who made me a judge or a divider over you?' And he said to them, 'Take heed, and beware of all covetousness; for a man's life does not consist in the abundance of his possessions.'" Then he told them a parable:

"The land of a rich man brought forth plentifully; and he thought to himself 'What shall I do, for I have nowhere to store my crops?' And he said, 'I will do this: I will pull down my barns, and build larger ones; and there I will store all my grain and my goods. And I will say to my soul, Soul, you have ample goods laid up for many years; take your ease, eat, drink, be merry.' But God said to him, 'Fool! This night your soul is required of you; and the things you have prepared, whose will they be?' So is he who lays up treasure for himself, and is not rich toward God." (Luke 12:16-21)

It would be interesting to know how this reply struck the man who had quarreled with his brother over their patrimony. If he had expected this for-the-moment popular Galilean to act the magistrate for him without the bother of formal litigation, he was disappointed. Jesus was no judge or divider. What the man needed was not a division between him and brother, but a union between them. Covetousness was a judge and a divider, and it was so dangerous an arbiter that a wider warning was advisable. Hence "beware of all covetousness."

[1]

But to get on with the parable. There is nothing about this certain rich man that is particularly odious. He enjoyed food, drink, and entertainment and looked forward to the day when these three perquisites of wealth could be guaranteed for life. Who, indeed, doesn't? So far as we can infer, this average man was neither glutton nor drunkard, nor was his merriment much more disreputable than merely taking his ease. He was rich, to be sure, and to some of his poor and covetous neighbors that might have been odious, but up to the point of the telling of our story his local credit rating seems hardly to have been a problem to him.

When, however, he became suddenly richer, too rich, in fact, for his storage space, he found himself in difficulty of an unexpected sort. The problem posed by his unbudgeted dividends was not unwelcome and he doubtless tackled it with zest and efficiency, to both of which qualities he would have modestly attributed his good fortune. His solution was exemplary, a fact supported by the consideration of other alternatives to be examined before deciding to enlarge his barn. What alternatives?

Well, he could let the bumper crop rot in the fields. This, while saving a good deal of bother, would have been improvident and appeared lazy, and would have outraged the sensibilities of his neighbors and his own pride in his reputation as a successful farmer. Or he might harvest it, sell it for the low price offered in the glutted market, and take the loss in his stride. Then he could even boast a bit in the city gates about the licking he was taking. Or he might give it away or sell it for a trifle. This latter would avoid beggaring the poor. It was risky, to be sure, but since it was not likely to be incorporated into a community plan that would radically alter the existing economy, it might benefit some of the worthy poor. There is no harm in being generous, he would have reflected, though care must be taken not to consolidate the lazy in their indolence or to upset the economic balance by reducing the proper social quantum of the unemployed. It might, furthermore, aid in the distribution of wealth in a quite simple way. There were those who said this would abate social restlessness and cure almost any imaginable economic trouble. The worst that could be said of these plans was that after all they looked rather foolish. Other farmers who had also prospered would think their neighbor had lost his mind or was up to some sort of trick to beat the market.

[2]

No; rather than do any of these things, he would provide more storage space, harvest his crop, and keep it for himself. After all, God had prospered him, rewarded him even. It were poor gratitude to spurn this divine compliment to his enterprise and honesty. God had given him the crop because he wanted him to have it and to keep it. This was beyond dispute, for God also had a way of blighting the grain in the fields of those who displeased him. And, since one must provide for one's future (had not the lesson of the provident ant been dinned into his ears since childhood?) here was his opportunity to out-ant the ant; for whatever the modest satisfactions were that rewarded insect frugality, he could now be assured of aliment, potable, and respectable entertainment for the rest of his mortal days. It was a thoroughly good choice—the obvious one, since everyone who could made it. It was thrifty, honest, pious, responsible, and above all it was what the economic order demanded. Yes, after careful reflection this was the smart thing to do.

But God called him a fool. This is a shocking judgment. Was God jealous, or angry, or irritated, or hasty, or misinformed? Would He have preferred the alternatives that had been carefully considered and conscientiously rejected? Certainly not the first; that was sheer waste. The second, perhaps; but to make part of one's excess fortune available to the poor did not necessarily conflict with his decision to care adequately for his property. The poor man is God's way of providing exercise for the rich man's charitable impulses. Prosperity trickles from the top down. What was God thinking about? Doesn't God need full barns to feed empty stomachs?

Observe that God did not call him a sinner, a miser, a cheat. This is somewhat surprising since covetousness (to illustrate which the parable was told) was one of the thou-shalt-nots upon which the man had been raised. "Thou shalt not make a fool of thyself," would have simplified the Decalogue, since sin always turns out to be stupidity; but the fact remained that covetousness which had once been a sin, was now called folly. Had God changed His mind, or was His indictment of the man incorrect? If he was a fool, what was the evidence that established it?

Folly, we assume, is a matter of the head rather than of the will. The man, therefore, was mistaken, not perversely malicious. Is there any way of knowing what God would have said had He been asked to specify? It is, we think, hardly necessary to ask, since if we consult so lowly an oracle as common sense, we get pretty clear answers.

[3]

First: The man in all likelihood thought his bulging barn was a reward for his virtue as a responsible citizen and farmer. He might have got very moralistic about this. The manner in which free enterprise today is credited with the high standard of living (more correctly the high standard of luxury) enjoyed by North Americans is the modern counterpart of this. It ought to be obvious that our living standard is due primarily to the wealth of raw materials on our continent. The freest and most enterprising free enterpriser could do little in the Gobi desert to create a luxury economy like ours. In so far as we have been economically free and enterprising we have achieved spectacular results, but the moral superiority we claim for this is quite blind to the basic fact on which every economy rests—raw materials. There is another way of putting this: "In political economy the meagerness of our understanding is especially remarkable; we have not yet grasped the obvious fact—a fact of immeasurable import for all the social sciences—that with little exception the wealth and capital possessed by a given generation are not produced by its own toil but are the inherited fruit of dead men's toil—a free gift of the past. We have yet to learn and apply the lesson that not only our material wealth and capital but our science and art and learning and wisdom—all that goes to constitute our civilization—were produced, not by our own labor, but by the time-bending energies of past generations." [1] This fortunate man thought he was solely responsible for his wealth; God's share was merely recognition of what he had done.

[1] A. Korzykski, *Manhood of Humanity* (New York: E. P. Dutton & Co., 1921), p. 104.

Therefore he was responsible for what was to be done with it. Talk about unearned increments and suchlike was nonsense. Those who were too lazy or incompetent to raise spectacular crops could disparage at will those who did; but let them be warned by wisdom older than his own: "I have been young and now am old; but I have never seen the righteous forsaken, nor his seed begging bread." But God still insisted he was a fool.

Secondly: He honestly thought he was the boss of his possessions. The right to own private property is almost universally recognized in all societies from the primitive to the most complex. The hunter owns his bow and arrows; the clerk his home, the banker his estate. At the same time it is quite as universally recognized that society can set a limit on the amount of private property an individual may own. In the days of our rich fool, Rome was siphoning off 60 per cent of the wealth (private property) of Palestine in tax levies. In our own day a graduated income tax tells us to the exact penny how much of our property in earnings we can keep for ourselves. In a way, of course, the man in the parable was boss; but in a deeper sense, he was the slave of his wealth. When he decided to keep the stuff, the stuff told him he would have to readjust to its demands. Not that he minded, particularly, but the orders were unequivocal: you pull down your little barn and build a bigger one, or else——. But the things he possessed in such abundance did not stop with ordering barns built; they had the final word to say about his most precious thing—his soul. Weymouth gives sharp emphasis to this in his translation of verse 20: "This night *they* are demanding your soul from you." The man was figuring his life expectancy in terms of many easy years; his possessions gave him less than twelve hours. Only a fool could miss a calculation that far. Here again the universality of this man's predicament is apparent in our modern life. That what a man owns owns the man is one of the most puzzling of paradoxes yet it is so apparent as to need no documentation. The United States owns a 250 billion dollar debt; that's quite some credit. But the debt owns us and exercises dominion over us in ways that are too numerous and perhaps unpleasant to recount.

His third mistake was in thinking that his security and his guarantee of comfort were vested in his possessions. Life is like riding wild horses, to be sure, but money makes the mare go. But the basic feeling of insecurity which is both the strain and stimulus to life is not completely relaxed by the possession of things that also are basically insecure. This misplaced trust is the subtlest of errors and for that reason, perhaps, is made oftenest both by those who have much goods and those who have little or none. The poor, no less than the rich, believe that security is a matter solely of much goods. Furthermore the misfortune that robs the rich of proper enjoyment of his wealth does not necessarily pass it on as fortune to others. "The things you have prepared, whose will they be?" Whose indeed, and how, and for how long; and for what good or evil?

His definitive folly, however, was that he thought more of his crops and barns and goods than he did of people. He would have honestly disputed this, and, if pressed, asked impatiently, so what? He might even have admitted that to think more of property than of people was morally dubious. But foolish? Never! Look at people in general—disorderly, shiftless, stupid! Look at that field of wheat—uniform, erect, golden! Don't be a sentimentalist! But is it sentimentalism to say that a covetous man loses what makes life worth living—friends? The rich have money, the poor have families. This is old and veritable wisdom, against which our choices are still judged. It would almost certainly have been unconventional and foolish and even dangerous, in the opinion of the other members of his income bracket if he had given his bumper crop away, but it could conceivably in the long run, have been smart. For all we know it might have saved him worry, made him friends, and extended his life. He chose to hoard it for himself, and God said he was a fool.

[4]

This parable, we have said, is properly and fully understood only within the context of a great concern. The man who asked for Jesus' help in the settlement of a brothers' quarrel, coveted what was not his. Maybe he was better off without it. Presumably the older brother was, in his way, no less covetous, and he was certainly in trouble. But Jesus was occupied with something more significant than a domestic feud; he said to *them*, meaning those who had doubtless overheard the brother's request, "Beware of *all* covetousness." The defrauded brother typified a danger of formidable proportions: the avarice that lay at the heart of the disintegration that was evident in every aspect of the personal, social, religious, and political life of the day.

Why, we may ask, did Jesus say "*beware* of covetousness" instead of "thou shalt not covet"? Why a warning instead of a command? Cupidity had been included in the sins prohibited by the Decalogue because long experience in social intercourse had proved to the desert wanderers that it was socially demoralizing. The man who coveted the wife, the cattle, the slaves, or the chattels of his neighbor was as intolerable as a liar or a thief. So far as we know, the moral status of covetousness had never been officially changed from sin to folly; yet Jesus represents God's judgment of the covetous man *who coveted his own goods and not his neighbor's,* as folly. It would seem that in the evolution of the social code, covetousness, the sin, had become avarice, the folly. Was this, as in another instance, divorce, an accommodation to man's hardness of heart? We can not be sure, but this we can confidently say: such is not infrequently the case with law—moral and civil. Sin tends in the common mind to moderate into imprudence, and as protection against sin's risk is developed, it tends to become more or less the pattern of conventional behavior. "Thou shalt not commit adultery" has become "Watch your step." What will this ancient proscription become when prophylaxis is foolproof? It may be that man's heart *is* hardened. Many today would wince at being called a fool who would smile at being called a sinner. After all, sin gets some applause if it is indulged with *élan;* but the fool, no matter how colossal his folly, at best gets a laugh, at worst, disdain.

Was it to this broad and deep condition our Lord was speaking? Again we must confess to uncertainty, but the likelihood is that what immediately confronted him was neither broad nor deep. Here was a great multitude of people. Why were they thronging him? It would be reassuring if we could say they found in him the answer to their spiritual yearnings; but if what Jesus talked about to them indicated what they were after, they were a covetous mob. Most mobs are. This one-time sin and latter-day folly of covetousness festered in the ambitions of his closest friends. Two of them coveted privileged seats in the kingdom they thought was coming. The authorities, civil, ecclesiastical and political, were covetous men. The cupidity of the high priest was as open a scandal as the unsatisfied greed of the Roman tax collectors. All the big fools were building big barns and promising themselves ease for many years. Jesus knew *these things* were asking for the souls of all of them, so he warned: Beware of all covetousness, including that miserly and stupid satisfaction in the abundance that they thought belonged indefeasibly and entirely to them. They thought they were clever and rich. God said they were fools.

There will be opportunity later to point out the timelessness of Jesus' warning. We too are living in times of great tension, and suggestions for the meaning of the Christian testimony for our day must be attempted in some detail. For the present, however, it will serve our interests to point out three facts. First: The tension under which we live is largely caused by the struggle between the haves and the have-nots. However oversimplified this may appear, it is still the rudiment of our stress. We in

America have always been relatively rich, but this has not prepared us to accommodate our prodigious new power and wealth. The rest of the earth is poor to the point of desperation while we don't know exactly what to do with what we have. Second: The pattern of Western society has for a century been correctly described as acquisitive. Once, in the early days of Western Christian culture, covetousness was a sin; then it became a risk. When we got strong enough to take calculated risks, acquisitiveness became the political, economic and social norm. Third: Like the genial plutocrat in the parable we are facing alternative choices as we survey our wealth and the poverty of the world. We want security and ease, and to live a long time. But some are beginning to see the folly of covetousness. Less and less do we believe our security lies in bigger barns; less and less are we the confident boss of our possessions. We are caught in the vicious capitalist circle: more wealth to create more power to protect ourselves against our covetous enemies, to create more wealth to create more power to protect ourselves ad infinitum. We, as a people when times get tough, think more of crops than we do of folks, and the sure result of that is the loss of friends. Are "these things" requiring of us our souls? After World War I we were called Uncle Shylock. Shylock was a rich man. After World War II we are being called Simple Simon. Simon was a fool.

This parable, it must be pointed out, ends with what would be called a negative proposal. To call the man a fool and predict his death in the night makes a doleful ending. Even the comment, "So is he who lays up treasure for himself, and is not rich toward God" (Luke 12:21), lacks specific and appropriate proposals for action. This deficit, if such it be, is repaired in the parable that follows, and this will be the subject of the next chapter. In the meantime, however, to indicate that the parable we have been studying cannot be left with a multitude thronging the highway to Jerusalem in the year 31, we quote from two fairly recent news items, the significance of which lies not in the date or the effort to predict a dismal future for rich America, but in the discovery in our century that bumper crops are just as dangerous as they were in the first century.

The first is taken from a reprint of an article by Professor Fetter of Princeton, that appeared in *The Saturday Evening Post* in July, 1946. Dr. Fetter is a political scientist, and he says under the caption, "Inflation's Cause: Too Much Money":

The real cause of inflation is well known alike to students of theory and to practical financiers. Without a shadow of a doubt that cause is the enormous increase of money and of bank demand deposits. . . . Nothing comparable to it has ever occurred in our financial history. Nearly all prices and wages . . . are still rising toward a peak not yet attained. That is the impending catastrophe. . . . To deal with the real cause, anything and everything must be done that will reduce the excessive amount of money in circulation and will check the inflationary rise of bank deposits. . . . Inflation is winning by default. Unless Washington does something effective to stop inflation the nation is headed for the greatest financial explosion in its history.

"And the things you have prepared, whose will they be?" (Luke 12:20). The other quotation comes from *Time*, July 15, 1946. The caption is: "High Price of Success."

Farmer Anderson is also a hard-headed businessman and he is not going to sell his wheat right now—not before January if he can help it. That is one reason why he built his own elevator. What about the Government's order to farmers to sell half the grain they bring in for storage? The stock answer of Ford County farmers: "Nuts to that." If the Government tried to put a penalty on everybody who does not comply, it would have to move against about 95% of the wheat belt's farmers.

Frank Anderson's decision to hold his wheat has nothing to do with that order against withholding wheat for "famine prices." As a matter of fact, he thought the $1.70-a-bushel ceiling under OPA was a mighty fair price.

His trouble and the trouble of all good wheat farmers is success. Last year he cleared $10,000. So far this year he has sold $15,000 worth of wheat and cattle. Said he: "I know there are people starving in Europe, and I'd like to help them. But this is a business. If I sell even half of $13,600 worth of wheat I'll get into a higher income bracket and my tax will go sky-high. Besides, I've got to stay in business; I've got to hold a lot of wheat as insurance against a poor crop next year." In rich Ford County it was a good guess that nine out of ten of his neighbors were in Frank Anderson's fortunate fix and had made the same decision.

It was 9:45 p.m. and Anderson's frank, blue eyes were heavy with weariness. Ahead of him were more days like this one and the dozen that had preceded it. He stretched his wiry arms, scratched his thinning brown hair and allowed that he had better get to bed. He sighed: "It's beginning to catch up with me. These last few years have been awfully hard. I'm tired, all my machinery is tired, and my land is tired. Sometimes I wish I could take it easy. I'm tired of worrying."

[5]

It is not ours to pass judgment on this man but we wonder what God would say about the situation in which he was caught. Clearly he was in what we call a tension situation. He wished he could take it easy. Why can't he? It is at this point that the pattern of one of the universal tension experiences emerges, the pattern to which Jesus was addressing himself in the first century. It arises out of man's relation to property. Here surely is no interim problem to be settled by *ad hoc* ethical maxims. So long as man finds the things he possesses necessary for the support of life, so long will he find himself in a tension situation. It may be alluring to think on a posthistory escape from it but we must take care lest such an engaging prospect create another tension of its own.

That organized society allows private property as a necessity for the spiritual and social advantages it provides does not abate the tension it creates. On the contrary. The man who has what he regards as not enough is anxious about what he shall eat and drink and wherewithal he shall be clothed. He who has too much is anxious about storage space for the safe containment of his much goods. When he says to himself: "Soul, thou hast much goods laid up for many years," he may be trying to persuade himself that he really has nothing to worry about, but worry he will. In between the poor man and the rich man is the man who has just enough. How much just enough is, is generally decided by the poor and the rich, for the middle-class man rarely agrees that he is secure from possible descent to poverty or that he should not essay the ascent to wealth. He has his worry also.

Man's efforts to deal with the property-versus-personality tension have been haphazard and heroic. It is the story of movement between laissez faire on the one hand to austerity on the other. He has devised systems, he has maintained his own right to determine what he shall do and he has invited the good offices of an arbiter. "Teacher, bid my brother divide the inheritance with me." "Man, who made me a judge or divider over you?" And we see here the shrewdness of the approach that Jesus took in this specific instance. To have arbitrated would not of necessity have settled the quarrel between these brothers though it might have settled the inheritance between them. To abate the tension between them and within each of them it was necessary to achieve a higher level of apprehension and action.

For this reason he told the story about the man—a good man by conventional standards—who was caught in a dilemma essentially the same as that which vexed the contending brothers. In both cases the property held by one was wanted by others because they thought they needed it. The brothers were already quarreling openly; the rich man was quarreling inwardly and, we may assume, there were poor neighbors who were grumbling either about God's apparent partiality or the big man's apparent indifference to social need. Jesus proposed simply that the man should have made himself "rich toward God." Failure to do this created his tension and precipitated him into a foolish method of solving his problem. This is what makes the crux of this parable a matter of good sense and not of good morals. He was a fool, more to be pitied than blamed.

Just how persistent our tension is and how foolishly we seek to abate it needs very little elaboration here. As these words are being written the United States Senate is having what is called a full dress debate on the Atlantic Pact. Who doesn't feel the tension created by the current struggle for power among the nations? Who does not know that it stems from the necessity for property—using the word in its broadest connotations—and the desperate concern for its protection. The military pact is a device, it is a big barn, bigger and better than the smaller barns that have hitherto been adequate for containing what we rightly (morally) regard as our own. That we will mount heavy armament on the big barn and protect it with radar and runways and suchlike military contraptions does not obscure the basic fact that we are dangerously tense because we—and this is the sedate voice of America speaking—have the highest standard of living and must protect it against the neighbor countries who, with their bizarre and messianic notions about economics and totalitarian government, propose to take it from us. Is the Atlantic Pact wicked? The prior question, in the light of our study would seem to be: Are we making fools of ourselves? To adopt the language of Jesus that introduced the parable of the fortunate farmer: a man's standard of living does not consist in the abundance of his possessions. Until we agree to that, we are certain to invoke the mechanisms of folly to settle our problems.

Just what it means to be rich toward God has been the subject of endless and detailed discussion elsewhere. It is, as a matter of fact, what the religious experience is all about. In the context of this study however, it may be given a more limited focus.

The tension situation we have been describing is that created by the personality-property nexus. We cannot solve it either by renouncing personality or property since, oddly enough, they—while different—are integral. The only solution must be found in a higher level of experience. Jesus calls it "being rich toward God." There is no indication in the parable that this meant smaller barns or no barns at all. Impoverishment or pauperhood is not necessarily godliness. The ascetic's rigor may, in its own way, create a tension that excludes God quite as completely as the prodigal's debauch.

It is easy to say that Jesus solved this tension, and let it go at that. Maybe leaving the carpenter shop—which represented property interests to the Nazareth home—was his way of becoming rich toward God. But we suspect it was not so simple as that. For this reason among others, we do not think that abolition of private property would necessarily be compensated for by collateral grants of God's riches. Unless, however, Jesus' perspective on life was grossly distorted by romantic notions about personality or irrational prejudices about property, his proposal to solve a universal human tension pattern by seeking a higher focus of interest and devotion is at least plausible. This is a very condescending way of regarding his suggestion about how the rich fool might have solved his dilemma and we are properly rebuked for it by the psychologists who assert that tension is creatively resolved only in a higher focus of attention. In this case, being rich toward God must be regarded as a higher focus of attention than big barns for bumper crops. At least if we do not so regard it we cannot easily escape the indictment of our folly or—and this is a more dismal prospect—the ultimate loss of our soul (personal demoralization) and the ultimate dispersal of our properties.

CHAPTER III

Citizen I and Citizen II

WE SAID that the parable about the man and the barn ended negatively. More accurate perhaps would be the statement that following God's summary and shocking judgment of the man, there was only a general observation about the likes of him that lacked directive. "So is he who lays up treasure for himself but is not rich toward God." The rich man's dilemma had been sketched, his choice registered and his status announced. That's the way it is with such people; but he who wants to escape the stigma of being a fool—an opprobrium in the shallow minds of many more grievous than being a sinner—needs clearer guidance. How is he to escape being a fool by making a wrong choice or from frustration by making a right one? It needs no argument to establish the fact that had the rich man accepted any of the possible alternative courses open to him he would, in his own opinion and in the judgment of his fellows, have knowingly accepted the frustration of his business. This still is a dilemma; none of us feels that its twin horns have been blunted by the passing of the centuries. If anything they seem to have acquired keener and more threatening points.

That his hearers were not unaware of the dilemma is indicated by Jesus' solicitous word about their anxiety. If laying up treasure for one's self was folly, was improvidence wisdom? No, he answered; life is neither the abundance of things nor the lack of things; it is *more* than things. The charming lyric about ravens and lilies follows; words as often quoted and as completely ignored as anything he ever said. It is easier to read poetry about birds that always seem to have abundant crops but no worry about barns to store them in, than to "consider" them, as his quaint suggestion has it. The same is true of lilies; they make lovely decorations, we know, but dubious teachers. Birds but not ornithology, lilies but not floriculture. Jesus was sure the fool was less resplendent than a field flower (there is evidence that for all his vaunted wisdom Solomon too was a fool), but how much his friends shared his judgment is not disclosed. It would appear that he felt it important not only to abate their tension about "things" as they related to common life but to reassure them about the good pleasure of their Father who was going to give them the Kingdom (12:22-32).

But this was still short of a positive directive, however lofty its charm and promise. They had been warned against folly: death in the night is the wages of the fool; and his recompense could only be avoided by the wisdom that was "rich toward God." Could one be rich like that? How?

[1]

He told them another parable.

"Let your loins be girded and your lamps burning and be like men who are waiting for their master to come home from the marriage feast, so that they may open to him at once when he comes and knocks. Blessed are those servants whom the master finds awake when he comes; truly, I say to you, he will gird himself and have them sit at table and come and serve them. If he comes in the second watch, or in the third, and finds them so, blessed are those servants!" (12:35-38).

He was interrupted by Peter who wanted to know whether this parable had general or limited reference. Without answering his question Jesus repeated the importance of the steward being wise and faithful and added that such conduct would positively be rewarded by the householder: "Truly I tell you, he will set him over all his possessions." Unfaithfulness also was requited:

"But if that servant says in his heart, 'My master is delayed in coming,' and begins to beat the menservants and maidservants, and to eat and drink and get drunk, the master of that servant will come on a day when he does not expect him and at an hour he does not know, and will punish him, and put him with the unfaithful. And that servant who knew his master's will, but did not make ready, or act according to his will, shall receive a severe beating. But he who did not know, and did what deserved a beating, shall receive a light beating. Every one to whom much is given, of him will much be required; and of him to whom men commit much they will demand the more" (12:45-48).

The contrast between the two men in the two parables could hardly be more sharply drawn than by the decisions they made about their use of their property. The rich fool had said to himself: I have much goods, therefore I shall eat, drink and be merry for many years; the other said: I have much goods; therefore much is required of me. This is all the more striking when we discover that except for this important difference they might, in other matters, have been much the same sort of person. Both were wealthy and well-served by many menials. Socially, we assume, they were at least respectable; and without too great use of our imagination we can believe them to have had and exercised a genuine sense of community responsibility. There are further facts about our latest acquaintance, Citizen II, that deserve emphasis. Rich though he was, he was also what is commonly described as democratic, a quality not always associated with affluence. Dangerously democratic, some might have said. Off to a wedding banquet he leaves his fortunate servants in a dither of excitement about his return. It made no difference if he came back early or late; they would be eager to greet him and tend his wants. But his most urgent need when he was home again was to share something of the hilarity of his evening with those who could not go. They had no invitation to the wedding feast so he would serve them a feast at home. Imagine that! He is hardly inside the house before he orders his servants to dispose themselves at the table that he may serve them. Such conduct was perhaps thought *infra dig.* by his substantial neighbors, but it did not breed the contempt among his servants that familiarity is said to cultivate. His menial friends knew they could not presume upon it to be slack or dilatory in their obedience. There was reward for diligence and measured punishment for defection. The affairs of the menage must be effectively administered and the boss knew co-operative and cordial good will would produce the best result. He could not afford to be either excessively austere or indulgent: to him much had been given and of him much was being required. Therefore his attitude toward people and toward things should be such as would enable him to fulfill his obligation.

This makes him out to be a very different person from his contemporary, Citizen I of the other parable. Had he been a farmer confronted with a bumper crop he would not have decided as did Citizen I. The fact of a bulging barn would have been to him a moral mandate, and by accepting it he would also have avoided the fatal folly of the other man. Unlike the luckless miser he would have been the boss of his goods; he would have been secure; he would have been free of silly moralizings about God's special and unqualified favor toward him. Beyond that he would have had friends, even among his servants, and, above all, preserved his soul. If God had passed audible judgment on his success it would have sounded a note in sharp contrast to the other's doom.

We have then in these two parables two ideas about the use

of possessions that stand in different categories, though it is not
true to say that they are at opposite poles to each other. Citizen
I decided to hold what he had for himself; Citizen II decided to
use what he had for others. These can be called different economic philosophies if we wish to use grandiose terms, but not,
we repeat, conflicting philosophies. If Citizen II had taken the
position that he had no right to hold his personal property for
any reason, and enlarged his notion to include the abolition *in
toto* of all private property, he would have taken a stand clearly
and uncompromisingly opposite Citizen I who would part with
his property for no reason whatever. Citizen II was, we think,
wiser than Citizen I whose decision won him the title "fool,"
and none the less wiser than a possible Citizen III who would
have abolished the private ownership of grain, barns, and goods
in one sweeping and irresponsible gesture. Such a man too, we
suggest, would have been something of a fool in his own right!

[2]

What we have then, in essence, is one of the possible creative
resolutions of the tension that arises because of man's need to
possess things. There have been efforts here and there to appease
the behavior of man and his goods by allowing covetousness on
the one hand, or encouraging indigence on the other. They both
stand condemned as foolish because of what happens in each
case to both property and owner. Between them stands the democratic householder, Citizen II, who keeps his property but holds
it under a compelling sense that he is required to use it for
others.

Too much must not be made of mere words, but there are
two other hints in the formulation of the economic philosophy
of Citizen II that deserve note. The share of the community in
the good fortunes of this good householder is clear. "And of him
to whom *men commit much*" sounds to modern ears like talk of

unearned increments and the place and share of society in one's success. In many ways "men commit much" to the successful. No man makes his fortune unaided. It is no new discovery that this is so, though there is many a modern man who does not include it in his inventory. This fact, however, does not stand alone; it is the cause of something even more striking. The complete sentence reads: "Of him to whom men commit much *they will demand the more.*" Here was something Citizen I had not thought about when he made himself comfortable for his otiose days, and forgetting it was one component of his folly. It is, indeed, the sure nemesis of covetousness, whether of individual or nation; and the more convinced common men are that their share in the prosperity of the privileged is not duly acknowledged, the more insistent or even threatening will be their demands for their proper share. Only those who are blinded by avarice will fail to see this. It has been clear to the wise for centuries.

The economic philosophy of Citizen II is not only a suggested mediation between the two extremes of economic folly; it is, we are convinced, what our Lord meant when he spoke about being rich toward God. We might paraphrase it thus: He is a fool who lays up treasure for himself; he is wise who, realizing he has much, recognizes a proportionately greater demand upon him.

Being rich toward God is a saint's investment and since few of us are in that bracket, we invest in insecurities and discuss the saint's fortunes frivolously. The world is full of memorials which are the efforts of philanthropic souls to be rich toward God, to become saints by indirection. They are not to be lightly regarded nor can it be said they have always failed to enhance their Godward holdings. But there is downright pathos in many of their efforts and sheer hypocrisy in not a few. If the rich fool had been reprieved for a decade he might presumably have endowed a pew in his synagogue or a chair in the temple college,.

not to mention a memorial window to himself. This he would certainly have felt enriched him toward God, even though that undeserving deity called him a fool. But if this is the sort of behavior that accumulates true riches toward God, then Citizen II has cast false light on the matter. We are sure, on the contrary, that he has by example presented us with authentic and elemental wisdom about being rich toward God. In three distinct entries his balance is to be added up. First: He was rich toward God in his recognition of the fact that far beyond any share he had in winning his own fortunes was the basic fact of the hand of God. Much had been given him, and to accept that fact alone was to enrich his soul. Here we are reminded again of the folly that claims the free enterprise system as the basic factor in the standard of living in the United States and overlooks the primary fact of the fabulous supply of raw materials found within our borders. Every enterpriser is God's beneficiary and must be man's agent: these, we insist, are the two first items to be entered into any trial balance when one casts up one's account with God. Second: He was rich toward God in the good will and hearty cooperation of those who worked with him in his household. He did not buy their good will by serving them an occasional midnight snack; he won it by the orderly management of his business and the just and impartial rewards that followed the performance of his servant colleagues. There were stripes for the malingerer as well as promotion for the faithful. Third: He was rich toward God in the uses he could make of his good fortune for the advantage of others. It is no mere coincidence that when Jesus spoke of the ultimate judgment, a man's credits—often to his great surprise—were based upon an act of compassion to a needy one who mysteriously turned out to have been God himself. So is he who lays up treasure toward God.

[3]

Was there a need for saying this as Jesus moved onward to Jerusalem? We need only ask whether there has ever been a time when it was not urgently demanded. The wisdom of Citizen II who was a wise steward in the household of God was needed to offset the folly of Citizen I suffocating in surfeit. The negative comment that summed up our first parable needed a positive emphasis to give certain direction. Here we have it all: the tension of the situation to which Jesus responded, and the clear light upon the synthesis by which the tension was to be made creative—a co-operative use of possessions.

There will be more to say on this presently, but another observation is important at this point. It was immediately following his statement of this creative synthesis that he described his own inner tension in the strongest terms. "I came to cast fire on the earth; and would that it were already kindled! . . . Do you think that I have come to give peace on earth? No . . . but rather division" (Luke 12:49-51). The sequence may be without design and hence without significance, but it cannot, for all that, be without interest. Was his effort to break the constricting grip of covetousness by what was a truly radical proposal, to be described as casting a firebrand? Did he see with sharp, pragmatic clarity that his word about Citizen II would not bring peace, but division? What arouses quicker resentment among the big-barn gentry than the suggestion that they might have no barns at all but for the generosity of God and therefore they should behave like adults and share their wealth lest it destroy them? We may still read his words and wonder. The last twenty-five years have seen fire cast upon the earth. It is already kindled, and there are those who, repeating the manifest folly of Citizen I, are ready to build higher the next and most ominous pyre. Peace? Nay, rather division. The dismal predictions in verses fifty-two and fifty-three are the frightened words of no ancient and forgotten prophet. Their sound is no distant echo; it is an alarm on our street!

He also said . . . "When you see a cloud rising in the west, you say at once, 'A shower is coming'; and so it happens. And when you see the south wind blowing, you say, 'There will be scorching heat'; and it happens. You hypocrites! You know how to interpret the appearance of earth and sky; but why do you not know how to interpret the present time?"

Are we still nonchalantly gazing at the sky? The cloud of covetousness rises in the west. Do we feel the breath of the south wind upon us? Citizen II shakes his head apprehensively. It will be hot tomorrow!

[4]

There is another relevant aspect of this story that must not be overlooked. It arises out of the fact that in modern society the feeling still lingers that those who work for us belong to us. There was time when this was literally true, when slaves were property. It was only slightly less true in feudal days and now, even after decades of struggle to win for the worker the independent dignity of a free man, vestiges of the slave-system mentality persist in the conflict between management and labor, or owner and employee, or capitalist and worker. Such tension as exists in this nexus is therefore part of, or parallel to, that which is implicit in the man-property tension discussed in the preceding chapter. What a man is to do with his laborers when they increase is as crucial a problem as what he is to do with his grain when it bursts his barns. It is perhaps more subtle, however, since while grain can be put up in bigger accommodations, dealing with human personalities in large numbers is a much more complex operation. This is particularly true when the labor quotient of a man's wealth has appropriated to itself the fact that since the worker has contributed to the wealth of his employer he is entitled to more than mere wages. "To him to whom men [the men who work for him] have committed much, of him will they demand the more." This is a more radical doctrine now than when it was first announced. One does not have to be a Marxist to see that in the theory of surplus value there is something disturbingly reminiscent of the word of Jesus just quoted.

There is important guidance for those who seek to abate this tension and it is found in the parable we are studying. This citizen had many associates in his household. They were called servants though in all likelihood there was nothing odious in the name. It seems that there were varieties of responsibilities: foreman, steward, factotum, helper, and so on. And they represented every variety of personal reaction to their respective jobs. Some were diligent, some were dilatory and some were—during recess periods—drunk and disorderly. There may have been chislers and sychophants too. In general, however, they seemed to get on well with the master; were even fond of him since, if we scrutinize the record, he was no stuffed shirt, no stickler for the invidious conventional master-servant amenities. He was democratic, friendly, shrewd, successful, serious-minded.

We must assume that the relationships which held his menage together were not haphazard or improvised. They rested on principles which are deducible from the parable. Let us suggest four of them.

There was a difference of status but equality of dignity. It was the master who was the guest at the wedding feast in the city and it would never have occurred to him to take along a group of his servants, or to encourage them in an access of egalitarian enthusiasm to crash the gate. But the satisfaction he enjoyed at the feast as a guest might be shared with his servants, whose social status had not entitled them to invitations. One's imagination is enlivened by the picture of this fine man coming home long past midnight and proposing that those of his household who had not been able to go to the party should have a party of their own at which he was to be host and caterer and flunky. If such behavior represents a state of mind, or better perhaps, a spirit, it would be stated in some such proposition as this: No status in life can derogate the essential dignity of the individual or deny him his basic rights. In this case, obviously, it was what we call familiarly the inalienable right to the pursuit of happiness. This is important.

The second principle: There was a difference of work but equality of responsibility. The master of the household had his own work cut out for him. He had to maintain the property he felt he held in trust. It had been "given him" and his associates had been gathered about him to help work out his responsibilities. He could treat neither his money nor his menials irresponsibly. His servants had lesser duties, more modest jobs to do; but it seems that they were quite as fully responsible for doing their jobs well as was the master. Again, if this can be thought representative of a spirit, it may be stated thus: The character of one's accepted or appointed work does not affect the measure of one's responsibility for its performance. The member of the road gang who drives a spike is just as responsible as the man in the tower who throws a switch.

The third principle: There was a difference of reward but equality of liability. This is clearly set forth in our parable. The men were recompensed for their work in terms of their responsibility, skill, and diligence, but they were all equally held accountable for their failures, whatever the reason for them.

"The master of that servant will come on a day when he does not expect him and at an hour he does not know, and will punish him, and put him with the unfaithful. And that servant who knew his master's will, but did not make ready or act according to his will, shall receive a severe beating. But he who did not know, and did what deserved a beating, shall receive a light beating" (12:46-48).

We are not concerned here with the propriety of corporal punishment in such cases; what interests us is that liability is a part
of the contract and ignorance can no more escape penalty than
willfulness. Again if this is representative of the spirit that informed this master-servant relationship it may be put thus:
There is an inviolability of contract that is supported by reward
for good performance and by penalties for nonfeasance.

The fourth principle: The positions of highest responsibility
and reward come to those who perform their duties with diligence and good nature. These last two words are synonyms for
the words "faithful and wise" in the parable.

"Who then is the faithful and wise steward, whom his master will
set over his household . . . ? Blessed is that servant whom his master
finds so doing when he comes. Truly I tell you, he will set him over
all his possessions" (12:42-44).

The spirit represented by this proposition is: The roadways to
advancement are faithfulness and wisdom. Nowadays we would
call it enterprise and know-how.

[5]

If there is need of further clarity as to what this parable is all
about it can be seen if it is told in reverse. Suppose the servants
had all been lazy or sullen. Suppose the man had been arbitrary,
irresponsible, inhuman, greedy, partisan. The picture we would
have had would have presented chaos, or, if we put it in modern
terms, we would have a story of the worst possible labor relations
in an enterprise that was sure to be plagued with every imaginable personnel and technical difficulty and quite as certain to
end up in the boneyard of bankrupt businesses.

Here then are four principles, by which, we propose, the tensions between labor and management can be creatively resolved.
In so far as they have been resolved it has been along these lines.

Conversely where they have not been resolved it is due to failures in these four areas.

Let us look more closely at this latter fact. Where there has
been an unwillingness to accept the principle that in wholesome
labor relations a difference of status does not mean a difference
of dignity, the fault has largely been that of the master of the
house. Class distinctions among us are real even though they are
concealed. There is a psychological hang-over from the days
when classes were thought a fixed part of an immutable order
of things. It is also a matter of pride. Fingernails are as clear an
index of status and dignity as a white collar or a mahogany desk.
Our fondness for Abe Lincoln the rail splitter is an afterthought.
He was called a gorilla even after he had achieved the White
House. Obviously it is to the advantage of the privileged to maintain their status, and too often weighting the scales in their own
favor lightens it for others. Too many masters of the house, beguiled by their success and importance, have denigrated the dignity of those who have shared their enterprise. "In all the strug-
gles for power in human history, those who have been powerless
have been able to see the evil that is done to them; whereas
those who have power both cannot and will not see the evil." [1]

The second proposition—that the character of one's job does
not affect the responsibility for its maximum performance—has
been more generally contradicted by the worker than by the employer. There is a factor here that must not be overlooked: in
general the more important job carries with it the greater concern for top results. This is not wholesome, for a finished product may be only as strong as its weakest production operation;
nevertheless it is difficult not to feel that the big job demands
a better qualitative performance than the little job. There are
charming little myths about chimney sweeps and other low-
bracket performers who gave their last ounce of energy to do an

[1] Daniel Day Williams, *God's Grace and Man's Hope* (New York: Harper &
Brothers, 1949), p. 172.

immaculate cleaning job that no human eye would ever see, but somehow they do not have the force of a moral imperative. The grease monkey in the ship's bowels may be as important as the skipper on the bridge but the comparison sounds more moral than material and it is not difficult to be disdainful of the exhortations to the skipper to emphasize the point. To be sure the lord has often made it hard for the serf to believe in his dignity and the importance of his job and thus has encouraged malingering or even sabotage. Conversely, when the master believes and practices Proposition I, he has made it much easier for the worker to practice Proposition II.

That reward is commensurate with responsibility and performance has rarely been successfully challenged. This is Proposition III. But that failure to work should be penalized has not infrequently been denied or overlooked. This is one aspect of the problem of the strike as it is the whole problem of the loafer. Nowadays we do not beat the indolent or disorderly servant. The record (verse 46) quaintly expresses the fate of the idler: "Put him with the unfaithful"—a euphemism for our more economical phrase: "You're fired." It cannot contribute to the lessening of the manager-worker tensions to protect, by law or union code, the workers who do not perform according to contract. The moral attitude that supplies us guidance here does not fall short of the manager or the moneylender who, in his own way, strikes against the laborer or fails to fulfill the letter and the spirit of his commitment. Penalty for failure is as important as reward for service. This is the clear instruction of the parable, and its application must be over-all to be morally defensible.

Proposition IV is the core of industrial democracy. The roadway to advancement is open to all who—as the record states it—have faithfulness and wisdom. Know-how and industry, as we have observed above, is the way we put it. Cinderella stories and Horatio Alger heroes are less absorbing to our sophisticated age than to former times, but it is still true that while the master occasionally unwisely gives his worthless son a cushy job and big pay, the boss's daughter can still marry the ambitious foreman of Plant II and the immigrant's son can become the top research specialist in the giant industry.

[6]

These propositions, we have been trying to say, represent practical ways in which the master-servant tension (which derives essentially from the owner-property tension) may be abated. It can even be said that it has already been abated, for the process of achieving equilibrium in this field has been by following these lines. It has taken a long time but the logic of this Christian dynamic can be seen to have moved from the master-slave to the lord-serf relation, and on to the employer-employee contract. The origin of this could not have arisen in an interim ethic, an *ad hoc* improvisation. Indeed its final stage has not yet been reached though the tendency is clearly seen. The only way in which the four propositions are likely to be fully operative is in an advance from employer-employee to partnership. It is going too far to say that the household described in the parable was a co-op. Is it too much to say that the ultimate fruit of the householder's social or economic or moral philosophy was to be a cooperative fellowship? The accommodations that capitalism has had to make to a changing world have been in the direction of co-operativism. How much farther it will go time alone will tell, but only those who are quite blind to what is going on in the world will fail to see the enormous shift in that direction. Call it C.C.F. or Social Democracy or Christian Socialism as we will. There it is and no amount of regret or reaction will deflect or deter it forever.

This causes great searching of heart among those who invest our present precarious social order with special sanctity and hope that the divine hand will stretch forth to steady it. But the

hand of God is impotent to stay the processes of social change
that the hand of God has initiated. The logic that moves toward
co-operation is inescapable and it is supported by forces that will
not be denied. Already partnership is common on the top level.
Hart, Schaffner and Marx; Carson, Pirie and Scott; and so on
ad infinitum. Why not also Bank, Factory and Worker; or Mor-
gan, G. E. and Murray?

From the distinctly Christian perspective there is one further
factor in the total equation. It is too much to hope, human
nature being what it is, that the tension situations in the capital-
labor nexus will be abated simply by the working out of the
propositions we have been discussing. Long before the need for
lessening our tensions was foreseen the formula was found. "We
are workers together with God." Here owner and property, or
capital and labor are coaxial. Together with God, that's the
pungent phrase. It raises ethical obligation to its highest level,
to fellowship with the Divine. Here the moral urgency becomes
the religious impulse; here the man-thing tension becomes the
man-God tension. This is the ultimate experience with which
all serious reflection about human destiny has to do. This is what
being rich toward God means. It may come as something of a
surprise to worried and tense people today to discover that this
was all prefigured nineteen centuries ago.

CHAPTER IV

Two Men and a Tree

THE episode (Luke 13:1-5) which introduces the next parable is obscure and it is odd that this is so; odd, that is to us. It may be that such atrocities were a fairly regular program with Pilate so that the author felt that a mere reference to it was adequate. Since we do not know, the slaughter of the worshipers seems a frightful thing. That Pilate was capable of acts of this sort blackens his reputation even more deeply than ever. For our purposes the Procurator's act has particular interest. It is obvious that these hapless Galileans had died very recently. The story is brought to Jesus as a bit of news. Jesus and many of his followers were Galileans and were on their way to Jerusalem to worship and, perhaps, to offer the conventional sacrifices. If the crime of the dead victims of Pilate's bloody act was only that of coming to Jerusalem to perform the ritual sacrifices, Jesus and his friends were clearly asking for trouble if they insisted on doing the same thing. That the dead Galileans had been guilty of nothing more blameworthy than ritual observances seems clear from the remark that they were not "worse sinners than all the other Galileans." Their suffering proved no special guilt. Furthermore there was a clear warning to those who had thus far escaped Pilate's cruel caprice. "Unless you repent you will all likewise perish." This was both a confusing and a frightening word. How repent? Was not the act of sacrifice the perfect sign of repentance? If this incurred the possibility of death, what sort of repentance, ritual or otherwise, could avert it? Here was a real dilemma. They were going to Jerusalem to observe the Passover feast. A part of the celebration involved acts of penitence. Performance of these rites had already cost the lives of some Galilean worshipers. There was a real possibility that others might suffer the same fate. Should they therefore stay out of Jerusalem to save their lives and thus imperil their souls, since faithful sons of Israel were expected to observe the festival? Or should they risk death as a testimony to their faith?

It is possible that this dilemma is one that is apparent only to us who read the story at this late date. Jesus did not deal with the problem in the terms we have outlined. He offers a peremptory comment about the need for repentance and sets forth clearly his idea that there was no correlation in this case between the fate of the victims and their state of grace. This latter emphasis he goes out of his way to make explicit by referring to another episode. It was not an atrocity, it was an accident. The collapse of a tower that killed eighteen dwellers in Jerusalem proved nothing about their moral character. They were not "worse offenders." The general deduction Jesus made on both of the tragic events was that his hearers must repent if they wanted to escape a similar fate. But this seems to be an observation so general as to lose its specific relevance to the two incidents.

There is a condescending attitude that has no doubt been expressed toward these impenitent victims. A later sophistication may say that those who have mistaken ritual observances for essential religious experience deserve, in one form or another, some such summary rebuke. Similarly we might insist that those who have no better judgment than to get in range of a precarious old structure have no one but themselves to blame if they get crushed when it collapses. This however has nothing to do with repentance as such unless it be an ex post facto regret.

[1]

And yet the emphasis of Jesus is very positive if not altogether clear from the response he made to the tragic occurrences. Here was tension of a very acute sort. We have suggested it above in the dilemma that confronted the Passover pilgrims. But was he concerned with a deeper and more elemental and perhaps more timeless tension situation? It is possible that a study of the parable that follows may expose the outlines of something of greater importance than the deaths at the altar and the tower.

And he told this parable: "A man had a fig tree planted in his vineyard; and he came seeking fruit on it and found none. And he said to the vinedresser, 'Lo, these three years I have come seeking fruit on this fig tree, and I find none. Cut it down; why should it use up the ground?' And he answered him, 'Let it alone, sir, this year also, till I dig about it and put on manure. And if it bears fruit next year, well and good; but if not, you can cut it down'" (Luke 13:1-9).

The story involves two men and a tree. Why the owner of the vineyard had planted a fig tree among his vines is no great matter. He may have had an eccentric fondness for figs, or simply liked a variety of fruits. We resist, of course, the inclination, indulged by some ancient expositors, to find a spiritual meaning in this fig-grape cohabitation. The proprietor of the place was, however, both a patient and a realistic man. Since he had been disappointed for three years in the performance of the tree he ordered his gardener to cut it down. There was no reason why the place it occupied should not nurture a more promising plant. The gardener in the story exhibits that fondness for growing things that is characteristic of those we say have a green thumb. He thought, maybe, that the tree, having symmetry and shade, had something to its credit even if it showed no fruit. In any case he seems to have accepted part of the blame for its plight. He had not tended it with sufficient care. Another year might produce fruit if the soil about the roots were properly broken

up and fertilized. It was worth a try. But the sentimental attachment of the gardener for a fig tree did not disqualify his own or
his proprietor's sense of economy. Try it another year; that was
his plan, and if it didn't show results, he (meaning the owner)
could cut it down. The pronoun may be important. It may indicate his own reluctance to cut down a living tree even if it was
barren; or it may be a deferential expression of confidence in the
owner's superior right and superior wisdom.

This is the story and it strikes us on first reading to be little
more than a common-sense tale adorned with a proper moral.
The tie-in with the foregoing events is not immediately obvious.
There the emphasis was on repentance as an escape from danger;
here the point concerns fruitfulness as an escape from death.
The relation between repentance and fruitfulness is not altogether clear and yet, upon reflection, it may appear to be both
germane and profound. Indeed, in this brief nine-verse parable
Jesus comes as near giving a meaning to history as in anything
else he is reported to have said. In general terms it may be said
to exhibit an approach that was both genetic and eschatological.
This means that there are two judgments that fall on history.
One is immanent in the processes of history itself. Growth is the
basic fact of organism; death is the suspension or cancellation of
growth—disorganization. The other is transcendent to the processes of history and becomes operative after the immanent judgment has been rendered. Here we encounter the tension man
feels because he is a creature of time.

This requires some background that may be briefly supplied.
The fondness we all feel for places where we have lived is a real
factor in the tensions arising from our relation to space. Local
pride and interurban feuds are a part of every normal, growing
social experience. It was a group of Galileans who had been
killed by Pilate. This brutal act was compounded in the minds
of Jesus' friends by the fact that many of them were Galileans.
The affront to the simple piety of Temple worshipers was ag-

gravated by the affront by association to all residents of the north-eastern corner of Palestine. The reference Jesus made to the accident in Jerusalem may have been subtly designed to point out that Galilee was suffering from no deliberate discrimination.

[2]

Now it is generally felt that the parables of the fig tree as reported in all three synoptists have reference to Israel and they have been so interpreted. It is therefore no strange thing that when Jesus spoke about the need for repentance, both in Galilee and Jerusalem, his mind should have moved into the broader perspective that included the whole land and destiny of his people. He too had a fondness for Galilee but it was not a fixation. He could not but think in terms at least as spacious as the whole land and people who, perhaps because of the need of repentance at that hour, stood in jeopardy.

It is therefore plausible to assume that this parable is an allusion to a national situation. The figures—the two men and the tree—may be taken to refer to two of the forces contending for the destiny of Israel, one demanding fruit or else——, the other seeking further reprieve with the promise of amendment. This, in a quite elemental way, is descriptive of the dynamic struggle at the center of every culture. High expectation is met by meager productiveness or complete sterility and there follows the threat of doom. Fruitlessness is the precursor of death, always and everywhere, in individual cell or social complex, yet the execution of the death sentence is always intolerable. The tolerance that life seems sometimes to show toward moribund organisms is amazing. Similarly, societies that have ceased producing the things by which they must live, stay on long beyond their expected demise. There is always the prophet or special pleader who asks for a reprieve and, within a limited historic interval, he nearly always seems to win it. But the prophet never asks for a stay of ultimate justice. If he does, he is a false prophet or a fool. Doom will finally fall but he wants it deferred in order that he may "dig about it and put on manure."

This, to one who like Jesus, seemed able to transcend measurably the space or local limits of his relation to Israel, was the way the great epic of his own people had been spelled out. Times of great planting and great hope had been followed by barrenness and despair and the word of doom had periodically thundered at them in natural portent or the word of the prophet. Exile and return, sentence and reprieve, Antiochus Epiphanes and the coming of the Son of man—these alternations must have been clear to all sensitive Israelites and were certainly agonizingly clear to the Israelite in whom there was no guile. Though he was hopeful, he was beguiled by no false hope. Faith in the ultimate victory of God beyond history stirred no blind optimistic impulses in his heart. "If it bears fruit next year, well and good; but if not, *you* can cut it down." Here the force of the pronoun is evident. It was not the vinedresser who would execute justice, it was the owner of the vineyard. Some such background must have given sharp point to the parable when it was first spoken, though we may properly wonder whether the first hearers understood it or accepted its meaning any more readily than the centuries that have been hearing it told since then.

The matter of repentance, which represents the tie-in between the altar and tower stories and the parable, needs further clarification. What does repentance have to do with the processes of history? John the Baptist demanded reformation of life and society and asked for fruit mete for repentance. In the Jordan valley repentance was to be followed by fruit. John used also the imagery of our parable as he warned that the ax was already laid at the root of the tree. They called John a demon and the Son of man a drunkard yet wisdom was justified by all her children (cf. Luke 7:33-35). The impenitent and the unproductive still think they can deactivate the dynamics of history or deflect the judgment of God by abusing the prophet as a devil or a degenerate. This has always been pride's way of evading the ancient demand for repentance and fruit mete for the same. The relation therefore between Jesus' admonition to the frightened and puzzled Galileans and the parable should be clear: death is the nemesis of fruitlessness; repentance is the prerequisite of spiritual productivity.

If we are right in saying that Jesus in this parable comes nearer than anywhere else to an adumbration of a Christian meaning of history, our first point is that while productivity is the intention of history or of man and society in history, this cannot come about without a preliminary dealing with the problem of sin in the act of repentance.

The second point deals with the relation of fruit to history. Fruit is both the criterion of value and the defense against death. Certainly within history there is no such thing as agelessness and yet, on principle, we have no reason for assuming that a fructiculose culture can or will die. The plea of the gardener was only for time in which fruit could be induced by diligent husbandry. He was content to see death supervene if life was forfeited by fruitlessness.

[3]

In this parable then we see emerging this second factor in the historic process. Fruit is made possible in moribund fig trees by a radical treatment. Here the word radical means exactly what it originally did. The tree was not to be trimmed; its roots were to be dug about. Such vitality as was left was to be exposed and to it was to be added the nutriment the soil lacked, ". . . dig about it and put on manure." In other words, there is in history always the contest between the radicalism that will dig in order to encourage fruit and the conservatism that will exhaust itself simply in hoping that fruit will appear. This latter is a form of impenitence. Since it will not repent it can neither bear fruit nor endure seeing others digging about the roots. Very often this "radicalism" is denounced by them as impiety. This is the most odious sort of pride since it equates its conservatism—or futile and inactive hope—with piety. It is God's tree; if it bears no fruit, that is His concern and not ours. Diggers and manure spreaders are messy and unpleasant people and most of the time are interfering in matters that are none of their business.

The evidence that Jesus encountered this tension between radicalism and inactivity is almost too obvious to delay us. It was what set him over against the Pharisee and the ruler. It greeted him in the bill of indictment before the high priest. This radical was going to destroy the temple, they charged. Destroying the temple is as good a metaphor for radical action as digging about the roots so long as the purpose was "restoring it" in one case as it was encouraging fruit bearing in the other.

It is at this point that the genetic symbol of fruit has special interest for the understanding of the historic process. Fruit provides at once both the utility of the tree for human sustenance and the continuity of the genus in the fertilization and nurture of the seed. It is to be expected that Jesus would see the fig tree as having been planted by a specific act. Whatever the reason for it, the owner had it put in the vineyard. There must be some purpose in history but it cannot become operative without the processes immanent in experience within history. To use the parable's idiom: the owner could not have had figs without a fig tree the function of which was the production of this specific variety of fruit. Or to put it more simply: the business of fig trees is bearing fruit and the energy of production is growth.

But not growth alone. The fig tree could grow without producing fruit and thus falsify the meaning of its life as a fruit tree. When its immanent powers faltered or were prostituted, what might be called a genetic judgment had already been passed upon itself. That would be judgment enough, perhaps. Surely

a fig tree that is figless is only a tree, no matter how it may be
still classified by the horticulturalist. But there follows what is
properly called the transcendent judgment by the owner, who
in the interests of the economy of space orders it cut down and
replaced by a fruit producer. This is no arbitrary or angry judgment; it is the contingency that awaits every genetic judgment.
A tree blossoms, is fertilized, grows, matures its fruit, which is
gathered or drops to the ground to make a new tree. This is what
we call the natural process. So, in our parable, a nation goes
through what is called the historic process, paralleling the natural cycle of the fruit tree. When the natural process is diverted
or denied, the fruit that is the nexus between the generations of
growing trees disappears and the tree (or generation) dies. After
that it is cut down while still living impotently, or its lifeless
stump stands in mute and unprotesting witness to the judgment
that has been laid against it. The failure of the impotent tree is
not followed by a universal debacle. Its own life is forfeit—and
no more. Again using our parable as our guide we may say that
the idea of a general *eschaton* or judgment against all trees at a
specified time and for a just, though inscrutable purpose, offends our sense of common justice. "If *it* bears fruit next year,
well and *good;* but if not, you can cut *it* down." After the genetic
judgment the transcendent, but never universal.

[4]

We must be careful that we do not establish too exact an
analogy between nature and history. Nature has one direction;
an organism grows, matures, and dies. Once set on its course,
death, however infinitely deferred by our limited schedules
(some organisms alive today have direct genetic continuity of
millions of years), is inevitable. History is multilinear and indeterminate. This is why man can subvert it by sin or sublimate
it by repentance, and it is in the decisions men make that man's

historic, not natural, destiny lies. At the same time, however, God is transcendent to these processes of nature and history. No event, therefore, is merely natural or historical. There is no judgment in history or nature which is wholly in its own right an immanent judgment. So, a fig tree—to use our present symbolism—which is barren will, in due course, die, as will also one that bears fruit. This is a kind of "judgment" imposed by the laws of *natural* genesis and death. But a fig tree which is cut down is subject to a *historical* judgment which means that the owner may destroy it or not; the gardener may seek a stay of execution or not. In other words, the act of the will as it impinges on nature is possible in indeterminate history as it is not in determinate nature. The judgment of the owner of this fig tree was therefore as much on the gardener as on the barren tree.

This understanding of the parable is not explicit in its brief and simple words and we are far from saying that Jesus was consciously aware of the subtleties and overtones of the little story. But that what has been said was implicit in the scene upon which he looked is not to be gainsaid. We have, moreover, every right to assume that he looked more profoundly into the historic situation of which his generation was a part than those with whom he shared so simply his immensely pregnant insights. History turned out to be on his side. When Titus put Jerusalem to the torch in A.D. 70, Jewry was already a spiritually barren tree. The genetic judgment had been rendered; Titus simply spelled out in a historic act what immanent processes had already wrought.

This understanding of Jesus' interpretation of history—to give it a somewhat prestigious title—is what Toynbee has proposed in one of his most engaging observations in *A Study of History*. A society is already in an advanced state of disintegration when its creative minority has become merely a dominant minority. The former is that small nucleus in every group that blossoms, fertilizes, fructifies, and provides the continuity of vitality. When it ceases to bear fruit, or when its creative impulse

and energies languish, it becomes the latter. Jealous of its former status as creator it seeks arbitrarily to maintain that status
though it is no longer creative. Creativity which has a genuine
right to dominance gives way to the sheer exercise of power which
may have no rights at all.

When Athens, after a period of great creative activity, saw
her strength being dissipated in wars, the aim of which was to
extend her holdings and thus augment her diminishing supplies
of foodstuffs, she turned to the creative development of the olive
oil industry and eventually found herself developing a mercan-
tile culture which saved or at least reprieved her life. Sparta died
because she could make no such accommodation to changing
situations, and because she had ceased to bear fruit. She was cut
down, Athens acting as the agent, at fatal cost to herself. This
is only one of the multitude of illustrations of this historic process adduced by Professor Toynbee in support of his thesis. He
therefore deduces the general proposition that civilizations (or
societies) are not killed; they commit suicide. This is only another way of saying that fig trees are not cut down until they
have proved themselves impotent. When Jesus said that vultures
gather where there is a dead body was he not also saying that
carrion birds do not kill; they spiral down to their meal after
the victim has already died from other causes.

[5]

It is a simple transition that brings us from the parable and
its deep-level understanding of history and judgment to the
times in which we live. Modern efforts to find meaning to history
have engendered what is thought in certain secularist groups to
be undue pessimism. It is un-American they say, to set our contemporary scene within the perspectives of a long view of history.
We have no dearth of those who on the one hand say everything
is lovely or on the other ask for a reprieve. There are some who,

convinced on solid grounds of the basic soundness of our culture (our fig tree) are unready to view its current fruitlessness as irremediable. They ask for a reprieve in order that radical measures may be employed to restore fruit to barren branches. They encounter two difficulties: they think that all that is needed to enrich the soil about our roots is an undiluted confidence in human nature and in the mechanical toys our ingenuity has produced. These are the "higher standard of living" enthusiasts, who see in the lifting of the material level of life here and around the world a rejuvenation of our industry and guarantee of our ultimate security. There is no harm in this in so far as it is not proposed and accepted as a panacea for the sickness of our times. Their second difficulty is the frustration that overwhelms them every time the economy is momentarily depressed.

To those who more realistically understand the illness of our civilization to be primarily spiritual, there are also lions in the way. The radical nature of our crisis, or our critical illness, demands radical methods for diagnosis and cure. Of all forms of radicalism, spiritual radicalism is the most suspect. There was bewilderment when Einstein radically revised Newtonian physics but no one got angry about it nor was he suspected of sinister designs on the universe. But in the area we describe as spiritual, which means broadly that which is not physical, the radical is a dangerous person. This is true in politics and economics, which are, in a deep sense, spiritual matters. In the specifically religious field he is doubly suspect since he is thought both to be tampering with man's soul by asking him questions and to be meddling with God's plans by examining them. It provides a bit of comfort that our parable represents the owner of the vineyard as agreeable to the root-digging the gardener advised. We could wish sometimes that those who have subleased the vineyard were as tolerant.

The religious component of our culture cannot escape radical criticism. It is not welcomed either in Protestantism, which had its historic origin in radical root-digging, or in Roman Catholicism, where the roots are protected by an infallible husbandman who is alleged to know—without looking—what the trouble is and have all the remedies for spiritual infertility. We have no difficulty in seeing that in the areas of life we call by the much abused and misunderstood word "secularism," our culture has ceased being creative. For most of our century the creative genius of the West has been concentrated on what are ultimately instruments of destruction. There are derivative civilian benefits from research in medicine and mechanics and nuclear physics, but they would not have come about had not we bent our wealth and brains to the primary task of being physically powerful against enemies, real and potential. To criticize this fact radically, to call men to look at the roots of nationalism, militarism, and monopoly capitalism to see whether they are viable in terms of their bearing anything but the Dead Sea fruit of suspicion and possible world destruction, is an unpleasant task and invites unpleasant consequences. But to keep silence, even though our concern be no more elevated than mere physical survival is to turn affairs over to those who, no longer creative in terms of fruit that is nourishing and capable of sustaining and passing on the seminal genius of our culture, are merely dominant in terms of residual physical power. Professor Toynbee has cited chapter and verse in his warning against allowing that to happen.

That our spiritual situation is under a dominant minority instead of a creative minority can be endlessly argued and will not be attempted here. It is enough to indicate that the history of Christendom does show great creative periods, times of prodigious fruit-bearing in terms of the things that nurtured and fertilized all life, personal and social, and even created new patterns for the ordering of groups as large even as nations. This is a familiar story. Equally familiar is the fact that there was always radicalism at the point of origin, though this is less generously conceded. We want creativity, but we hope to get it without radicalism. We want our fig trees to bear fruit, but we think that digging about the roots (radix) is strenuous to the point of endangering the tree. Still the word of the parable comes to us: radicate or eradicate.

Living within history creates the tensions involved in time and space limitations. There are ways of escaping it: that of the hermit or the suicide for those who take matters into their own hands; that of the bloody altar and the tottering tower for those whose piety is fierce or whose aimlessness is blind. Such folk, following our story, are perhaps originally no more wicked than their fellows and ultimately no less tense than we. We have tried to point out that Jesus, reaching down to deeper levels of thought, sees the connection between repentance (a change of mind) and the redemptive processes of human life in history. These redemptive processes are immanent in life; they are the ability to bear fruit and thus continue history, but they do not operate without repentance. But it is repentance plus: the plus is the understanding of the summary judgment of nature if fruit-bearing languishes and the ultimate judgment of the owner if fruit-bearing fails. To avert the former, radical digging and the application of proper nutrients are necessary, but if these fail, nothing will avert the latter. "If it bears fruit, well and good; but if not, you can cut it down."

One wonders what fancy can, with propriety, make of the undisclosed denouement of this parable. It is ingratiating to imagine that the diligence of the gardener (which we might properly call faith) was rewarded with a bumper crop of figs. Sometimes things like that do happen and this allows us a discreet and sober optimism about what may go on in the world. And when it does, the owner must relax and the gardener feel himself momentarily free from anxiety once more. The tree? It never was more lovely to look at or more promising.

CHAPTER V

The Narrow Door

THERE are two minuscule allegories that occur in verses 18 to 21 of the 13th chapter which repeat two of Matthew's sententious parables. They refer to the Kingdom of God as a grain of mustard seed and as leaven. In this respect they are similes rather than parables. They also deal with things instead of people. More properly perhaps their central reference is to process. Since they are not characteristic of the Lukan method of treatment we shall not make a detailed study of them. At the same time it is useful to indicate that they do represent an important factor in the thought of Jesus.

The last chapter has dealt with an understanding of history in both genetic and eschatological terms. History is a process (*saeculum*) which can be correctly understood as growth. If the liberal optimism of the last century misunderstood this to mean that it was ageless growth, we must not for that reason overlook the fact that immanent in the historic process there is the dynamism of progress or, to satisfy the less sanguine, of growth. Growth might conceivably be in a direction away from progress but it would take a somewhat perverse pessimism to see it that way.

These two similes are references to the dynamism immanent in the order of the Kingdom within the historic context. What it is that makes a seed grow comprises the fascinating mystery of life. The invisible energy that stirs within and breaks open the spore case and finally produces a tree contains in miniature a paradigm of history. Few things are more mysterious or exciting. Similarly the action of a yeast cell. It grows by fission within its host, develops or increases by the mysterious energy it contains and proceeds until its ferment has pervaded everywhere— as Luke and Matthew put it, "till it was all leavened." Again the energy is immanent and not transitive. Thus far liberal optimism was right. It would have been mistaken in saying that there was no life cycle in a mustard tree which could run out; or that there was no limit to which the yeasty ferment could not go. There are other elements in the process of history, whether . of the Kingdom of God or the kingdoms of this world, that debilitate its dynamism and incur the judgment of God. At the same time we must not overlook the clear fact that in the mind of Jesus there was that dynamic factor in the historic process. Leaven has been used by some interpreters to mean the dynamism of evil in the world. There is no objection to this concept except as it is used to explain the explicit words of Jesus. These two similes—seed and leaven—are clearly a pair with a single identical emphasis. Unless the tree is an evil growth, it is difficult to see how the leaven can be taken to be an evil energy.

The record which follows these brief verses presents Jesus and his crowd moving in a leisurely fashion, from town to village, on their way to Jerusalem. There must have been something, either in the gaiety or the sobriety of the crowd—it could easily have been either mood—that inspired a question. "Some one said to him, 'Lord, will those who are saved be few?'" Jesus' reply takes the parabolic form though it is not called a parable. This question is one that grows out of a sense of personal deficit or danger, and out of a sense of group insecurity. It is therefore both an individual and a class question.

And he said to them, "Strive to enter by the narrow door; for many, I tell you, will seek to enter and will not be able. When once the householder has risen up and shut the door, you will begin to stand outside and knock at the door saying, 'Lord open to us.' He will answer you, 'I do not know where you come from.' Then you will begin to say, 'We ate and drank in your presence, and you taught in our streets.' But he will say, 'I tell you, I do not know where you come from; depart from me, all you workers of iniquity!' There you will weep and gnash your teeth, when you see Abraham, Isaac and Jacob and all the prophets in the kingdom of God and you yourselves thrust out. And men will come from east and west, and from north and south, and sit at table in the kingdom of God. And behold, some are last who will be first, and some are first who will be last" (Luke 13:23-30).

[1]

The question which introduced the parable is basic to human experience on almost every level. After a manner of speaking all human experience is the business of being saved. We are born that we may be saved from suffocation in the womb; we die that we may be saved from intolerable physical and mental senile disintegration; we eat to save us from starving and bant to save us from obesity. Thus education, work, and play; and hospitals, banks and churches are components in a vast soteriological enterprise. Peace saves us from war and war saves us from peace and diplomacy saves us from both. So goes the endless rune.

This is not frivolous; nothing is more serious than the saving process and few things exercise one's concern so deeply and so relentlessly as the question, "Am I saved?" It is basically the question of security, a matter that touches both the minutiae and the profundities of mortal life. It will be seen from this to be one of the major tension situations in which every man is caught. The tug between security and insecurity, between being saved and lost is of the essence of life. This means, of course, that it can never be wholly resolved within the context that produces it. Hence the beatific vision of an eternity in which "all sorrow and sighing shall flee away." At the same time it can be creatively employed. While the perfect security of the rich fool brought its dire consequences, and the complete insecurity of his opposite would be equally dire, there is a point at which the tension between the extremes can be made to yield something better than complacency on the one hand or despair on the other.

It would be interesting to know who put this question to Jesus, and what lay behind it. The popularity of the Galilean was momentarily resurgent. This had created opposite reactions. The dispossessed, whose hope of salvation had been crushed or vaguely sublimated, might have seen in his concern for the multitudes an augury of better days. Incredulous but daring, they might have defied the current notion of their hopelessness to ask whether, after all, the idea that salvation was the perquisite of an elite few was really true. Social revolution has turned on that pivot before, indeed it is turning today among those who have come to realize that salvation—using the word in its full connotations—is the right, if not indeed the destiny, of every man.

Of course the question might have been put, not by those who hoped that salvation was for the many, but by those who feared it might be. Nothing so easily disturbs the sense of security among the elite as the realization that security is the right of all. Paradoxically those often feel least secure who realize that security belongs by right to all. This is one of the quaint perversities of pride: it actually persuades itself that it is best for all that only a few be saved. This is a repetition of the idea expressed in the previous chapter that the best way to guarantee a solvent economic order is for an elite to possess its wealth and to distribute it judiciously to the lesser breed. "Let it trickle down," some put it.

It is our surmise that this question emanated from those who feared that salvation was for all rather than from those who feared it wasn't. The reply seems to point in that direction. The first comment of Jesus lifted the whole question out of the area of the factitious or arbitrary and put it solidly down in the area of experience. Salvation was not a matter of few or many, of privilege or discrimination, but of striving. "Strive to enter in by the narrow door." Whatever one means by salvation, it is an enclosure, not an open field. One enters it by a door, one does not ramble over it. And the door is narrow, not to debar, but because salvation of every sort is restricted to those who meet its demands. It is open to all, but not entered by all. Many will seek to enter and not be able, but the narrow door will not be what excludes them; they will exclude themselves.

[2]

This recalls to us the point previously made to the effect that immanent in human life and its initiative are saving forces. Man is not condemned by his nature or by the historic process to miss the narrow door. For any number of reasons he may refuse to "strive to enter." Perhaps the most conspicuous reason is that he feels he is already in or can take care of himself on the outside. Nevertheless the door is still there for those who strive to enter.

On the other hand, we are also reminded that as the vital properties in the fig tree do not guarantee its fruitfulness, so also does a judgment supervene when fruit is forfeited. In the former parable the figure was an ax cutting down a tree; in this story it is a householder shutting the door. This is the judgment of God, but it comes only after barrenness is final and after striving has ceased.

The panic of those who face ultimate insecurity, which may be only another way of saying damnation, of whatever sort— and we must be careful not to shrink the word salvation to fit our limited understanding of it—this panic of the unsaved is observed as the story moves along. There is noisy knocking at the closed door and a voice, at first touched by surprise that the door should have been closed against them, and then by confidence that it will be opened to them. The answer of the house-holder is devastating: the worst thing that can be said to the elite is that they are unknown. Next to that, the worst thing is to tell them that one somehow fails to remember where they came from, for one's pride in one's place is secondary only to one's pride in one's self.

We come now upon one of the most discerning of comments about those who have believed that because they are what they are, all doors are open to their knocking whether or not they have striven to enter. The knock, to them, is the measure of their total efforts to get in. They make themselves out to be the patrons of the strivers and assume that this bland patronage of the striving of others to win salvation is entitled to the same reward.

Consider: It was something conspicuously virtuous to the patricians to consent to eat and drink in the presence of the salvation strivers. They overlook, for the moment, the insult implied in the householder's response to their knock. Wounded in their pride, they whimper their credentials. It is an old device of the prideful spirit, of the condescending. We, they say, are tolerant people. Tolerance is the gratuity the proud toss to the under-privileged. We did not follow, they went on to say, the unreasonable taboo about eating with the vulgar rabble. Eating is an amenity which determines social stratifications, to be sure. But we felt it important to defy occasionally these restrictions on free social intercourse. Society should, well, be fluid, somewhat. So when one judiciously steps over the barriers and sits by those who may be flattered by one's generosity and elevated by one's gentility, is there not virtue in the act? To be sure we did not invite you as guests into our homes. ("We ate and drank in your presence," not you in ours.) That would clearly be going too far at this time. But taking everything into consideration we feel that we not only jeopardized our security but offered the strivers a sense of security by holding lightly what is to many an important rule of etiquette.

This was the first item of credit offered by the disappointed and the damned. It was not all, by any means. They had deliberately gone beyond the breaking of a taboo; they had risked the aristocrat's chief guarantee of his security: they conceded the right of free speech to those they despised and feared. "You taught in our streets." This jeopardizes the inherent "right" of the privileged to censor the utterances of the vulgar, the contentious, the ambitious. Particularly in the light of the fact that this so-called prophet had preached dangerous nonsense about the gate of salvation being open to all who strove to enter in, their concession was generous to the point of being prodigal. This had caused raised eyebrows and table-drumming. Such preaching and our attention to it sows discontent among those who have hitherto been satisfied with the lot God has assigned to them. We are frankly not pleased, nor are we sure that truth will prevail by such lenience with error. Nevertheless we have not taken counsel of our fears. Despite warnings, we gave you the forum to present your ideas. That they were both perverse and dangerous is now clearly proved by the way in which you have shut the door in our faces. Think for a moment, they might have truculently added, what would have happened to you if we had slammed the gates of our town in *your* face!

The report indicates that the householder behind the door was unrelenting. Their tolerance in the matter of eating and their condescension toward the preacher of "equal reward for equal striving," were unimpressive. He says, with an emphasis they cannot miss: "I tell you, I do not know where you come from." Somehow he has forgotten the experience when he was formally presented to these elegant folk who thought that slumming was a benefaction and free speech the final achievement of forebearance. But more than this: he dismissed them, ordered them away from the door and settled the matter with a stinging indictment. "Depart from me, all you workers of iniquity." This, we are reminded, is the transcendent judgment that is imposed after man has given up his own efforts to enter the door of salvation.

[3]

Was not this too much? One may call condescension odious and patronage offensive, but to call the practitioners of these dubious arts evildoers seems too severe. Call them mistaken, call them stupid, call them pitiful, but why call them evil? It is just at this point that the insight of our Lord plunges into depths of understanding that we have not yet been willing to accept. The attitude of these who believe salvation to be a special privilege, the result of the fortuitous accident of race, status, or endowment is not only *mistaken,* it is *evil.* It has been easy to get on with it so long as it has been thought to be nothing more dangerous than an error. Now that it can be seen as an evil so malevolent that it can plunge a world into war, it must be dealt with for what it is. For fascism is the modern dress that privilege wears, and its instruments are those that help preserve a status that will protect it. Not always tolerance, to be sure, but *always* tolerance if that serves its selfish ends. Not always free speech, but *always* free speech if its opposite threatens the status of the censors. Let us suggest two reasons why the credits offered to satisfy entrance requirements at the narrow gate were disallowed. Why, in other words, those who offered them, were evildoers.

In the first place they were evildoers in what they did to themselves. It is not seldom that attitudes and practices we accept with the best intentions corrupt our souls with evil. Why this is so could take us, if we allowed it, all the way back to a discussion of the nature of evil. We have more immediate and practical interests here, and they can be put in a fairly simple proposition. The error in the attitude of patronage or condescension lies in its negativism. It allows us to think that to do nothing to disparage the "lesser folk" is a sure way to applaud them; to make them the beneficiaries of our generosity is the way to fulfill their highest destiny. This is an error; nothing is more clearly documented today than the fact that such a spirit, however acceptable in the past, is repudiated today. Thus people who, in their understanding of life, have consented to this error, have done evil to themselves. Without realizing it perhaps, they have paralyzed the impulses of human brotherhood; they have substituted for positive action the luxury of pride; they have said to themselves that since God is partial to them it is not asking too much of them to be kind to those He has dispossessed. When one has allowed such a mood to possess his soul, he has done an evil thing to himself. The mistake has subtly turned into a poison that ministers on the one hand to his pride in himself and his crowd, and on the other hand to contempt for others. This is evil, gross, palpable, destructive.

Yes, it is not only an error, an error that mistakes inaction for creative good; it is an evil. These people were called by our Lord evildoers, not ignoramuses. The mistaken mind becomes the cruel heart, and class distinctions, invidious and disruptive, are forthwith supported by prejudices that lie deeper than the surface of our thoughts.

In the second place, they are evildoers because of what they do to others. Perhaps if the privileged could isolate themselves, as they seek in some ways to do, we could let them alone. They are willing to run with their set, and to keep others in their place. Why not let them? Time was when such was the pattern of society. One born to the purple wore it; one born to rags aspired to nothing better. But that world is now done for, at least within that area we call the West; and what is happening to us will affect the rest of humanity sooner than we think. The smugness and pride that we have exhibited has injured our souls and we need cleansing, but it has roused anger and bitterness in the souls of others, and that means revolution! Listen: "And men will come from east and west, and from north and south, and sit at table in the kingdom of God. And behold *some are last who will be first, and some are first who will be last.*" That is the formula of revolution.

Revolution of the sort that was let loose in Russia in 1917 was against the evildoers who thought patronage and condescension were the way to keep the people immured in the degradation to which centuries had consigned them. Whatever may be said about the ultimate good that violent revolution has achieved, bloody revolution is a hideous and evil thing. However it may be argued that at times revolution is the only expedient of the disinherited, revolution is still a ghastly instrument of social change to be avoided as much for the havoc it works among those who invoke it as for the moral obliquity into which it plunges all those who are involved. This is no place to analyze the techniques of radical change by peaceful methods; democracy rests on presuppositions that should make violent revolution unnecessary. It is to point out first that the error and the evil of the privileged in our story were the prelude to their expulsion from the Kingdom of God, and second that there is nothing in the story that implies that violent revolution is the method of their banishment.

[4]

Here is something for modern Christendom to ponder. In the political field, revolution both violent and orderly is in the making and we shall see much of its excesses and achievements in the next century. But revolution—or if a more gentle word be preferred—change must come in the heart of the Christian community. Recall that Jesus was talking to respectable people, people of culture and substance, people who crowned their "evildoing" with a nimbus of sincere, if half suspicious, faith. It was shocking to be told they were shut out of the banquet, the banquet that was being prepared for them, prepared for those who were accustomed to napery and a row of forks. It was preposterous that welcome should be offered those who might fumble with the accouterments of gentility.

Nor is such a mood alien to much of our respectable Christian fellowship, and consequently it is shocking to be reminded of it. It is not so much the ill-mannered antics of avowed anti-Semitic and anti-Negro and antidemocratic groups that imperil us. We can deal with them overtly. We know almost nothing of such folk within the churches. But there is a genteel anti-Semitism, a respectable white racialism that rarely rebukes itself because it thinks it is at most conventional and at least tacitly supported by ideas that have been thought to be Christian dogma.

Are we willing to go beyond eating and drinking with those whom taboo has relegated to segregation? Dares the Church repudiate the easy tolerance that Jesus excoriated as evil? Do we think it is enough to be "liberal" in the allowances we grant to those who differ with us? Is free speech enough? Politically that may be as far as we can go, but even then it is no end in itself but a trusted device for achieving a truer democracy. How far has the tolerance of our upper middle-class churches, a tolerance that prides itself on allowing its minister to speak boldly and withholds its discreet judgment that he is something of a crackpot—how far has this "evil thing" corrupted vigorous church action?

These are questions that cannot be answered here, but the mind of the Church must address itself to them. For here is a quality of evil that is widespread, subtle, and vitiating. And unless we accept the searching insight of One who twenty centuries ago put His probing finger on the tender spot that indicated dangerous corruption, we may find ourselves shut out of the banquet that is, even now, being thronged by those who come from the areas where hitherto we have thought the elite did not exist!

The sense of tension in this story is acute. The universal sense

of the need for salvation is compounded among the "few" by
the sense of frustration that follows their pretentious and unrewarded attempts at goodness. Once the doom has been pronounced they are vividly presented in an agony of desperation,
not alone because of their exclusion but because of the ultimate
insult to their pride in the spectacle of heroes and prophets *and*
alien folk from the four corners of the earth, sitting down at the
table. One may imagine that had they stopped weeping and
gnashing their teeth for a moment they would most certainly
have said: "So he didn't know where we come from? We wonder
if he knows where this striving rabble comes from!"

[5]

There is a further tension stress indicated here but since it
will be discussed elsewhere it need only be pointed out. Class
tension is the source of revolution. The Marxist heaven is a
classless society to be achieved by revolution that reduces all to
the dead proletarian level. This is one way of abating class tension but we foresee that it will be costly in the beginning and
futile in the end. Such tension as exists between classes is inescapable within a historic context which makes classes inevitable.
This is not to say that class tensions are ineradicable. It is to say,
from the Christian perspective as distinguished from the Marxist, that they may exist and serve creatively the wholesome development of society. Class tension does not, *ipso facto,* have to
be destructive. "And behold, some are last who will be first, and
some are first who will be last." This is very different from saying
behold, there will be no first or last—which is the Marxist dogma.
The question for the Christian conscience to face is: How can
class tension be sublimated in creative living? This is as stubborn
a question as can be asked. The effort to answer it is, indeed, the
very essence of the striving by which the narrow gate will be
entered.

What did his generation do? It is not a pleasant thing to remember, but our episode supplies it. Some Pharisees warned him, so the story goes, that he had better get out of the neighborhood; Herod was unpredictable! "Get out of here," they said in effect, "get out of here and keep going." An old trick. It was not Herod he had spoken against; his quarrel with officialdom was over other matters. But it is always easy to warn those who point out our sins to us that if they are not careful some Herod —he may be a deacon, an industrialist, a Legionnaire or an ecclesiastic!—will make trouble for us.

What did Jesus do? "Go," said he, "and take this message to that fox: See, today and tomorrow I drive out demons and effect cures . . . yet I must continue my journey today and tomorrow, and the day following. . . ."

It is a tribute to the vitality of the Christian testimony that though it has faltered, been falsified and smothered, been caricatured and condemned, it still has the power today to "cast out demons" and to "effect cures." What is needed is more disciples who will walk with him *today*. Others will walk with him tomorrow, and others the day following. Our only chance is to walk with him now. His is still the narrow way and it still invites all who choose it and strive earnestly upon it to move toward the narrow gate. Those who will enter it have no credential but their courage and no merit but their devotion.

CHAPTER VI

The Man Who Came to Dinner

WAS it lawful to heal on the Sabbath, or not? It should
have been easy to get an answer to that question from
a lawyer. In the circumstances which invited the
question the answer should not only have been positive, it should
have been ready. Clearly this unusual dinner party was something more than a social occasion. It almost appears to have been
a ruse. The host was a ruler and a Pharisee; the former title indicates that he had certain responsibilities for preserving order.
It is unimportant what they were. The latter designation identifies him with a class who were bound by a sense of responsibility
for a culture. The chances are he was first a Pharisee and second
a ruler, by which we mean that the preservation of a culture was
his primary concern; his official job provided him one of the
ways by which he could exercise his cultural influence.

That Jesus should have been invited to such a gathering is in
itself somewhat puzzling. By this time he had achieved a reputation of being something of a problem to those who were responsible for civil order and the culture of Israel. Not that he
was disorderly although on one occasion he had been disdainfully called a glutton and a drunkard (Luke 7:33). Perhaps it
was his influence on the crowds who thronged him, and since a
crowd is always a threat to civil order, he was, in a way, a threat
to peace. Nor had he set out to destroy the cultural pattern of

83

his people. He was anything but a boor. And yet it had been observed (cf. Luke 11:38) on a former occasion that he had accepted an invitation to dine with a Pharisee and had caused no little astonishment by failing to wash before dinner. This indicated no indifference to personal hygiene; it was disregard or defiance of ceremonial, and it was largely through the maintenance of ceremony and amenity that the culture of his people, already effete within the "barbarian" culture of Rome, was trying to preserve itself.

One Sabbath when he went to dine at the house of a ruler who belonged to the Pharisees, they were watching him. And behold, there was a man before him who had dropsy. And Jesus spoke to the lawyers and Pharisees, saying, "Is it lawful to heal on the sabbath, or not?" But they were silent. Then he took him and healed him, and let him go. And he said to them, "Which of you, having an ass or an ox that has fallen into a well, will not immediately pull him out on a sabbath day?" And they could not reply to this (Luke 14:1-6).

[1]

We have here a clear picture of the unresolved struggle between legalism and normal human impulses. The humane feelings that make possible the organization and maintenance of the human community tend to be suppressed sooner or later by the legal structure that the community erects. There is a general uniformity in human reactions to the circumstances of life but there is also sufficient variety of reaction to make necessary the establishment of normative patterns lest the community be eroded by outer influences or crumble by lack of inner cohesion. The silence of the legalists in this story was due to no lack of knowledge of the law. The answer to the question about the legality of healing on the Sabbath was clearly "No." It was illegal. Similarly the propriety, indeed the clear duty, of relieving an animal that was in distress on the sabbath, was manifest even though disallowed by the law. The silence that met Jesus' two questions was due either to the artifice by which they sought to trap him, or to the struggle in their minds between humaneness and legalism. In this instance legalism won, for their refusal to vote for the healing of the dropsical man or for the rescue of the hypothetical ox amounted to a vote against them.

This tension exists in all organized societies. It cannot safely be resolved either in the direction of pure sentimentalism on the one hand or by excessive legalism on the other. Humane sentiments are the creative basis of community, a profuse or Draconian code of law is the sterilization of community. This is what Jefferson meant when he said that that government is best which governs least. It was necessary on another occasion for Jesus to explain that his interest in reference to the established law was not its destruction but its fulfillment. The traditions of the elders which had achieved the sanctity of law were suffocating the humane sentiment without which law easily becomes tyranny. The originality of Jesus was rooted in that universal sentiment for one's brother man that made fresh growth in orderly society possible. It is this that was the ground of difference between Jesus and his host and the other guests at this dinner. There is little wonder that they were watching him; that they were silent when he asked the first question on a point of law and could not reply when his second question raised the issue of the correct humane attitude toward a beast.

[2]

They were watching him, the story goes. But the next paragraph, in which the parable appears, indicates that he was doing some looking about on his own.

Now he told a parable to those who were invited, when he marked how they chose the places of honor, saying to them, "When you are invited by any one to a marriage feast, do not sit down in a place of honor, lest a more eminent man than you be invited by him; and he who invited you both will come and say to you, 'Give place to this man,' and then you will begin with shame to take the lowest place. But when you are invited, go and sit in the lowest place, so that when your host comes he may say to you, 'Friend, go up higher'; then you will be honored in the presence of all who sit at table with you. For everyone who exalts himself will be humbled, and he who humbles himself will be exalted" (Luke 14:7-11).

If it were not for the profound generalization with which this parable ends it might be regarded as little more than a bit of friendly advice on etiquette. The matter that had just engaged them dealt with the relation of law to culture. Here we seem to be concerned with the relation of culture to amenity. There is a relation, and it is important. Amenity is to culture as characteristic is to character. One does not exist without the other. For this reason they are often thought to be identical. Hence one who never offends the *ipse dixit* of Emily Post in our times passes for a cultured person when, as a matter of fact, he can very well be a lacquered boor. He may take a high polish and be rotten underneath.

A more careful look at this parable will, however, disclose something more important than a lesson in good manners for wedding guests. Had it been no more important than that there might be good reason for thinking that Jesus, himself a guest, was showing bad manners by openly rebuking his fellow guests for their efforts to seat themselves in the places of honor. Surely protocol here would have demanded that any necessary rebuke should have been administered by the host. It is just because the matter was symptomatic, not of bad manners but of bad morals, that the comments of Jesus were not impertinent. On the contrary, they were extremely pertinent.

The story is not without its overtones of whimsicality. The sight of a pompous person, fastidiously clad in his most impres-

sive wedding garments, stopping at the door for a hasty performance of the ceremonial foot bath, keeping an eye cocked the
while in the direction of another arrival who, by skimping the
ablution might move in ahead of him, and finally, the minimum
ceremony duly done, scrouging past more leisurely guests and
plumping his resplendent bulk into the seat of honor—this is
amusing to those who have an eye for the extravagances of the
proud. We may find malicious delight in what follows. The host,
with no pretense at civility, orders him curtly: "Give place to
this man," and offers the seat of distinction to one who looks
quite undistinguished, one who, indeed, protests modestly of
his unworthiness to be so honored. Thereupon the crestfallen
self-appointed honoree begins "with shame to take the lowest
place," and there is a hint that the process was both slow and
painful and infinitely humiliating. The suggestion follows that
a reversal of the process would have brought more pleasing results to this gaudy man who hungered and thirsted after recognition. We must not allow the notion that Jesus was encouraging
a disingenuous humility in order to win the place of honor. He
was stating a common-sense fact. The pompous gentleman would
have given himself away quite as quickly, sitting in mock modesty in the lowest seat, fidgety with fear lest the host not see him,
as he did when he shoved his way rudely to the head of the table.

The amusing aspects of the story must not preoccupy a more
serious understanding of what was being described, for here is
one of the common life situations in which tension is all but
universally present. We say almost, because there have been
saints who have apparently divested themselves completely of
the wedding garment mentality and the seat-of-honor desire. But
there is a tension situation that has its origin in something proud
(and this time we use "proud" without any invidious meaning)
in the human spirit: the wish to improve one's self.

[3]

If one wished to establish by the canons of natural science the one datum that clearly sets man in a category distinct from his humbler cogeners, it would be the innate urge to self-advancement. It has been advanced as the basis for a universal morality, since anthropologists, psychologists, and sociologists agree that in this faculty for self-improvement and in its exercise lies the basis of moral and social organization. It reduces morals to a simple mechanism: that which improves the individual is good. Extended to society it substitutes the group for the individual and regards that which improves society as the good. There is much to be said for this though no one who advances it is naïve enough to think that simply to state the fact clarifies all the questions arising out of the operation of the factor in the individual and the group. The fact as it stands, however, is definitive. Those to whom a naturalistic approach is inconclusive feel it important to go further and say that this is the response of the human spirit to all the creative (improving) energies in the universe; those who believe in God as the central datum of all experience will insist either that it is the essence of the divine in the human soul, or that it is one aspect of the profound experience of man confronting God. For two of the elemental factors in this confrontation are: the realization within one's self of one's capacity and one's need and therefore one's wish for self-improvement; and the effort to use this capacity to supplant God or to make Him serve our wish; in other words, the desire to be God. This has of late been called original sin. It misses the point however to call this sinful if sin is to be thought of in voluntaristic terms. More correctly can it be called the original self or the original sin potential. Without it man would not be man. It strains credulity too far to say that the potential of sin is the essence of sin. It is both a metaphysical and a practical question as to whether God could have created man without endowing him with the dangerous power that can seem to come so close to usurping the prerogatives of God. To have created him thus and then invested that very power with the essence of evil, just because man does and will forever pervert it, would have come close to having been either a cosmic hoax or a divine sin itself. For mortal man to try to *be* God is the open road to sin; for him to try to *be like* God is the narrow pathway to holiness. Both impulses spring from the same source. To the familiar question of the Apostle James (James 3:11) "Does a spring pour forth from the same opening fresh water and brackish?" we would have to answer "Yes." At the same time we would insist that the law of gravity that makes the spring pour forth is neither sweet nor brackish.

We may seem to have strayed pretty far from the parable but we have by no means lost sight of it. These men who were guests at dinner are representative of their fellows to a degree they never dreamed. To have been invited flattered them and supported their sense of status in their community; to have been warned against immoderate indulgence of the heady wine of presumption supports our sense of their importance for our community.

It is commonplace now that one of the basic psychological drives is the wish to achieve status, the desire to belong and to have a secure sense of belonging. How the frustration of this drive in early life has created an inordinate subconscious pursuit of it in adulthood has been endlessly documented. The scrougers, the shovers, the pushers whom we so cordially dislike, are overcompensating for frustrations experienced in the family, the gang, the grade school, or elsewhere. It is good to know this for it is possible to cultivate in practical ways during the formative years of young folk the sense of being wanted and of belonging and thus avert measurably the spiritual trauma that tries to heal itself by overaggressiveness in later years. It is a highly deceptive thing and can rationalize its action in most plausible ways. The pretentious man in the parable would have been pained deeply if he had been told his garish wedding gown with its outsized tassels and glittering ornaments adverted his subconscious sense of alienation from the other guests and a desire to overcome it. Similarly his aggressive push to the seat of honor was no doubt regarded by him as a token of high regard for his host instead of a subconscious low regard for himself. Let those of us who are addicted to the loud tie or the glittering bauble be duly admonished.

It is not enough to point out the difficulty of the man who came to dinner. It is not even enough to indicate that he, in a way, is Everyman. It is important to see how his difficulty was to be overcome, his tension abated, his wardrobe refitted with more modest clothes. His aggressiveness was the source of great humiliation; but humiliation often curdles into anger, and anger into vengefulness, and vengefulness into destruction. We have had enough of that sort of thing to last us till the end of time.

[4]

To this problem Jesus gave his attention. That he thought it important—though in terms far less elaborate than have been outlined here—was the reason for his assumption of the right to rebuke the man publicly. The formula was a very simple one: Don't shove! It arose, however, from no simple— that is to say, superficial—understanding of human nature. On the contrary! It is very clear that he recognized that there are seats of honor and that they are to be occupied. He did not tell the man to go home; he simply told him to take his turn. For the nub of the problem was that the seat of honor belonged first to the host and second to the man to whom he wanted to offer it. He could have occupied it himself or awarded it to another, but no one could seize it for himself.

We have already pointed out that one can "go and sit in the

lowest place" with just as much ostentation as the one who rudely crowds to the highest. There is little to choose between the shover and the sycophant for in essence they are the same thing. To the negative word—don't shove—it is necessary then to add a positive one. There must be no scramble for the lowest seat, nor is there to be servility. What is indicated in the parable as a positive guide and as something that promises release from the tension suffered by the frustrated guest at the world's table?

We do not think it relevant in this discussion to undertake to set forth a discipline by which the growth of personality can be directed in its formative stages. Jesus was dealing with a mature man here. We are mature and in so far as this is a tension problem for us, it will be dealt with in mature terms. There are three intimations in the parable that are suggestive at this point. The first is that honor among one's fellows is important and therefore desirable. In the story there were guests of honor and seats of honor, but there is no indication that the elevation of one guest implied any lack of appreciation of the others. At this point the second intimation appears. They were all friends. There is an appealing sort of gentility in the words that are used here. Jesus has just rebuked the man in the story, and he has taken his demotion with confusion and shame. But as the comment continues and he is advised what would have been a more correct procedure, Jesus has the host say—and he is still concerned with the bumptious man—"Friend." The third intimation takes us down to deeper levels of experience. It is the lot of man to be exalted and humbled. It is the host's business to do the former, the guest's to do the latter. To put it another way, God exalts man, man humbles himself. The importance of this is seen at once when it is reversed and the agencies are exchanged. Then man exalts himself and humbles God. This is not merely misbehaving at a banquet; it is committing the unpardonable sin of setting one's self in the place of God. Correctly enough Jesus is reported elsewhere (Matt. 20:23) to have said to one who sought places of honor for two of his friends in the coming Kingdom: "To sit at my right hand and at my left is not mine to grant, but it is for those for whom it has been prepared by my Father."

These three intimations are clear; they might even be accorded the status of moral principles. That there is no false or arbitrary egalitarianism which refuses to recognize either levels of distinction or the innate wish to reach them is, if not a moral principle in itself, a circumstance upon which the moral quality of our behavior often depends. It would be a strange thing if man's ineluctable wish to improve himself could go no further than bringing him up to a dead level of equality. There can be no virtue in equality per se. Virtue lies in a man's "wish exceeding his grasp" on the one hand or his willing abasement in the service of others, on the other. Mere equality is regimentation. This is the subtle error at the heart of the Marxist dream of a classless society. "There is one glory of the sun, and another glory of the moon, and another glory of the stars; for star differs from star in glory" (I Cor. 15:41).

The danger here is as patent as the principle. It is that man, recognizing the principle, should exploit his fellows or regard himself as God. This is due, when it happens, to a misuse of a proper function because of a misunderstanding both of the nature of man (including himself) and of God. And no error is more dangerous than to assume that since egalitarianism is not of the order of nature, those on the higher levels have a natural right to exploit those on the lower.

It is at this point that the second principle can be brought to bear. The man who in the parable furnishes us the model by seating himself in the lowest place is as much a friend of the host as the man who seated himself in the highest. It is that magic word "friend" that converted him to the man of distinction. We may correctly assume that the deposed and shamefaced man who had been asked to descend to a lower rating was also—and still—a friend of the host. If this circumstance is to be shaped into the substance of a moral principle it says: The fact of inequality is what gives fluidity to society; the fact of friendship is what gives it solidity. Here we discover the moral evil that hides in the act of discrimination. Discrimination is the exploitation of a factitious difference or unequal status. It argues that since God ordained races or classes which are different and unequal, the strong should possess or dispossess the weak. This completely ignores the fact of friendship which is the method (or one of them) by which the inequalities of nature are compensated. This allows nothing of condescension or patronage, for those twin snobs having nothing in common with genuine friendliness.

Friendliness, we hasten to observe, is not enough. From our Christian perspective we must insist that the third intimation provide us with the third moral principle which is our ultimate safeguard. The high seat belongs to the host; the pride that seeks to possess it is the sin that sets off the evil impulses toward discrimination just referred to. Can the Marxist dream of a classless society come true? We undertake no prediction but the present tendencies do not promise much hope. Their efforts to end exploitation in the interest of equalitarian society not only tend to a reduction of all to mediocrity but are, in themselves, exploitative of other social groups. With due humility and an honest effort to avoid cant we may say to the Marxists that what God says is still important. "Friend, come up higher" is a more promising word than any formula for world revolution that is based on expunging God or putting class or nation in His place.

[5]

We can close this on a much simpler note. Again we wish we knew what the reaction of the pompous man was to the host's rebuke. Maybe at the next feast to which he went he spared himself humiliation by following the advice his previous *faux pas* had evoked. If so he was converted. We are not too hopeful that this was his good fortune. Reorientation—which is not a bad synonym for conversion—comes hard to the pushers, the climbers, the gate crashers. The impulse that drives them comes from deep down in their subconsciousness. The tension that tortures can, however, be somewhat abated, but only by the three principles we have found in the parable, and not without great and deep humility and constant discipline.

Alas that the world has its own way of treating the bumptious. It too says "Quit shoving!" There is a point of tolerance beyond which an unpleasant person or nation cannot safely go. When an individual begins to throw his weight around, there is someone—to continue the idiom—who will undertake to cut him down to his proper size. This is the cause of much social friction and conflict. When a nation indulges in what Professor Toynbee elegantly calls "the idolization of the ephemeral self," there are other nations who at never-mind-how-staggering-the-cost will combine to destroy it utterly. This is the essence of war. Thus it is difficult to imagine a maxim that is more universally recognized as true than "Everyone who exalts himself will be humbled, and he who humbles himself will be exalted." Must we add that few maxims are more universally resisted?

That the truly humble man is exalted can be proved by citations from history. So far as we know no nation has been cited to support the principle. The authentic saint, wherever and whenever he has appeared, has proved that humility is exalted. We cannot forget that it was said of Jesus that he humbled himself and "therefore God has highly exalted him and bestowed on him the name which is above every name" (Phil. 2:9). Is the Kingdom of God the "nation" that will prove the rule to be true of cultures also? We shall have to wait for that. In the meantime we cannot think that this principle Jesus propounded at the end of a delightful story was an interim order. It was a recognition of a universal fact; not an accommodation to a limited period. Somehow we must learn to take it seriously.

CHAPTER VII

The Big Banquet

THE banquet motif that has carried along the parable discussed in the last chapter continues for a brief but significant comment in verses 12-14 and extends to another parable. It is important to consider the homily that joins the first and second parables of this general theme.

He said also to the man who had invited him, "When you give a dinner or a banquet, do not invite your friends or your brothers or your kinsmen or rich neighbors, lest they also invite you in return, and you be repaid. But when you give a feast, invite the poor, the maimed, the lame, the blind, and you will be blessed, because they cannot repay you. You will be paid at the resurrection of the just" (Luke 14:12-14).

This is a suggestion about the amenities of social feasting which apparently has never been taken seriously, either because it is thought to be trivial or because its basic meaning has not been grasped. If there have been church suppers organized on this basis we have never heard of them. To be sure all such convivial gatherings are ostensibly unrelated to any hope for a reciprocal invitation. Indeed we would be pretty quick to deny that any dinner invitation, either given or accepted, carried with it the necessity of a return courtesy. For this reason it is easy to dismiss these words as relevant only to a society in which the social code provided that a chain reaction of feasting episodes would be started off by one invitation to a banquet.

The important emphasis here, as is so consistently the case in what Jesus said, lies on a level deeper than amenity. It is interested in two of the giant concerns of any social order and, similarly, of any responsible individual. These are felicity and justice. Our record refers to the former as blessing. It is obvious that these are basic social and personal desiderata. No society is so mean or impoverished or so disordered as not to seek them. In fact it may fairly be asked whether social or individual life are possible without them. For clearly justice is the base on which a secure and permanent order rests, and blessedness is the superstructure that men erect on the base. It can be put otherwise: Felicity and justice are the warp and woof of human life; or justice is the tree, happiness is the fruit of the social organism.

It is Jesus' unique use of these two concepts that is arresting. He says "You will be blessed *because* they cannot repay you." This is very different from saying "You will be blessed *in spite of* their inability to repay you." The cause of felicity would appear to be not in the possible aftermath of an act of generosity or courtesy, but in the act itself. Reduced to a simpler statement it would say: True happiness comes from uncalculating kindness. This is a dictum the hedonist does not dispute. If an act of generosity is principally a means for securing an act of generosity, the nature of the act is conspicuously qualified. It ceases to be generosity and becomes a bargain and the happiness that should come from pure kindness is lost in concern over the likely return on the investment. It almost reduces generosity to a gamble. Gamblers, we are confidently informed, may be carefree people, but they are not happy ones.

We cannot resist pointing out that this is another illustration of the way in which Jesus saw the tension aspects of human life. If, as he says, felicity is uncalculating kindness, then the tensions

that seize the host whose generosity is designed to elicit reciprocal consideration and who cannot be happy until his hopes are
realized—such tensions do not disturb the truly kind, the truly
generous. This has very real parallels in our society. The frustrations of the social climber who has had a big party in an
effort to crash the higher society brackets, and who discovers
subsequently that her guests during the social season have forgotten her, must be cruel indeed.

This does not say kindness is unrecompensed; it says if it is
to bring happiness it must be uncalculating. "You will be repaid
at the resurrection of the just." There are aspects of the term
"resurrection of the just" that are somewhat unclear. Why, we
ask, did he not say at the resurrection of the dead? It is apparent,
however, that in the mind of Jesus there was a correlation between an act of uncalculating generosity and justice. It was
those who acted generously as an end in itself who were to be
compensated in the final recognition of the just. We cannot
fabricate a philosophy of justice out of such meager materials.
On the other hand it is important for us to realize that uncalculating kindness and justice are not as disjunct in the thought
of Jesus as they are in the mind of the jurist.

The meaning—we might even say the radicalism—of this
brief comment was not missed by at least one of the guests.
"Blessed is he who shall eat bread in the kingdom of God," he
ejaculated. Quite so. There alone we may assume will come the
true happiness that because it is uncalculating is tantamount
to true justice. Certainly our mortal time-bound perspectives
do not allow us to expect this sort of thing this side of eternity.
But there is patent danger in becoming ecstatic about categories
of post-mortem generosity and justice, lest we fail to face realistically the need for a proper response to generosity within the
circumference of the now. It is this fact which supplies lively
interest to the sixth parable in this series. There are some to
whom invitations to dine at the great house are issued in the

expectation that they will, in due time and with equal elegance, reciprocate. There are some, though as we have said we have never heard of such parties, where guests are invited on the grounds that they cannot reciprocate. In the first of these cases, the host's happiness is partly due to his expectation that he will subsequently be a guest; in the second, the host's happiness is due to his certainty that he cannot be a guest. There are some, however—hosts and guests—who cannot get together at all. This creates a sort of situation in which unhappiness is mutual. Here is another interesting tension situation. In general it may be described as that which pulls one between two types of obligation, each of which is altogether respectable. It is to this that our study now turns.

[1]

But he said to him, "A man once gave a great banquet, and invited many; and at the time for the banquet he sent his servant to say to those who had been invited, 'Come; for all is now ready.' But they all alike began to make excuses. The first said to him, 'I have bought a field, and I must go out and see it; I pray you, have me excused.' And another said, 'I have bought five yoke of oxen, and I go to examine them; I pray you, have me excused.' And another said, 'I have married a wife, and therefore I cannot come.' So the servant came and reported this to his master. Then the householder in anger said to his servant, 'Go out quickly to the streets and lanes of the city, and bring in the poor and maimed and blind and lame.' And the servant said, 'Sir, what you commanded has been done, and still there is room.' And the master said to the servant, 'Go out to the highways and hedges, and compel people to come in, that my house may be filled. For I tell you, none of those men who were invited shall taste my banquet'" (Luke 14:16-24).

There are two ways of approaching this familiar story. We remember that in the exhortation to his host Jesus was proposing a banquet for the ragtag and bobtail of the community with the promise that it would be an experience both gratifying and unique. At the end of this story this happens and as unconventional a crowd of guests as can be imagined files into the banquet hall. People of the highways and the hedges, the paupers, the cripples, the stumbling blind, fill the place. It is surprising that this scene has never caught the imagination of some great artist. What a mural it would make for a cathedral!

But this striking circumstance had come about not because of an original impulse of kindness in the host's heart. He had experienced what was an embarrassing frustration if it was not indeed a deliberate slight. The persona of the story are familiar people all the way from the man who "gave a great banquet" to the last highway straggler who came in. They are to be seen in almost every community. The slight the host suffered may have been deliberate, a conspiracy such as has not infrequently developed in order to put a crimp in the ambitions of a social climber. We are told that "they all alike began to make excuses." This sounds like collusion, particularly in the light of the fact that they had already accepted the invitation in obvious good faith. Was he a social climber? Was he simply repaying his social debts to those who had formerly entertained him? We do not know; but the point raised in the previous verses is sharpened into a story that is as full of drama as anything Jesus ever said. The men of distinction in his city were all on the roster of the bidden. They had all been formally notified and had accepted. When reminded by a messenger, they unanimously declined, giving excuses that on the face of them were neither sincere or substantial. The frustration of the host turns to anger and his anger induces him to do a penurious and petulant thing. He is not moved with compassion for the poor; he is indignant at his absent guests. The latter needed nothing of his magnificent spread, to be sure, nor were the former accustomed to it. It looks like an absurd social tour de force. He will not waste the food; rather than that he will spread it before the pariahs who will perhaps wolf it down without grace and leave without appreciation. Once he has been put off by his proper guests, he is determined that they shall be unanimously excluded. "I tell you, none of those men who were invited shall taste my banquet." Here is sheer and unmitigated bitterness. There is no intimation that he is satisfied that his bounty should go to those who could never repay him, or that in some post-mortem resurrection of the just he would be reimbursed.

This understanding robs the story of any elements of nobility. A man suffered an affront; he paid it back in the only way possible; by an eccentric and impulsive act, he gave his enemies to understand that the rabble in the streets were as good as they were and as deserving of his patronage. His concern for the poor was simple spite for the rich. It was not that the worthy and dispossessed people would at last have a chance; it was that the *haut monde* should for once get their deserts. No; we must look elsewhere for a more satisfying understanding of the parable's intention.

For the most part the great banquet has been regarded as symbolic or typical of the Kingdom of God. Here the host is God whose invitations are sent abroad and rudely spurned. Whereupon God, in His wrath, turns to the outcasts and invites them to the feast. If we are to salvage any valuable suggestion here, we must first absolve the Divine Host of the ill temper and manifest partiality He shows for the important people in the community. Nor does it satisfy us that the Kingdom is seen to operate in any such hit-or-miss fashion. If the peoples of the north and south, east and west, are to sit down with Abraham, Isaac, and Jacob, we hope it is not just because the people from Main Street reneged on their promises to come. Status in the Kingdom of God must be on a much more solid basis than that. There is nothing redemptive in spite; the salvation of one man cannot depend on the rudeness of another. One is not saved by default. That would be not an order of salvation, but the disorder of personal capriciousness. Jesus meant nothing of the sort. We incline to think that the central concern of this story is not different from that of others we have been studying. It has to do with the experience of redemption and judgment and the manner by which the first is complicated by the second. Salvation, we have said, is the total business of life. Birth and death are both its effective agents. We need sometimes to be saved from our friends no less than from our enemies. In this particular story, redemption is represented by an invitation to share in a great banquet. We overlook, for the moment, the fact that the inviting appears arbitrary and limited to a special group, because we shall later discover that this seems less so on closer examination. But the judgment that is laid on those who are finally excluded from the feast is one they have rendered on themselves. This is the same crowd that thought it unnecessary to strive toward the narrow door in our study of the fourth parable. To be sure the door was finally barred against them should they for any last-minute reason have relented; but the exclusion from the feast was their own doing. Men make choices they think will best serve their interests. Sometimes it is pride that compels the selections; sometimes a bauble, a field, a pair of oxen, a wife. There is nothing reprehensible in the choice. It can be made with civility and even frivolous unconcern, but the choice is theirs and the barring of the gate is no more than a baleful epilogue to the tale.

In the relatively uncomplex society of Jesus' day there were three social factors about which life moved. One was money, a second was manufacture (on a small and highly personalized scale), and a third was the home. One might even make a case for these being the basic social components of which all others are derivative. Professor Toynbee describes a fully mature society— one moving into a preliminary stage of disintegration—as having four essential components: a money currency, a military organization, an elaborate administrative setup and class of public

servants, and the refinement and monopoly of propaganda.
These are ways, both simple and involved, of implementing the
three factors enumerated above. There must be a medium of
exchange, whether it be coinage or some other token of value;
there must be a way of getting things made for human use,
whether by an artisan or a production line, and there must be a
nucleus that is permanent even though factitious in which society can cohere, whether it be a home or a parliament. The
money changer beside his counter, the shoemaker beside his
bench, the mother beside her table; these, with the ramifications
that are implicit in each, and greater or less in terms of the
simplicity or complexity of the social order, are the foci of social
power, and the promise of social continuity.

[2]

It is interesting then to observe that in our parable those who
were first invited to the feast represented each of these social
nuclei. The man who had bought a field without ever having
seen it (since he gave as his excuse a desire to see his newly
acquired property) was a man who had money. There was
nothing bad about this. His money had both personal and social
utility, and by increasing it through shrewd buying and selling
he was contributing to social stability. He was, in our way of
putting it, a capitalist, which means simply that he was a man
who had used capital and claimed for himself the gain as readily
as he also absorbed the loss he incurred in his trading.

The second man was a manufacturer. Our use of this word
to call to mind huge plants throbbing with machines tended
by skillful fingers and turning out bales of goods or a parade
of vehicles must not obscure for us the fact that in an elemental
way, this man was making things and that oxen were his machines. Now that manufacture no longer necessarily means mak-
ing-by-hand, we shall not be too fussy about using manufacture

to designate making-by-oxen. His wish to be released from his promise to come to the feast was due to having bought a new machine. We would call it an improved process, a labor-saving device. Presumably if one yoke of oxen had saved two or three men from pulling a plow, five yoke of oxen would save five times as many, or even more since the ratio of labor saving is generally considerably higher than the simple multiple of the number of machines would indicate.

The third had married a wife. This, on the face of it might be nothing more than the happy conclusion of a romance. It was at least that, we assume, and we are all for it. Yet marrying a wife is a good deal more than a romantic episode. It involves a great many more than the two contracting parties. It will certainly involve, biologically, the countless human beings who will be the physical issue of the union. It should certainly involve the most important experiences of those committed to them by birth—discipline in the manner of living with its correlative justice, and teaching in the meaning of life. Here in the home we see the nucleus and pattern of social control, of the school, and of the court. How often, without thinking what we are saying, we speak of the paternal aspects of government. It is a simple, unconscious recognition that the control aspects of society in discipline and instruction and law are rooted back in the family. This man asked for no excuse from his host. It is an amusing omission. Perhaps the capitalist thought he could extenuate his refusal by speaking of a new piece of land and the manufacturer by his wish to see a demonstration of a newly installed five set ten ox-power multiple processor. The man who was newly wed simply stated the overwhelming fact and added he couldn't come. That, we assume, foreclosed any further concern the host or his hurrying emissary may have had in his attendance at the party. Perhaps, in those days, a man could not bring his wife along. Perhaps, indeed, she had given him a curfew hour he was loath to violate.

It is obvious at this point that this simple social paradigm—capitalist, processor, family—is not in any explicit way oriented toward what we call spiritual values. There is truth in saying that man being what he is touches everything he does with spirit. In this sense there is no such thing as pure secularism or pure materialism. Spiritual and material values have continuity; they are not completely disjoined though they can be differentiated. Thus the capitalist in this story may have loved land with the fondness that the good earth has always inspired in those who live close to it. On the contrary he may have been a land speculator whose sole devotion was to acres that could be turned to profit by a sale. This was loving the profit the land brought him, not the land itself. Similarly the manufacturer might have been a lover of beasts. There is a spiritual quality to this. Nothing could have so delighted his eye as the powerful sinews of an ox bent to its prodigious labors; but again he may have loved a great beast solely for the acres it could plow in a day. Cattle were not a hobby with him; an ox was a machine. As for the man with a wife: something inherent in our Christian view of marriage and the family makes us see a spiritual glow about the happy pair. From our perspective the family is perhaps the most spiritually exacting and rewarding of our social experiences. At the same time we are not so sure that this comes without conscious and continued effort. Certainly the basic components of the family represented by discipline, justice, and instruction, as they have expanded into great social enterprises on their own, need to be constantly guarded against their complete separation from the spiritual values that give them unique value and significance.

To put it bluntly, the three guests asked to share the abundance of the great feast may be taken to symbolize and severally to represent a society that was secularist—not purely so; that we believe is not possible, but in its orientation, predominantly so. It was a society without religion, religion here meaning the vehicle of specifically spiritual values and interests. By the same token then the great feast itself was, in the image Jesus chose, the Kingdom of God, again to be understood as the vehicle or instrument of spiritual experience. To Jesus and to us who are the inheritors of the Christian testimony, it was something more than that: the great feast was the redemptive opportunity set down in the midst of the tight little society that is covered in the parable. By acceptance of the invitation to the feast, the capitalist, the processor, and the *pater familias* could, each one, redeem, so to speak, their particular interests from the blight of secularistic preoccupation.

[3]

A part of the tragedy, for this story is a tragic one, is that they came so close to redemption and yet missed it so completely. These great refusers were not, we think, evil men determind to destroy a socially ambitious man in the community or indifferent to social obligations. We have abandoned that notion already. They were not only respectable folk, they were the solid substance of the town without whom there would have been no social structure or cohesion. At first, when they accepted their invitations they did so in good faith, but when business interfered with pleasure—which means that material concerns superseded spiritual concerns—they turned back to the former as the more pressing. They accepted the invitation in good faith, but their faith in their own private affairs was better.

The host, so the story goes, was very angry. We have said we find this detail of the symbolism distasteful. The smugness of the might-have-been guests was, on the other hand, enough to infuriate their would-be benefactor. His judgment on them was summary, but as we have pointed out before, it was rendered only after they had judged themselves. It is in this context that the relevance of this tale for our contemporary scene is made apparent.

If it is true today that society is dominantly secular in its orientation, this condition has come about through its own choice. The reasons for secularism are not quite so simple as they are often thought to be, but even the most exact analysis could not eliminate the element of choice in the direction our culture has taken. Certainly in the West, at one time seriously called the Christian West, religion has hitherto provided orientation to all the factors in society and invited them to partake of the great feast. This is, in itself, an interesting story that cannot be retold here. But certainly within the last century, the invitation (and it is perpetually extended to every generation) has been pretty generally spurned.

When in Amsterdam in August, 1948, the World Council of Churches refused to assign to laissez-faire capitalism or Marxist socialism a position of preference in a putative Christian social order, it created a great pother in some circles. What right had the Christian Church to pass judgment on—or more specifically against—Free Enterprise Capitalism? The right to judge its opposite was hardly disputed, but to condemn capitalism——? There was a flurry of explanations but the sense of shock in some sensitive quarters has not yet been healed. The answer, however, may be made in terms of our parable. Capitalism has judged itself. It does not have, nor does it want, a primary spiritual orientation. It has been invited to the great feast, but it has a business deal pending and begs to be excused. Not that there are no capitalists who have urgent spiritual concerns, but that the system that goes by that name is deliberately and shamelessly pagan. "After all these things do the pagans seek" is the source of our descriptive word.

Much the same strictures are to be made against industry. Great improvement is to be noted in industrial relations over the past twenty-five years, but it has been due to the pressure of the folk from the highways and hedges who have been brought into manufacturing plants. To be sure they may have no greater concern for spiritual values than the men who own the oxen.

Again that is another story, but modern industry has almost completely refused to orient itself to the spiritual values that work, as a divine gift (cf. the great Genesis *mythos, in loc.*), was supposed to provide and protect. It has followed the capitalist lead and has stayed away from the feast.

What of the family with its social derivatives? The home is still the first school and the first court. The same dispiriting comment must be made if we are to look at the general tendencies in our western culture. We have judged ourselves. Little as a family, less as a school, least as a court do we want to go to the feast. We have wives and children and schools and courts, but they are touched by the same perversity that refuses a spiritual orientation. Let the man have his feast! Let the Kingdom of God offer its redemption; we'll take care of ourselves. We aren't even interested in making excuses. "I have married a wife and cannot come."

These are peremptory and perhaps presumptuous indictments but they are not, for that matter, unsupported. The cause of the tensions in the modern world between rival economic orders, between employer and employed, between the compulsions of the family bond and the impatience with them, are all, in the language of our parable, due to their refusal to accept the invitation to the great feast. The proximate judgment has been laid against them by themselves, the ultimate judgment (*eschaton*) has been rendered by their exclusion by the host. What right has our socio-economic order to be angered by the indictments laid against it by the spiritually sensitive? It has already judged itself, and the door has been shut.

[4]

It is not alone that our culture no longer moves within the orbit of idealism and action described by the Kingdom of God that causes the tensions of our time. The feast will not be adjourned for want of guests. Into the places of the elect, the indiscriminate crowds will pour. To those who have refused the feast, this is a frightening sight. We have seen it before in parable four. There was weeping and gnashing of teeth then; now the fear is noiseless and for that reason more terrifying. It is not reassuring to see the spiritual values of a culture abandoned by its most substantial elements. To see it appropriated by the maimed, the blind, the crippled, and the vagabond is both a sign of hope and of despair.

No spiritual vacuum can long remain empty. God will have guests at the great feast in spite of the genteel withdrawal of those first chosen. That is our hope. Who will fill the vacuum? That is for time to reveal. We wonder what will happen if the vacuum becomes a vortex.

CHAPTER VIII

The Contractor and the King

IT IS not surprising to find that the paragraph that follows the final judgment that had been passed on the might-have-been-guests at the great feast, opens with the report of great popular response. The big banquet story had been told to a party with whom Jesus was sitting at table. It is possible that outside the open portico where the meal was going on there was something of a crowd assembled. This was not uncommon. It is also possible that the story was overheard by some in the miscellaneous audience. It is even possible that the story, heard by the small company at meat, had been repeated with relish or disdain to the outsiders. Whatever the way in which the parable got around the response to it seems to have been immediate and extensive. "Now," says the record, "great multitudes accompanied him." The "now" is hardly the meaningless verbal gesture with which a sentence is often begun. It clearly has a right to more solid emphasis. In Luke 12:1 we were told that "many thousands of the multitude had gathered together." Exaggerated, perhaps, and not intended as an accurate census, but it gives to us who read the impression of the one who saw. The thronging crowd is again a "great multitude."

Now great multitudes accompanied him; and he turned and said to them, "If any one comes to me and does not hate his own father and mother and wife and children and brothers and sisters, yes, and even his own life, he cannot be my disciple. Whoever does not bear his own cross and come after me, cannot be my disciple. For which of you, desiring to build a tower, does not first sit down and count the cost, whether he has enough to complete it? Otherwise, when he has laid a foundation, and is not able to finish, all who see it begin to mock him, saying, 'This man began to build, and was not able to finish.' Or what king, going to encounter another king in war, will not sit down first and take counsel whether he is able with ten thousand to meet him who comes against him with twenty thousand? And if not, while the other is yet a great way off, he sends an embassy and asks terms of peace. So therefore, whoever of you does not renounce all he has cannot be my disciple" (Luke 14:25-33).

[1]

It is neither honest nor reverent to try to disguise the feeling that this is, by any interpretation, both difficult and dangerous doctrine. If Jesus was undertaking to screen out of the crowds those who had not the hardihood to accept and practice such rigorism, it seems to be an unnecessarily strict test. Furthermore we are not comfortable in the presence of the demand that hate be made the basis of discipleship. The word cannot be softened or silenced. It stands in almost truculent contrast to the new commandment, "that ye love one another," or the old one that we should love our neighbors as ourselves. One will not love his neighbor very convincingly if he hates his family nor would any decent neighbor feel safe in accepting the love of so sinister a person.

Furthermore there is what appears to be a disturbing *non sequitur* at the close of the passage. Why the important "so therefore" at this point? There never has been any serious dispute about the importance of renunciation as the spiritual exercise preliminary to any great act of dedication or discipleship. Colin Kelly's renunciation of life in order to destroy the Japanese warship *Haruna* was as real and complete as Dr. Schweitzer's renunciation of life in Europe to heal the black folk at Lambaréné. It is the "therefore" that puzzles us. If renunciation of all is to follow the careful calculation suggested in building a tower and fighting a war, then the contractor would renounce his plans and erect nothing and the king would disband his army and fight no one. Jesus had been talking about careful planning for aggressive action, and then seems to dismiss it all with a "therefore" that cancels any need for it. One might even go further and say that the familiar saying about insipid salt falls awkwardly into the pattern of this passage. Consistency would seem to expect that salt that had lost its savor—which is all that salt has—might be commended instead of consigned to the dunghill. Surely if men are to renounce all that they have, even for the lofty end of discipleship, they will bring to their discipleship nothing. It helps little, if at all, to say that certain magical processes will reward such asceticism with new and better virtues. But in that case should not they too be renounced? Of one thing we may be sure, whether we approve it or not: the Christian movement has never taken this *extreme* statement of the requirement for discipleship seriously. One may even ask whether it is physically possible or morally edifying when it is tried. No; we must, for the good of our souls, confess that discipleship that begins by hating and matures only by total renunciation is too hard a saying. This is not because men are willfully perverse but because such an extremity of self-denial would become nihilism even if it were physically possible. Most of us find it hard to *renounce* hate in the interests of discipleship. To *incite* it in the interests of discipleship gets us nowhere. If we cannot erase the words "hate" and "renounce all" or spiritualize or dilute them until they have lost their savor, we can at least face the fact of our bewilderment honestly and get on the best we can with it.

We are not, however, abandoned entirely to such a mood.

In our efforts to understand what is said to us in these parables we have been emphasizing the place and profound significance of tension. We have also made the important point that the spirit of Jesus was taut with tensions during the portentous days in which he told these stories. Is it not plausible to assume that at this point we have what may actually have been the moment of greatest tension that came to him? If this is so, it may soften somewhat the shock of disillusionment and repudiation that has often followed a serious study of the words we have just been reflecting upon.

[2]

Of one thing we may be sure: Jesus was not bemused by the multitudes just because they represented a considerable statistical proof of his influence. A multitude following a leader generally lays on him a sense of crushing responsibility that is in direct ratio to his sense of satisfaction. In the case of Jesus we think he was more oppressed with the former mood than beguiled by the latter. From the two little parables about the contractor and the king we may properly assume that to his searching and anxious eye, this great multitude was aimless. It was not following him, it was just following. And this sort of thing put his whole program in jeopardy. Paradoxically, the more people who thronged him the safer he was from the authorities but the more imperiled was his movement by the crowd itself. What was he to do? He could not renounce the crowd for obvious reasons. The situation was tense to a disturbing or even distracting degree. Was the extreme and impractical stringency of his demand for discipleship the reflection of the tautness of his own soul? Here indeed was a baptism to undergo; how his soul was straitened until it be accomplished! What was to be done with the multitudes?

Nothing is so infuriating to a desperately serious person, bending all his interests and energies toward a great end, as the self-satisfied aimlessness of those who follow him largely because it is momentarily the popular thing to do and they have nothing else to engage them. There are occasions when a crowd must be shocked out of its meandering mood. The inclination to agree with the leader, no matter what he says is no compliment to him. It may indeed turn out to be their undoing and his. Jesus seems never to have lost his sense of balance in a crowd. A large following made him think no more of himself, a sudden defection, no less. If this is kept in mind the disturbing passage we have been studying comes into clearer perspective. Was he not undertaking to jar the aimlessness of the crowd into directed and considered action? The dullness of their unconcern had to be matched by the sharpness of his demands. They hear the staccato word "hate" and the gruesome word "cross" but this shock treatment is followed at once by an ingratiating question: Which of you desiring to build a tower does not first sit down and count the cost? Here was the opposite of aimlessness; here was something that appealed at once to that modicum of creative appetency that is latent in every soul.

To the simple mind, life, if one wants to talk about it seriously, can be best described as a growing or a building process. Of these, building is easier to understand since at the heart of the growing process is mystery. How common are the references to building a life, building a career, building a fortune, etc. It is to this elemental and yet important fact that Jesus appeals. There is no subtlety here; he could risk no subtleties on this multitude; it is an interest to which even the children in the crowd could respond. Building involves three preliminary operations: deciding what is to be built—tower, barn, house; checking the materials; estimating the construction costs. The presumption is that once these three steps are taken, average industry, guided by the plans, will get the tower built. The alternative is equally clear. Without thoughtful planning one might, to be sure, bring measureless optimism to a project. The foundation could be laid with odds and ends lying about, since no one sees the foundation once the structure is complete. Optimistic beginnings are, however, no guarantee of a job well done. It is likely to subside once its ready-to-hand materials are exhausted. Then— and we are sure the crowd was intrigued by this suggestion— those that passed were to find great amusement in the optimist's discomfiture. There was the raucous laugh and the ribald taunt: "This man began to build but was not able to finish." More accurately, perhaps, their appraisal of the job would have included the man's disinclination to make his plans and count his costs before he set to work. Both his optimism and labor were wasted.

The intention of the little homily is manifest and there is no reason for thinking that it was lost on the audience. To the more sophisticated mind, however, life is more than building. Accurate as that metaphor may be, it fails to come to terms with a deeper apprehension of what life is. No mechanical process, adding of experience to experience as stones are imbricated in the rising walls of a tower, can really produce a completely built life. For life is a battle in which one faces imponderable odds against one's chances of victory. This dynamic, insurgent quality of life puts it on a level of nobility higher than building a tower, even the tower of a great cathedral. St. Peter's in Rome is a mechanical achievement of great beauty, but a tiny flower struggling for life in a glacier on Mt. Blanc has something of loveliness and meaning that outranks any building man has made.

[3]

That life, thus conceived, lies on a higher level is supported by the way in which, if it fails, its failure is indicated in the battle metaphor. In the case of the uncompleted tower there was the derisive laughter of the neighbors: in the case of the battle, the issue was, by inference, life for the victor and death for the vanquished. To build a tower one must deal with estimates fairly easy to arrive at; to fight a battle, one must deal with imponderables difficult to assess. Failure to build a tower is due to the folly or impractical enthusiasm of the builder; failure to win a battle is due to the superior assault of one who advances to engage his adversary with a determination to destroy him. His superiority may be discovered in unexpected qualities or places.

So the king, upon whom had fallen the necessity or desirability of making war on another king, would, like the contractor, sit down and do some figuring. His question is not whether he has money or material enough, but whether he has, in his army, shrewdness and spirit enough. A wise contractor can be sure of his tower if he has planned well, but even the wisest strategist in war cannot be sure of victory. The reason for this is that war is ultimately a contest of spirit. We may be reluctant to describe modern mechanized warfare in such lofty terms, but the point must be allowed to stand. The king in this story had ten thousand men and he was being advanced against by another king with twice the number. If wars were won by statisticians the odds would have been two to one, against the army of ten thousand. Gamblers might have offered bigger odds or—and this is what supports the fact that war is a matter of spirit—given no odds at all to the larger army: they might even have bet on the small one. For there is always the chance that the little man may have something the big man doesn't have—have just the thing that will bring him victory, and in victory win the greater glory. So the king sat down and took counsel *whether* . . . There was a possibility that he might win. His men could have been in better shape and higher spirits. They could have believed more thoroughly in their cause. Their morale, their mobility, their leadership; the advantages of terrain, timing, weather, and what not, could conceivably have weighted the chances in their favor. It was worth at least a council of war. And yet there was to be no wild boasting that would betray his careful assay of the total situation. It was not a matter of do-or-die for the flag regardless of what the odds were, for or against them. That sort of thing invites the same kind of ridicule that greeted the optimist's half-built tower, and the shrewd king in our story was going to risk nothing by blindness or pride. If, after taking account of all the elements involved in his materiel, morale, and possible strategy, he saw the contest was hopeless, he would send "an embassy and ask terms of peace." He was not one who wanted to fight for the fight's sake, or would throw away his life for an impossible cause. Peace may have been worth fighting for, but a king is a fool and a butcher who sends his men into a situation that he knows will bring only the peace of death for the slain. To be sure a refusal to fight is always liable to the charge of cowardice, appeasement, or sheer capitulation. That is one of the hazards that life, understood in dynamic—not mechanical—terms, must run. The bricklayer building a tower may be lazy but he is not likely to be accused of cowardice; nor will the brigadier directing a battle deploy men as a mason lays bricks unless he is an idiot. We must not forget that in this little story the king was debating whether he could make a constructive use of a situation by suing for peace. In this connection one recalls the "unconditional surrender" demand of the last war and what it seems to have done for the efforts to recreate a peaceful world.

We have no clear way of knowing how the huge audience that heard these parables about the contractor and the king reacted. At the close of the episode there is a sharp exhortation: "He who has ears to hear, let him hear." This may well be taken to be a rebuke to restlessness in the crowd, as if Jesus had detected that there was considerable inattention. All of them had ears but a limited number had ears to hear. This is true of all agglomerations of people. It would not be surprising then

to hear him address to the attentive and comprehending a word
that both reassured them and fixed special emphasis on what he
was trying to communicate. Such listeners, many or few, would
no doubt have understood that he was concerned with important
business—building and waging war—and that the issue of both
is always in doubt. Some, the more perceptive and concerned,
would have seen that he was inviting them both to serious
thought and to active participation in the enterprise to which
he was dedicated. To them the hard words about renunciation
might have seemed less shocking. Could there have been in his
cryptic reference to salt a reflection of momentary disillusionment? Was the salt losing its savor? Was his dream to be cast
out on to the dunghill? There was zest in struggle as there was
savor in salt. If the struggle lost *its* zest, or if these thronging
crowds lost *their* zest, was not the dunghill to be the end of
the whole business? These are questions it is proper to ask but
improper to answer, for they take us to the threshold of the inner
consciousness of Jesus beyond which we cannot go. The tension
which was pointed out at the beginning of this chapter might
very easily have expressed itself in such a mood as he faced
listlessness and preoccupation in his audience.

[4]

It is instructive to note that from this point on the narrative
does not refer again to large multitudes. There are crowds, to
be sure, but nothing like the pressure of sheer numbers impinged
upon him. The way chapter 15 of Luke's record opens, while
setting the mood for what will engage us in our next study, is
pertinent here. "The great multitudes" that "accompanied him"
(verse 25, chapter 14) appear to have been replaced by "tax
gatherers and sinners [who] were all drawing near to hear him."
There was a limited number of tax collectors and "sinner" was
specific rather than a generic term in this context. We assume,

therefore, that their number was not great. Whether this means that the apparent effort to screen out those who had ears but did not use them was successful may be debatable if not indeed dubious, but that there is, from here on, a new quality that appears in his stories is beyond question. It is not implausible to say that the tension that existed in the pressure and disorder of great crowds may have been measurably relieved after the telling of these two short parables.

But these stories have pertinence to other multitudes and other times. By an odd circumstance, our age is conspicuous by its preoccupation with building and with making war. What towers we construct! What wars we wage! It makes little difference, apparently, that our warring destroys our towers; we seem indefatigable in both building and battle. Now it is interesting to observe that, strictly speaking, there is no moral to these stories, moral, we mean, in terms of an ethical addendum or implication. We have already pointed out that what immediately follows the telling of the stories does not provide a logical sequence. On the other hand there *is* a moral in terms of the sure sequence that joins folly to ridicule and blind bravado to defeat. Put in positive terms the sequence joins foresight to success and prudence to peace. These sequents are timeless, of course, and their importance to the survival of our culture makes it possible if not indeed imperative for us to appropriate for the times in which we are living, the wisdom of these ancient homilies.

To comprehend rightly the nature of culture both the tower and the battle components must be given place. Or call it the complementary activities of contractor and king; or even more simply the material or building phase and the spiritual or struggle phase of the life of a people. It is the boast, as indeed it is the accredited accomplishment of Western culture that it has pretty well solved the problems related to the material aspects of life. Not that we use our wisdom wisely or share it generously; that is a moral problem. But we seem to be able to count the cost, to lay a foundation, and to finish what we started. Sometimes laughter greets our labors, but it is sardonic, not amused. It is not inspired by our failure; it is evoked by our use of our success. It is this fact that gives us pause. Our skill in putting brick on brick, in adding and subtracting molecular weights to create new compounds, our precision, our speed, our delving, our soaring—these all are the results of the prodigious figuring of those who "desiring to build a tower . . . first [sat] down . . . [to] count the cost." But are we as sure of the ends for which we are building as we are of the towers that reach the sky? To answer that, one needs only to consult the serious —one might even say appalling—studies recently made under the auspices of our government about possible ways of moving American industry underground for the new civilization of the Atomic Age. The tower in reverse is the burrow. Does one hear the sound of laughter at the thought of that? It might be argued by those who laugh that converting a tower into a sub-terranean labyrinth is greater folly than not finishing the tower at all.

More power to the builders! We would not tear down a single thing they have erected; but we may be allowed to warn them that before now other civilizations have builded towers, tall, sturdy, giant structures, proud, indestructible, and that today jackals laugh among their ruins? This is to say that all towers at best are only fragile instruments for living, not its aim.

At this point we pick up the second little homily about the beleaguered king. This is not a discussion of war; it was not so used by the parable-maker. It simply reminds us that culture, to survive, must have the dynamism of a struggle in which the *odds always seem against it.* The moment the spirits of men are sure no attack will be launched against them because their ten thousand are stronger than the enemy's twenty thousand—and we will let that figure of speech stand for every element and type of strength—at that moment they are exposed to man's most powerful enemy, the pride that deceives him while it commits sabotage with his defenses. It is the constant necessity for estimating our strength against imponderables and against odds that keeps alive and creative the spirit of man. More important this than building the highest tower or drilling the deepest burrow. This is the point of Toynbee's important thesis about "challenge and response" being the primary impulse that gave birth to the twenty-one cultures of which history is the record. It may mean that we, by virtue of spiritual qualities—represented as they may well be by a political system, an economic order or the verve of a still youthful country—can take on the world and do battle against it. Or we may see the wisdom of sending "an embassy and ask[ing] terms of peace"—political, economic, social, spiritual.

For all its difficulty and seeming impracticability this may require a reorientation of ourselves to father and mother, and even to our own total life. It may demand renunciation, yes, even of towers or of armies. Or even a cross willingly borne. Just that deeply into the soul of modern man can the probe of these little parables go. We may wince and turn away, or even laugh nervously. "But he who has an ear to hear, let him hear."

CHAPTER IX

Sheep and Coin

IT HAS already been said that the opening verses of chapter 15 indicate a change in those who attended Jesus' meetings. The "many thousands of the multitude," the "great multitudes," give place, as the record proceeds from this point, to smaller and more select groups. We have even suggested that this may have been due to a deliberate effort to screen out of his following those who had ears but did not use them. There is clear evidence that his new audiences had ears and made proper use of them. The hearing of the renegades who collected Rome's taxes for her was doubtless acute to the abuse to which they were endlessly subjected. They and the miscellaneous sinners with whom they were bracketed were for some reason drawn into his orbit. They were hearing things and to their surprise and perhaps momentary discomfort, they found that the Pharisees and the scribes were also bending an ear and cocking an eye. Whereupon the ears of Jesus, taxgatherers and sinners, all heard a murmuring the meaning of which was ominously clear to them.

Now the tax collectors and sinners were all drawing near to hear him. And the Pharisees and the scribes murmured, saying, "This man receives sinners and eats with them" (Luke 15:1-2).

This accusation was apparently made within the hearing of those on whom contempt was being cast, for the reply of Jesus is directed at his accusers and made in a manner that would be relished by those with whom he was scornfully identified. Tax-gatherers and sinners were social outcasts; the former had offended national pride, the latter had outraged moral respectability. The Pharisees and scribes had offended nothing, but their exaggerated self-regard had erected a barrier beyond which the exercise of normal humaneness could not pass. Both groups were drawn to Jesus; one wanted to trap him; the other was perhaps flattered that a figure momentarily so popular should take sides with them in a contest in which they almost always came off badly. Another matter: they may—these outcasts—have heard his difficult words about the renunciation of family and even of life, and the bearing of crosses. To such people ideas of that sort often have a reverse sort of relevance. They are the victims of renunciation and mistakenly appropriate to themselves the virtue that accrues to those who have renounced a lesser good for a greater. They had, they would have said, crosses pressed upon their backs and deserved some merit for bearing them. This is the perverse piety of the morally disoriented. They equate ostracism with distinction and the pity they claim for the redemption they scorn.

Oddly perhaps, and yet significantly, we have no record of the sort of things Jesus said exclusively to these outcasts, the parables he told them. We are sure that they were spared nothing of his indignation at their sin but he must have been able to convince them of the warmth of his attachment to them as persons. This is why they "were all drawing near to hear him." His severity toward the religious leaders was partly due to the fact that they had piety without pity. They resolved the universal tension between legalism and love by going all out for the law. The two parables that follow are clearly an effort to make them see the unnaturalness of their state of mind, to realize that the issue of sin and righteousness is not so simple as their categories set it forth, that there are reasons and responsibilities for lost people that their legalistic rigor had blacked out. It was to the murmuring Pharisees and scribes that he spoke, and they must have been shocked by the symbolism he used; a coin as the representative—shall we say—of a sinner, and a sheep of a tax-gatherer. Coin and sheep—tokens of value, not of loss, in the economy of the day.

So he told them this parable: "What man of you, having a hundred sheep, if he has lost one of them, does not leave the ninety-nine in the wilderness, and go after the one that is lost, until he finds it? And when he has found it, he lays it on his shoulders, rejoicing. And when he comes home, he calls together his friends and his neighbors, saying to them, 'Rejoice with me, for I have found my sheep which was lost'" (Luke 15:3-6).

[1]

This is a story of the way people get lost and found. It was put in the form of a rhetorical question to which the answer presumably was "Yes." Not certainly so, however. There might have been practical considerations in favor of writing off the loss of one vagrant sheep because of the obvious danger involved in leaving the ninety and nine unprotected in the wilderness. Shepherds, like all other businessmen, have to deal in net and gross estimates and there is a normal loss anticipated in every operation. That Jesus seems to have assumed an affirmative answer to his question gives generous credit to his Pharisee hearers that some of them may not have deserved.

The story has three simple elements: how the sheep got lost; how it was found; and what his friends and neighbors thought of the whole affair. So far as we know this was an ordinary animal; he certainly was not a *black* sheep. The trouble he got into was something of which he may never have been consciously aware. Sheep are not noted for a perspicuous sense of direction. Similarly he was quite undisturbed that he was getting himself into difficulty when he left the flock. What then inspired this ovine eccentricity, if that is what leaving the flock really was? Certainly no malign intent. What is more innocent than a lamb? Or what is less inclined to go off on its own? Sheep are notoriously flock-conscious, let us say. A bellweather can lead them unprotestingly anywhere he happens to go. All our traditional tenderness about sheep and lambs does not prevent our protest at the lack of initiative in people who, we say, follow their leader with the docility of a flock of sheep. The matter can be put thus: sheep get lost by following their noses, by normal preoccupation with what is immediately in front of them. The chances are that this famous sheep by sheer good fortune hit on a lush growth of grass and kept following it as long as it lasted. It must have been quite a growth and commensurate with the animal's hunger. Sooner or later, however, it was to become aware instinctively that it was alone, albeit quite solidly full and, for the moment, comfortable. That it was in danger in the wilderness was obvious only to the shepherd.

Of course it was just as certainly lost as if it had left the shepherd in obstinate revolt against him. Jesus was not excusing the taxgatherers and sinners and saying they were better off outside the fold than in. To be sure they had followed what to them were lush growths, and this had lost them from the fellowship of their own people. That they were lost in this way had nothing particularly to do with the question of their state of grace. Lost they indubitably were and no one knew it better than they did. This is, we insist, an important matter. It provides us with an understanding of the word "lost" that has nothing to do with the idea of sin. This, perhaps the most famous sheep in our literature, not excluding Mary's little lamb, has been made the symbol for perversity, profligacy, and revolt against the Divine Shepherd in thousands of discussions about man's perdition, and most of this has missed the mark completely. The tax collectors and the "sinners" were lost, make no mistake about it. But were

they, for that matter, any more unrighteous than the Pharisees
and the scribes? Or were they any more lost? We cannot forget
that Jesus, in another connection told the Pharisees that publicans and harlots would precede them into the Kingdom of God.
Was this because they were righteous? No; it was because they
had found themselves in a way and in a fellowship that the
Pharisees had missed. This indicates how deeply Jesus saw the
relation between goodness and self-realization; between lostness
and self-defeat. Of this more later elsewhere.

To be lost through innocence is none the less to be lost, but
it brings a different emphasis to the condition of lostness and to
the method of recovery. How was the sheep found? The initiative seems to have been entirely the shepherd's.

> Away in the desert he heard its cry
> Weak and helpless and ready to die.

Thus reads part of the most famous versification of this parable,
but it takes the full liberties allowed to the poet. Whether the
shepherd heard this cry or not, of one thing we may be certain:
it was not a cry of penitence. The initiative of the shepherd was
due to a sense of obligation to a lost sheep, his property, a sense
of lost value that was recoverable if he was willing to make the
effort. So he did. How easy or arduous the search is of no great
matter. He found the errant creature, hoisted it to his shoulder
and came rejoicing home. That the successful search was the occasion for great satisfaction among the neighbors is indicated by
the parallel Jesus draws with the heavenly satisfaction over one
sinner who repents.

It will be noted that Jesus seems to make an identification
here between the returned sheep and a repentant sinner. This
is more apparent than real. He had already abandoned the metaphor of the parable and was setting forth a principle, bare of
metaphorical embellishments. He was doubtless aware that there
had been nothing in his parable indicating that the neighbor-

hood rejoicing was over a *repentant* sheep; it was over a *found* sheep. The lost sheep was not a "bad" sheep anymore than the ninety-nine were "good" sheep. The difference was in the integrity of the relations of the ninety-nine within the fold, and the impaired relations with the one that was lost. This is a meaning of perdition that has all but dropped out of the language of preaching. We wonder why. Is it because a dissociated person is less dramatic than a violently wicked one, and is, for that reason, of less concern to us?

[2]

In understanding perdition in these terms the word "lost" takes on more spacious dimensions of meaning. What of the sense of lostness in our times? Here is a tension situation increasingly prevalent. It would seem that the larger a concentration of people gets, the more lost persons it contains. The number of lost souls is in direct ratio to the size of the city. Not primarily because cities are wicked places; that is beside the point, but because cities are lonely places and shelter with anonymity numberless individuals who belong to no fellowship. They have followed a lush—or in many cases—a niggardly growth of necessity or of promise and have come to a place where the throngs of their fellows are a wilderness in which they are hopelessly lost. Here is breakdown and heartbreak and the anguish of frustration. The efforts of those shepherds whose privilege it is to counsel such vagrants always take the form of urging that they establish themselves in a fellowship of some sort—church, club, or what not. This is the clear analogue of lifting a strayed sheep to one's shoulder and carrying it back to the community of its fellows.

It was failure to do this that was the "sin" of the Pharisees, always a pharisaical oversight. Perhaps the local renegades had forfeited their right to belong to the we-group; their ostracism was self-invited and deserved. Hence the rulers regarded it a proof of their own rectitude that they scorned them. But Jesus took an attitude that was the exact opposite. He sought these lost sheep out. Did he abuse them for their vagrancy from the fold? We have no record of it. What he sought to do was to restore to them a sense of fellowship. Loneliness is intolerable—as much so as sinfulness. Indeed sin in most of its commonest forms is an effort to avert the boredom or panic of being left alone. Playgrounds are the cure for the delinquency problem, which is another way of saying that fellowship or a sense of belonging is the point at which much sinning is to be averted. It is because man is a gregarious animal that he is in danger when he must constantly be denied the fellowship of his kind. How rich the idea of the fold becomes when set within this context. That it should have engaged the imagination of Jesus to such an extent that he is reported in the Fourth Gospel as referring to himself as a Shepherd in a sort of universal relation to all men, and the ultimate fellowship as being "one fold, one shepherd" is no accident. It followed clearly from the understanding of one aspect of the human problem that he caught in this ageless little parable. How generous—and unhappily how mistaken—was his assumption that everyone would act similarly in the same circumstances. His rhetorical question: "What man of you . . . does not leave . . . and go after the one that is lost?" implies an affirmative reply. If the Pharisees had taken pains to answer honestly—and our answer would hardly be different—they would doubtless have said: "No; let well enough alone; there is enough to be done taking care of the ninety-nine." In such a case what is to be said for the lostness of the Pharisee who answers thus?

[3]

There is a very practical matter that may profitably be mentioned before we turn to the next parable. We do not easily keep in mind the clear fact that we all can get lost by innocently following our noses until they lead us out of the fold of human fellowship. Making money nearly always does this. The rich often disfranchise themselves from the community and while their self-imposed ostracism may flatter their vanity, it just as surely starves their souls. They have followed the lush growth till it has led them into the wilderness of loneliness. This is equally true of the scholar whose fondness for his ivory tower costs him the companionship of his humbler fellows; the artist, the playboy, the politician—indeed is any one of us exempt from this tendency? It may begin in moral innocence but it ends in loneliness, which is a spiritual perdition of a sort often as deep and as dangerous, perhaps, as the sense of guilt. After all is there not basically a similarity? Of what is the sinner more aware than that his sin isolates him from his fellows and from God? These lost sheep should be as much the concern of the shepherd—whatever his official or vocational title may be—as are the dramatic sinners. After all, how much of overt and offensive sinning is an effort to overcome a sense of lostness from the fellowship of one's kind?

They were not given time to reply for Jesus follows the story of the sheep with the equally familiar story of the lost coin. The switch from the pastoral to the domestic milieu is ingratiating and adds charm to the famous pair. And yet the emphasis is not different.

"Or what woman, having ten silver coins, if she loses one coin, does not light a lamp and sweep the house and seek diligently until she finds it? And when she has found it, she calls together her friends and neighbors, saying, 'Rejoice with me, for I have found the coin which I had lost' " (Luke 15:8-9).

The silver coin, we are told, was a drachma, the equivalent of about sixteen cents. Ten such pieces represented a modest hoard of $1.60. What induced Jesus to change the metaphor in repeating the idea he had just finished presenting? There were taxgatherers in his audience, and sinners. Were there women in the latter group? Perhaps. Thrifty housewives? Hardly. Harlots? Most likely. Never mind. Once again he puts a rhetorical question and assumes an affirmative response. The assumptions which gave him right to expect assent were simple: coins have value; coins get lost; homekeepers are not indifferent to their loss; their recovery demands effort and provides great satisfaction.

How this coin got lost we do not know. It may have been that the woman was an untidy housekeeper and never knew where anything was. Or she may have been overly fastidious and put the coin away so carefully that she couldn't find it when she needed it. Or she may have been going over the needs of the family and in counting her resources carelessly dropped a coin that rolled, with the perversity of free moving objects, out of sight and came to rest in a dark, inaccessible and unsuspected cranny.

Whatever the circumstance of its disappearance, two things are certain: it was the woman's fault ("What woman . . . if she loses one coin"); and it was no fault of the coin. This latter fact has already been pointed out in our discussion of the lost sheep. In that case, however, there was apparently no fault of the shepherd in the loss. Innocent shepherd and innocent sheep compounded a loss and necessitated a search. Here, however, the culpability or the carelessness of the woman is both described and confessed ("I have found the coin which I had lost"). Innocence and culpability compounded a loss and initiated a search.

If there is uncertainty as to the way in which the coin was lost, this is not true of the way in which it was found. There is a capsule description of the great energy and intelligence with which the woman set about finding it. She lit a lamp, she swept the house, she searched diligently. We are dealing with parables, in these studies, and whatever other interest they may have for us must not obscure the fact that their symbolism, even in the details, is important. The lamp, for example. We shall not identify this as the light of truth or the gospel though within disciplined limits there is no objection to such use of it. The simplest understanding is, however, likely to be the most accurate. The woman knew that groping in the dark would reduce the chances of finding the coin to luck. She would rather trust a lamp. Similarly the sweeping of the house may be—as indeed it has been—used as a "type" of the besom of God finally exposing and gathering out of the dark places all hidden things both valuable and worthless. Again there is no very great objection to this, but the more elemental inference would seem to be that since a lost thing, whether a coin or a person, is simply out of its proper place, a general tidying up will both improve appearances generally and expose the things that are out of place. The suggestion of diligent application to her job needs no comment since however hard or long she worked, she was at length successful. There follows the neighborly sharing of satisfaction over the retrieved drachma and the parallel joy in heaven over the repentance of one sinner. As in the previous story there can be no intimation that the coin had offended the woman beyond having made a nuisance of itself by rolling under the sideboard!

[4]

The cause of the lost sheep's perdition was his having followed a lush growth. This was a normal thing for a healthy sheep to do. The nature of his perdition was separation from the fold. This was the wilderness. T. S. Eliot has written of it in obscure and sometimes irritating ways as "The Wasteland" in which mankind today wanders in isolation and loneliness. The cause of the coin's perdition was somehow connected with its owner, and the nature of its perdition was devaluation by virtue of the fact that out of circulation it had no real worth.

We do not need to speculate as to the reaction of the Pharisees and scribes to these stories. The next time we hear of them, after two more parables, they are scoffing at the parable-teller, and his reply is that they seek to justify themselves before men (Luke 16:14-15). Self-justification is exactly the reverse of the attitude of the woman who had lost the coin. She was quick to acknowledge her fault and quick to remedy it. It must have been intolerable to the Pharisees to have the clear implication laid against them that they were responsible for the lostness of the publicans and sinners and were doing nothing about it. This was unjust and therefore infuriating. They could agree when a sheep wandered off that it was in danger but that was no fault of the shepherd. But when the coin was said to be lost through carelessness, untidiness, or overscrupulosity—that was accusing them, by clear implication, of complicity in the perdition of the men and women they were ready enough to write off as loss.

Not only this: the searching mind of Jesus had gone deeper. The sheep was lost in the wilderness, but the coin was lost *in the house*. Here it could suffer no danger except devaluation. It was safe even when it was lost. What could such obvious impertinence have meant to the Pharisees? They were not only accomplices in the perdition of the outcasts, they—the outcasts—were lost right in the very house where they had lived all their lives. They could say a lost coin is not a coin, but could they say a lost son of Israel was no Israelite? What was wrong with them and with the house that these people could be lost? Was the house untidy? Were its custodians careless? That would anger a Pharisee, right enough. Had their overfastidiousness—mint, anise and cummin—pre-empted their concern for justice, mercy and faith, the three things that both illumine the house and make a thorough cleanup possible. And finally: Had they shown less than diligence in seeking the lost? Had they, in all honesty, shown any interest at all? It was a much simpler matter to write them off as lost coins, to treat them as outcasts and to find community satisfactions, not in the fact that the lost were found, but that they were quit of them. Little wonder that the Pharisees scoffed.

[5]

Let us, however, not be too ready to condemn the scoffers. The timelessness of this parable is, like that of its pair, not calculated to make us feel smug if we take it seriously. Once again it may be necessary to point out that whatever the moral condition of the outcasts who stood by and overheard what Jesus was saying to the lordly arbiters of society, there were certain circumstances involving their separation from their fellows which were innocent of moral connotation. We need not grow sentimental about the innocent qualities of bad people; but we do well to be realistic about the bad qualities of innocent people—meaning ourselves. If the lost sheep followed a normal animal impulse and got lost, are we so sufficiently aware of this very common human experience that we seek the lonely-lost, in our communities, yes, in our churches even? The sinners don't come to church much; the lost come every time the door is open. They may be unaware of moral defections but they know what it is to be lonely and all about the nagging tensions that drive them to seek association on any level that will satisfy their longing for the companionship of any fold.

It is hardly necessary to comment further on the sharply probing insights hidden in the coin story. For modern Christendom it has come as a shock to realize how it has been responsible for lost coins in its own house. Carelessness, untidiness, fastidiousness; how much of this has been the real cause of the innocent lostness of many within its own house it is as impossible as it is unpleasant to contemplate. It is not uncommon for some eloquent advocate of church efficiency to dilate on the hidden wealth of personality in our churches. Why hidden? Why lost? Very often, if this parable is to have any meaning for us, because

of the church leadership itself, that is, its disinclination to emu-
late the ancient shepherd and housewife.

The devotion of the shepherd and the diligence of the housekeeper are not by any means lost among us. But it is the lighting
of the lamp and the sweeping of the house that are our present
hope. Dare we turn a light on the inside of our house? We shall
not find the lost values without it; with it we shall find some
things that will make us ashamed. It is when we are ashamed
that we will begin to tidy things up, to repair the disorder and
indecency in some of the affairs that have made it easy for orderly
and decent persons to get lost in the house. Such details as are
involved in this sort of sheep-searching and coin-hunting are to
be found in endless studies elsewhere. Our concern is simply to
point out that the pungency of these innocent little stories is as
sharp today as it was when they first moved the Pharisees to scorn.
They had ears to hear; they preferred the lips that scoffed. He
that hath ears to hear, let him guard his tongue.

CHAPTER X

Three Prodigals

SHEEP get lost and coins get lost. Some people get lost like sheep and some like coins. But other people get lost too, and some of them get lost like people. We return to Jesus' audience again for a moment. Assuming that the parable teller always fitted his stories to his hearers, we may be sure there were some before him who, having heard what he had been saying, decided that he had spoken directly to their perdition. To become aware of this was the first step in their restitution. There were others there, however, who did not fit the lost coin and sheep categories. Perhaps there was a prodigal son listening to him and a prodigal father, and a prodigal brother. He may have known such a trio personally. Why not? In any case he certainly knew that wherever one goes one encounters such prodigal persons whether they can be identified or not. Hence we have the greatest of all his parables, if not indeed the greatest parable of all times. Its full meaning is not to be seen apart from its relation to the two that have preceded it or without a complete analysis of the three characters that appear in it—all of them, each in his own way prodigal in his use of something uniquely and superlatively worthful to himself.

We must keep in mind the sense of tension pervading the period in which these parables were spoken, tension which Jesus and those about him were experiencing, tensions which are pandemic wherever people are organized for living together. Where, so much as in the domestic unit, do we encounter more varied and more enervating tensions? Here they are born, nursed, and raised to wretched adulthood or, to vary the figure, they are ignited, fanned, and exploded into destructive personality conflicts. Here also they may be eased or employed creatively. It happens in the best of families and with consequences that are little less spectacular and shattering than when they happen in the not-so-good families. We have said that the sheep and coin were lost through no initiative of their own, nor was there a conscious sense of tension at separation from the fold or the purse. There was loneliness and devaluation which, interpreted in human terms, do cause anxiety and fretfulness. The communities seem to have rejoiced at the recovery of the sheep and the coin, but they themselves participated not at all in the festivities. To have abated loneliness and devaluation was a social gain which was generally recognized.

[1]

Now the situation presented in the story of the three prodigal people has significant differences. Here the initiative was never consciously or willingly surrendered by those who had it both by natural endowment and right and the satisfactions at the abatement of the tensions was intramural only. It is not to be wondered at that this story has been more widely and continuously studied and moralized about than any other in the literature of the West. Certain literary critics have even asserted that it is rivaled only by the Good Samaritan story for the position of the greatest short story of all times.

There seems to be nothing to support the notion generally held that this highly extroverted second son, known exclusively as the prodigal, was a rebel against the family—its traditions or its members. Too often he is pictured as a willful adolescent, bent on his own destruction and altogether heedless of the domestic and personal implications of his desire to leave home. On the contrary we have reasons to think that his request of his father was in no sense irregular.

"There was a man who had two sons; and the younger of them said to his father, 'Father, give me the share of the property that falls to me.' And he divided his living between them" (Luke 15:11-12).

Here was no wheedling teen-ager asking for spending money. There was a time at which the law provided that a son could make legal claim for the share of the family fortune that, in a real sense, belonged to him. "The share . . . that falls to me"; there can be no misunderstanding of these words. If there was a quarrel about it, we have no evidence in the record. That there may have been reluctance on the part of the father is undisclosed. Here is what appears to have been a normal situation in a family of substance that accepted the laws of the domain concerning the distribution of its property.

"Not many days later, the younger son gathered all he had and took his journey into a far country . . ." (Luke 15:13a).

We must not forget that the older son had also been awarded his share of the property. It was his right, by primogeniture, to have a greater proportion, and his right to use it as he wished. We may speculate all we want to about his use of his fortune, but we have no reason for thinking that he proposed more worthy or judicious use of it than his younger brother. All we know is that he stayed at home.

The second son was clearly inclined to no such demure use of his share. He was going to see the world. Why do young men leave home? There is, of course, the biological necessity for establishing new domestic units that operates powerfully to break up the family. It would be disastrous if this were not so. There is the psychological necessity for establishing one's self as an independent personality. It is also powerful in its operation in dissolving the family bonds. If it did not influence individual behavior in the growing person, he would not grow spiritually and a family would become a group of midget egos attached parasitically forever to the parent. There is also the normal friction between individuals in families, the fixations that develop and the irritations and alliances that they form within the family circle. These are all, to a greater or less degree, the growing pains of the soul and are to be cured by maturity alone. The mature stage will be reached, however, only by the exercise of one's own initiative in directions which are to him definitive in their promise of personal fulfillment. More often than not these factors also result in the fragmentation of the family.

Was the most famous—and, we think unjustly, the most infamous of these three persons—determined when he left home to cast away all his family had given him, including of course the money, in an effort at self-destruction? Was he unfilial, rebellious, sinister, roistering, escapist, irresponsible? We have no indication of any of these moods. Indeed, had the story ended at the point of his departure from home he could have quite as easily been the fair-haired boy carrying the family's good name to far lands in search of fame and fortune, as the waster he subsequently became. The point is that so far, he was simply exhibiting the initiative and adventuresomeness, the exploring and inquiring mind that has excited many a lad with dreams of what lay beyond the farm's fences and touched his soul with a determination to see the world. It is what has taken many an American farm boy off to college with his tuition fees carefully contained in his pocket. Equally true must it be said that beyond the fence such adventure is apt to encounter the roadhouse as well as the dean's office. But never to have had the urge to move toward the distant horizons was to have lacked either properly functioning endocrines or a properly activated soul.

So off he goes. There is no angry repudiation of father by son or of son by father. The record is silent on their separation. Separations are often silent. There is an inarticulate recognition of the portentousness of such leave-takings and it is often better so. Into a far country he went ". . . and there he squandered his money in loose living" (Luke 15:13b).

[2]

This is the point in the story where we discover he is lost. What had happened to him? We need not people the story with reprobates and playboys to explain what had come about. We can look inside his own soul. There is a point at which the inquiring mind becomes merely inquisitive, when the desire to know becomes simple curiosity, when the line from home to horizon loses its direction in aimless meanderings. Here the proud spirit that wants to know becomes the proud spirit that wants to show how much it knows, or pretends to know more than it does. Is this what happened to the younger son?

There is evidence that it was pride that was his undoing. Whatever accomplices it may have had—and they spawn wherever hubristic self-regard sheds its warmth—pride was at the center. This is shown negatively in his confession, along toward the story's close, that he had lost his worthiness to reoccupy his former status of sonship. Once upon a time he had been aware that he held and deserved this position. Had it not been inflated when he first found himself among strangers and had to be a strong friend to himself to get along? This is one of the subtlest forms of pride and the margin between it and self-confidence is always obscure and often inadvertently crossed. Once on the wrong side, one's mind becomes its unprotesting aid and proves by its ingenious legerdemain that because one must be one's self at all times, being one's self in all ways (good and bad, wise and foolish) is the primary demand and the perfect triumph of the soul. His sense of inner worthiness that he had brought from his family transferred itself by the subtlest of pride's tricks to everything he did. And also, by pride's unrelenting nemesis he came to lose utterly his sense of personal dignity and self-regard.

The positive way in which the change is detected is in his wastefulness and loose living. Waste is prodigality in its essence. He was throwing himself away and being proud about it; loose living is the irresponsibility that follows the casting off of all restraint. Now it is clear that these two qualities of human behavior have always been the marks of the proud man. He finds it necessary to prove his importance to himself and his fellows by his easy-handedness and free spending. He will commit any folly of prodigal waste or giving if he is sufficiently flattered by those he entertains or subsidizes. It may be the overcompensation we discover in one whose ego is weak, the sign of a deep-laid sense of inadequacy and inferiority. But such a morbid state—if such it be—differs very slightly if at all from similar symptoms in so-called normal people. The man who, shrinking from oblivion, perpetuates his memory by a building erected to his honor may only be more pretentious than his neighbor who assures himself of immortality by wild parties. We are not concerned here with the relative moral value of the one or the other; we are concerned simply with the way the pride of both of them will play tricks on them in spite of themselves.

The other side of this hubristic display which we call prodigality is the proud man's repudiation of all restraints. Loose living is living on-the-loose. For it is a corollary of the sense of pride that spends freely that it shall brook no interference with all other expressions of one's egoism. Earlier renderings of the words "squandered his property in loose living" put it: "wasted his substance with riotous living." The older brother is even more specific. He described the situation as his having "devoured your [the father's] living with harlots." He may have been right; certainly the casting off of sex restraint has in our culture been the perfect symbol of emancipation, and at no time does the pride of man submit more supinely to the arguments of his servile mind than when he is told that in casting off the restraints others have imposed, he is demonstrating his own "higher" restraint! This is ego-sufficiency of the most delusive sort because no man thinks he is loose. Whether he be puritanical or profligate, he is confident of the restraints on his behavior. For this reason the amplifications of this simple story have peopled it with all sorts of depraved characters among whom the prodigal was on-the-loose. This is what we are given imaginations for, but we must be careful that they do not go on-the-loose themselves. Since, as we shall see, the older brother exaggerated nearly everything else he said, he may have stretched the facts to suit his mood when he mentioned his brother's lady friends. There is, however, no doubt that the boy was lost. His initiative had taken him away from home, his pride had betrayed him into waste and unrestraint. If this wasn't perdition words have little meaning.

"And when he had spent everything, a great famine arose in that country, and he began to be in want. So he went and joined himself to one of the citizens of that country who sent him into the fields to feed swine. And he would gladly have fed on the pods that the swine ate; and no one gave him anything" (Luke 15:14-17).

This marks the low limit of his degradation. He had no money and no friends and no job. The anonymous citizen who gave him a chance to work may be the hero of the story, for in furnishing an opportunity to think about himself and pigs and to eat their discarded garbage, he started the process that led to his final restitution. The fact that emerges from the description of his complete abasement is that it was as much a reduction of his pride as it was of his physical well-being that was the overture to his return from the far country.

[3]

Before we look at the return of the younger prodigal a study of the older one may be helpful. The younger had gone into a far country and got lost; the older had stayed in the field back of the manor house and got equally lost. Not in the same way. Indeed it is one of the amazing things about this story that it shows two opposite kinds of perdition which threaten us. The one is self-pride, the other is self-pity.

When we first encounter this older son he is seen briefly with his brother as the father is dividing his fortune between them. There was apparently no trouble at this point. For reasons of his own the older decided to keep his share at home. It is altogether possible that filial piety demanded that he accept cheerfully the lot of the elder son to stay with his aging sire and relieve him ultimately of his responsibilities. The next time we see him, he has been surprised in the field by a servant who explains the noise of revelry emanating from the house as a party being given for his long absent brother. It would seem that the festivities were well under way when he heard about it. Maybe the party had been hurriedly organized but he had not been let in on the important family news. Quite by accident had he heard the sounds of revelry.

"Now his elder son was in the field; and as he came and drew near to the house, he heard music and dancing. And he called one of the servants and asked what this meant. And he said to him, 'Your brother has come, and your father has killed the fatted calf, because he has received him safe and sound.' But he was angry and refused to go in" (Luke 15:25-28a).

This anger reaction is clearly unnatural. He may have thought that he never wanted to see his brother again, reports of whose goings-on had doubtless reached the home. To be surprised by his unannounced return and to be affronted by this display of

welcome caught him off guard and revealed something significant about him. There follow certain intimations that give us a
clue to the nature of the older son's perdition.

He had not got on very well with his father. This was hardly
the father's fault; he had given him his share of the property
at the time of division and had later made him the sole owner of
what was left. "Son," he tells him in order to smooth his rumpled
feelings, "you are always with me, and all that is mine is yours."
But the son had spoken rudely to his father before this conciliatory reminder had been offered. When he was told, "Your
brother has come," he retorted, "This *son* of *yours*." When he
learned about the fatted calf, he countered with, "[He] has devoured *your* living with harlots." Observe that it was his own,
not his father's living, the younger brother had devoured. This
petulant remark poorly disguises a sense of resentment at the
distribution that had put money into the waster's hands. And
his accusation that the father had been niggardly in his recompense to his elder son for his impeccable filial devotion—"I have
never disobeyed your command, yet you never gave me a kid
that I might make merry"—seems in thoroughly bad temper.

How he had got on with his errant brother we can only guess,
but our guess is that it was pretty badly. Temperamentally they
were opposites, one activistic, the other phlegmatic. They might
have quarreled; brothers do, and that may be why the younger
thought it advantageous to find more spacious areas for making
his own way. That he declined to recognize him as his brother
when his father entreated him ("this son of yours") has already
been mentioned; and that a welcome party should have incurred
anger rather than delight reveals a good deal. Was he allergic
to all parties, or just to this one?

The basic fact is that he didn't get along well with himself.
The dead weight of his morose self-pity pressed heavily on all
his other moods. Note: To pity one's fellow opens the heart; to
pity one's self closes it. This is the explanation of the man's

anger. Not the justification he would have given, to be sure; his explanation would have flattered his sense of superior virtue, a sense that he thought was scandalized by the misbehavior of his glamorous brother. Was he really scandalized? No; he was not morally indignant; he was just plain sore. And he didn't know why. Do we? Well, it is altogether possible that he was jealous of his more spectacular brother. Secretly he would have liked to leave home himself, but he was held back either by obligation or lack of self-confidence. For all his preferred status in the family, he was insecure. He didn't like his father; he hated his brother; he pitied himself; but he had not openly disclosed these deep feelings. Such latent disorder in one's soul cannot forever be concealed, however, and when his brother turned up unexpectedly his subliminal hostilities exploded. His brother had dramatized himself in riotous living; he would dramatize himself in riotous anger. All his insecurity, his frustration, his self-pity were projected on his brother and directed at his father. At last, he subconsciously knew, he could draw attention away from his loathsome brother to himself.

Here was a prodigal if there ever was one, prodigal in the waste of the most precious things a man has—the inner securities within which his soul may relax. Here also was a lost man if ever there was one. Even within the external security of his outward circumstances he was lost—lost to his father, to his brother, and to his better self. The younger brother had, at the low level of desperation cried: "I perish with hunger." Had the elder brother known the low level of his spirit and been as honest, he would have cried: "I perish with anger." The younger brother, in seeking his freedom in the wide world, had got lost; the elder brother in trying to escape the risks of freedom by staying at home, also got lost. But the younger brother knew what the elder hadn't even suspected.

[4]

Since the final restitution of the younger brother is not to be properly understood outside a pattern of readjustment that involved both the sons and their father, it is important to consider the latter as the third prodigal. To refer to him thus is no novelty. Some years ago a pamphlet entitled *The Prodigal Father* was widely distributed. It made the point that the errancy of the famous son might have been avoided if the father had been stricter in matters pertaining to his use of money. This is all to the good but an effort to understand his complicity in the fortunes of both sons takes us down to deeper levels of character.

The story presents him as a member of the upper middle-class gentry of an average community of his time. Had he been interviewed by a modern feature-story writer after the return of his son he would have conceded that he was a modestly successful, middle-of-the-road, generous-spirited citizen. He was obviously a man of property. There are hints of luxury—hired servants, the best robes, gold ornaments, fatted calf, etc. Moreover he and his two sons apparently managed to get along pretty well together. He clearly had a sort of fondness for both of them as is indicated in his unqualified welcome to the younger and his affectionate entreaty to the older on the occasion of our story. This is significant, we think, for the way a man expresses his feelings of affection is an index of the sort of man he is. In this case it was an indication that his was, superficially at least, a generous spirit. Other facts support this: the readiness with which he complied with the request that his fortune be divided; the concern he felt for the restoration of the younger son to the full status of sonship; and the gala way in which he proposed to celebrate the return.

The influence of these qualities on his sons must have been considerable though it clearly was different in each case. When the younger was in the far country he realized he could have "bread enough and to spare" if he returned home; yet while the older brother stayed at home he felt abused because, as he said, he had never been given a kid with which to entertain his friends. This difference of attitude may mean that the father was partial to the younger. On the contrary it may mean that he was lacking in depth. This calls for further comment.

He was morally superficial. We might even call him something of a sentimentalist. All of us, to be sure, more or less fall into this classification, but he seems particularly so. As a rich man he made property the criterion of moral values. That this is sentimentalism is repudiated by men of substance. They like to think of themselves as realistic, hard-boiled, ledger-conscious, practical. To have thought he could discharge his obligations to his sons by giving them material security and that this was all they needed was the veriest sentimentality. Allow what we must for the adventuresomeness of the son who left home, we must feel that he left home morally unequipped to use his money. To go off on one's own is adventure; to leave with one's pockets full of gold is sheer moral hazard. The great pioneers have not started out with their fortunes; they have come back with them. The father's legal exactness plus his sentimental trust in the security money would guarantee constituted a definite moral handicap for the boy. The pride which toppled him to his downfall was abetted —if not indeed inculcated—by his fond father. This, we must unhappily say, is little more than we can expect from those whose outlook is limited by the sentimentalism of the materialist.

There is another element in his moral shallowness that is less apparent but even more dangerous. He held a cheap view of forgiveness. Here is sentimentalism again. His fatherly attachment to his son made him waive all the concommitants of restitution that give it moral dignity. The boy knew the abasement of sin but the father knew only the pains of loneliness and disappointment. These latter were to be cured by the simple fact of the boy's reappearance. Not so the son's deep sense of unworthiness.

He wanted to atone for his prideful waste of life and property by returning, not to the status of a son, but to that of a hired hand. Here is realism; here is moral penetration. And yet the father would have no talk of such nonsense. The most important thing for the son to do was to confess his sin; the next important was to accept its consequences, for forgiveness does not cancel the results of evil-doing. But the father would have none of it and thus, in effect, repudiated the moral relevance of his son's spiritual catharsis.

Furthermore, in the father's eyes the restoration of the son was primarily a matter of his immediate return to the propertied status he had lost. Ring, robe, and roast veal—this was the agenda proposed for one who had fallen into evil by means of, and largely because of, these three things. What reason did the father have for thinking the prodigal would not regard his escapade, once he was renovated externally, as far less serious than it had seemed in the pig sty? What was to keep him from squandering and loose living again? This sentimental father was restoring to his stricken son the things that had fed his pride of position and been the prelude to his downfall. It was as if to celebrate the cure of an alcoholic he was urged to solemnize it with a stiff drink.

Once more: The father's understanding of himself was shallow. Here is sentimentalism again and in its most dangerous form. When the older brother "refused to come in," "he went out and entreated him." This was certainly a conciliatory gesture but what he said was what was to be expected from a shallow mind. He insisted that they had always been together. That this was physically true was probably a part of the reason for the older son's neurotic anger; that it was spiritually *not* true was the reason for his frustration. Again: "All mine is yours" was a reference to the material goods they may have jointly owned, but what was truly the father's best wealth had never been given the son. Hence his sense of loneliness. Fields, robes, kids, rings

—these were his, but comradeship, deep understanding, and friendliness had been withheld from him. Did not this stem from the father's preoccupation with things as the basic values? This is the materialist's philosophy. What more, he might have asked, could be expected of a father than bed and board for his boys?

This man was first-century bourgeois. It is interesting to note the concern that Jesus exhibited for this type of man. There follow this story three parables about rich men. Why did he, who was concerned with the outcasts, exercise himself also over those who were substantially established? Was it not that they also were in perdition, all the more dangerous because they thought they were safe?

This is no judgment of moral obliquity laid against them; it is a description of moral shallowness. This father was not a wicked man or an undutiful parent; he simply suffered the spiritual disabilities of the comfortable. Had we no deeper insight into the moral problem of sin, guilt, judgment, penitence, forgiveness, and restitution than that provided in this story, we would exculpate prodigals as readily as this man did and miss the problem of the frustrated as completely as he did. He indulged in an emotional spree when his boy came home. No wonder; who wouldn't? But it could easily have had a deleterious effect on both the sons. The elder son's sense of estrangement from the family was apparently exacerbated by it. Unhappily the story has nothing to tell us of *his* restoration. Fundamentally this man's outlook on life rested moral judgments on very shallow foundations; deceived him and his sons as to the depth of his own moral stratum; and made everybody feel that the process of reclamation was much simpler than it really is.

[5]

These were three prodigals; three lost men. The father wasted his time, the elder son wasted his emotions, the younger his substance; the father was lost in the family circle, the elder son in a jungle of confused emotions, the younger in a world of evil companions. In the story, however, we have only the record of the youngest's salvation. He rarely lost the initiative whether in leaving home, spending his fortune, or returning. Even when he was tending swine he was able to think clearly about his inglorious state and to plan for, and take constructive steps toward, his rehabilitation. This is not to say he achieved this alone, but that he initiated the saving process. The light of self-improvement was at times dim but never extinguished. What happened to the elder son we do not know. It would be interesting to continue the story to an apocryphal conclusion in which the two sons became friends, one by the telling of inexhaustible tales and moralizing about the state of the world, the other by practical guidance in sharing the running of the family affairs into which he had been reintroduced. The unhappy fact is that the recovery of the elder was perhaps more difficult, if it was ultimately achieved. His anger shut him out of the family festivities when his brother showed up. Anger of the sort that possessed him is always a barrier to fellowship because it is the overt indication of a hidden feeling of frustration. It is a perverse form of self-praise in that it tries to project resentment away from itself. In finding a scapegoat, it deflects the blame it subconsciously feels and thus protects itself. Because he was too immature emotionally to take care of himself, he had long since surrendered his initiative to his father. Had he wanted to be saved from himself, neither he nor his father would have known the steps necessary to be taken. What of the father's salvation? Alas that we think of him, with all his excellent qualities and accomplishments, as typical of those to whom the idea of being lost is preposterous and the need for being saved is no less insulting than absurd. At the same time we are not left without suggestions about these two unsaved prodigals. Could the famous rich young ruler have been the prototype of the elder son? Was any one of the parables about rich men pertinent to the father's problem? We shall see.

In the meantime there is a final word about the trio we have been studying. It concerns the inclination to make the parable of the prodigal son a paradigm of salvation. The efforts to construct a soteriology out of it have been many. It is a tempting exercise because it seems so simple. The father, indulgent and generous and ultimately forgiving, is offered as the picture of God; the son, repudiating the protection of the father's care and falling into debauchery and disaster is presented as the prototype of the sinner; and the ultimate forgiveness and restoration into the family depict the completeness of the sinner's reparation and reunion. But if the rudiments of the Christian understanding of salvation are concerned with the nature of sin, the nature of judgment, and the nature of redemption, they cannot be skimped or dealt with superficially. It is clear that this story —if it is a pattern of the redemptive scheme—does just that. It is, to be sure, too much to ask a parable to say everything, to include in its simple pattern all the elements relevant to a situation it attempts by indirection to say. A parable is not a treatise. On the other hand we cannot accept the elements that appear in a parable as a perfect whole. To let it say too little is as much an error as to make it say too much. It is the former to which we have been prone in this story. We cannot believe sin is sufficiently understood as an amicable leave-taking from the father's house with one's pockets full of money. Nor are the demands of judgment met by an amicable reunion, nor is atonement made first by compassion, an embrace, and a kiss, and then by a robe, a ring, and a banquet. This makes the business much too simple and far too easy. Sin is rooted in man's prideful desire and effort to usurp the prerogatives of God; sin stands under the irrevocable judgment of God, and man must come to terms with it; sin, because penalty is correlative to judgment even where the grace of forgiveness is operative, must be atoned for. Except for the first, and even then not explicitly, these three profound factors are missing from this parable.

We are led therefore to understand both the intention and the essence of this most famous of Jesus' parables in other than simple soteriological terms. This is why we have undertaken to study it within the more general context of crisis and tension. For this reason our first look was at the group to which it was addressed. It is anything but fantastic to imagine that Jesus may have known personally prodigal sons and prodigal fathers in his audience. If so he surely knew of the tensions that tugged at their souls; if so he surely was concerned to make suggestions, hidden in a didactic medium with which his hearers were familiar, that would not be missed by those who had ears to hear.

It is, of course, the quality of great teaching, whether it uses a discursive or a narrative approach to its theme, that it is susceptible of both profound and simple uses, but it is never oversimplified or abstruse. To preserve, for our understanding of this story, the tension in the time context and the tension in the spiritual context within which we assert it was first told takes from it nothing of its simple profundity. On the contrary we believe it saves it both from oversimplification and overcomplexity and, at the same time enables us to see its proportions, and its dimensions and its timelessness. Little wonder that it has been the inspiration of art as well as religion. Is it not, after all, part of the story of each of us, a chapter, at least, in the epic of Everyman?

CHAPTER XI

Ends and Means

IF THE much advertised visitor from Mars were to find himself in church one fine morning, he would encounter many
things that would astonish him. To his naïve questions, however, he would find friendly and ready answers. He would be
told that he had made his way into a Christian worship service
which was a product of the Christian culture which surrounds
and gives character to all that we do. Hymns, prayers, exhortations, and so forth were simply an effort to follow the instructions
found for such exercises in a book we call the Bible. This book,
he would be told, was the basis for our way of life—civilization,
some bold parishioner would call it. He would perhaps ask for
a copy for further study and take leave, still mildly curious but
hardly mystified.

If, on the next day, he were to take himself to the temples of
trade he would discover practices quite different, and, taking
his cue from his experience of the day before, he might leaf
through the book to find, if possible, the explanation for the
ritual of the market place. Suppose he turned to these words:

"Make friends for yourselves by means of unrighteous mammon,
so that when it fails they may receive you into the eternal habitations" (Luke 16:9).

Some things there might not help him a great deal, but the Mar-
tian eye would undoubtedly light up with comprehension as he

pointed out to one of the priests of the stock exchange the exhortation: "Make friends . . . by means of unrighteous mammon." "These words," he would say, "explain this part of your Christian civilization. Here you are using something you call unrighteous to win something that is good—assuming that in your culture, friends are good things to have." Maybe the priest would demur courteously and try to explain, but the visitor, feeling that he had found the key to the curious behavior of the buying and selling operations he had encountered would with equal courtesy take leave, satisfied that the Book was taken quite seriously by these odd earth dwellers both in work and worship.

Here is the problem of ends and means which plagues everyone who thinks at all about the business of getting along with his fellows. It is set forth in a parable that presents two very common tension situations. There was a rich man who had a steward and tension had developed between them and there were debtors with whom the steward had to deal and there was tension there. Beneath and in great measure accounting for these tensions was the problem of means and ends.

He also said to his disciples, "There was a rich man who had a steward, and charges were brought to him that this man was wasting his goods. And he called him and said to him, 'What is this that I hear about you? Turn in the account of your stewardship, for you can no longer be steward.' And the steward said to himself, 'What shall I do, since my master is taking the stewardship away from me? I am not strong enough to dig, and I am ashamed to beg. I have decided what to do, so that people may receive me into their houses when I am put out of the stewardship.' So, summoning his master's debtors one by one, he said to the first, 'How much do you owe my master?' He said, 'A hundred measures of oil.' And he said to him, 'Take your bill, and sit down and write fifty.' Then he said to another, 'And how much do you owe?' He said, 'A hundred measures of wheat.' He said to him, 'Take your bill, and write eighty.' The master commended the dishonest steward for his prudence; for the sons of this world are wiser in their generation than the sons of light. And I tell you, make friends for yourselves by means of unrighteous mammon, so that when it fails they may receive you into the eternal habitations" (Luke 16:1-9).

Here, we submit, is as cynical a pair of operators as one is likely to encounter anywhere. Clearly there must have been reason for Jesus to tell a story about sinister people like these. It may have been an interest in the general problem of ends and means; or it may have been that the sort of thing described in the story was so common and acceptable in current practice that it needed a sharp rebuke. Whatever the reason, we have an insight into the moral problem that goes to its very heart.

[1]

Let us look at these unsavory characters. The rich man was a capitalist. He dealt in oil and wheat and made his living by crediting these commodities to needy borrowers for interest which, it is quite evident, was subject to no rates except those set by the inclination and shrewd business judgment of his agent. (We cannot forbear to point out the timelessness of a story that deals with oil and wheat as basic commodities in an economy, and credit for interest as its basic method.) There was nothing wrong in his owning wheat and oil or in lending it. On the contrary it might be argued that he sustained the business of his community and stabilized its economic life. Nevertheless he was, beyond his social utility, clearly a man without scruples. He fired his agent, not because he was dishonest (he commended him for his clever trickery later) but because he was wasting his property. This sounds like frugality but it more likely means that he was collecting too little interest or reporting too little of his earnings.

The steward (an interesting word from an Anglo-Saxon pair, "sty" and "ward"—watcher of the pigs) is described more fully. He is physically soft. Having graduated into the white-collar

class he had lost the calloused palms that once made it possible
for him to dig from dawn till dark. With this physical flabbiness
had come psychological flabbiness. Once it had been honorable
to work with a shovel; now, soft and fat, the idea of appealing
to the sufferance of others for a living was intolerable. "I am not
strong enough to dig, and I am ashamed to beg," he said to himself when confronted by his irate employer. But his wits were
still keen. Having lost the boss's confidence he turned in to win
the boss's creditors, and the method by which he did this was,
we may safely assume, a continuance of the way in which he had
already misused his responsibilities. The picture is an interesting
one, if not indeed amusing: The consternation of the debtors
suddenly herded without explanation into the compound; the
relief on the face of the first one as he emerged from his brief
("sit down quickly and write") and private interview holding a
bill that had been discounted 50 per cent; the others who followed with similar smiles and discounts. The steward was losing
no time making friends. This thing could not be kept from the
rich man's ears for long and he seems to have come into the office soon after the last radiant creditor had departed, and confronted his now ex-factotum. Instead of abusing him for further
wasting his goods by the extravagant discounts he had allowed,
he seems not a little pleased. It must be that his sense of appreciation for clever business rigging overcame what sense of out-
rage he might have felt for his compounded losses.

When these two men faced each other for what was perhaps
the last time they put on a shameless display of cynical amoralism.
Only a cynic could overlook personal loss suffered at the hands
of a former associate and turn to praise the shrewdness that had
defrauded him. The fact of the steward's dishonesty gave him
no concern. On the contrary, the prudence which used dishonest
methods in a polite sort of blackmail won his commendation.
What the factor had done was to put his master's debtors in debt
to him to such an extent that he could collect handsomely when

he needed to. By the generous disbursal of the boss's money he assured himself at least of a place to live in perpetuity. Little wonder the boss commended him; it was a smart trick. One wonders whether when he dismissed him, he did not ruefully watch him leave. An agent as clever as that might have been more useful to him than a scrupulously honest one. This episode in the story would seem to indicate that both of the men lived in an atmosphere of calculating selfishness that was so pervasive that trickery, one against the other, excited admiration instead of anger.

To show that his strange good will toward his agent was no sentimental aberration, the capitalist goes on to state what to him was apparently the cynic faith that supported him. There are two kinds of people in the world, he said: the sons of this world and the sons of light. The former are the smart operators. To be sure there is a place for the sons of light. They can be identified by their shining foreheads and bright eyes, their liberal optimism. They talk loftily about ideals and the ultimate victory of righteousness in the world. They are gentle and if let alone, quite harmless. Indeed one need not dispute their confident prediction that over the long haul, righteousness will pay off and evil will bankrupt itself. But the sons of this world are wiser *in their own generation.* After all, no one lives out the long haul; one only lives in his own generation, and in the short haul one has to be practical! "Take the cash and let the credit go," as Omar said. "Eat, drink and be merry," said an earlier pagan, "for tomorrow you may die." Why not? And there is always the chance that you may *not* die. While the sons of light talk of sobriety as an ideal, why not drink to their health with a cocktail? They are nice, clean, honest, determined fellows, sometimes a nuisance, to be sure, but never a menace.

Then follows the exhortation our friend from Mars found and thought so expressive of the modern temper he had encountered in the market. The master is so sure of his own cynical faith that he urges others to accept and practice it. "Make friends for yourselves by means of the mammon of unrighteousness (despite the warnings of the sons of light that this is ultimately futile) so that when it fails (as one must admit is a contingency) they may receive you into the eternal habitations." This is practical good sense, he would have insisted. More than that, it was suffused with a realistic aura of piety. The eternal habitations— what more worthy goal for the pilgrims on the mortal road? Here is an end the sons of light themselves are moving toward. Such an exalted end—if one is practical about it—may best be reached by the stages marked out by the sons of this world. In any case why quibble about means if the end is sufficiently noble? Let's compromise: we will let the sons of light point out the end; the sons of this world can choose the means. Fair enough!

[2]

There may be those who will disallow this understanding of the story. It is a puzzling passage. If the words just studied are taken to be representative of an attitude of Jesus, they are immediately contradicted in the following verses.

"He who is faithful in a very little is faithful also in much; and he who is dishonest in a very little is dishonest also in much. If then you have not been faithful in the unrighteous mammon, who will entrust to you the true riches? And if you have not been faithful in that which is another's, who will give you that which is your own? No servant can serve two masters; for either he will hate the one and love the other, or he will be devoted to the one and despise the other. You cannot serve God and mammon" (Luke 16:10-13).

Here is the definitive statement of the Christian moral ideal that the end does not justify the means. It is set in direct contrast to the cynic's ideal that one may win an eternal domicile by dishonesty, or any other worthy end by an unworthy means. There is therefore only one way in which we can understand the words in the ninth verse to have been spoken by Jesus. If he said them it must have been with searing sarcasm—an accommodation of his language to something he and they knew he did not mean. It is a common but dangerous forensic device. Irony not infrequently backfires, and what is spoken in sharp contemptuous words is often taken to mean its opposite. Did Jesus, looking about him at the cynical faces in his audience say: "Go ahead; get your heavenly habitations any way you can, by evil if necessary!"? Whatever we may think of this, there is no mistaking what his hearers thought. If it was sarcasm, they felt its sting. The Pharisees, who were lovers of money, heard all this, and they scoffed at him. Had they missed his meaning, had they thought him approving the use of unrighteous mammon to win the assurances of the custodians of the eternal habitations, they certainly would not have scoffed. On the contrary one can imagine them rubbing their hands with delight and saying: "Well; why haven't you said that before? If that's what you think, we can do business with you. We have never differed with your ends; it's been your means that have seemed impractical. There's no reason why we can't understand each other; in fact, from what you have just said, we see eye to eye perfectly." But they didn't say that: they scoffed, and the word is as vigorous and ugly as the mood it depicts. Scoffing, however, was his meat. He followed through:

"You are those who justify yourselves before men, but God knows your hearts; for what is exalted among men is an abomination in the sight of God" (Luke 16:15).

Is it the degradation of an exalted end by the use of evil means that is an abomination? This fits the pattern of Jesus' mind perfectly.

This makes the mooted words tolerable if they must be understood as spoken by Jesus. Thus they were sharp, bitter, barbed irony, and so understood. We incline however to the understanding that puts them on the cynics' lips. To do this requires no exegetical *tour de force;* a bit of punctuation with quotation marks will do it. This leaves the evil words where they belong and the angry recoil of the Pharisees is allowed to fall naturally at the point where he warns them that they could not serve God and mammon. That they could, was apparently a typical item of the Pharisees' faith. Furthermore, being lovers of money and adept self-justifiers, there was enough in his later stricture to incur their anger. There was enough indeed in that to keep them scoffing for a long time.

The issue it seems was clear: "No servant can serve two masters"; he cannot serve a good end and evil means, "for either he will hate the one and love the other, or he will be devoted to the one and despise the other." He cannot secure eternal habitations by dishonestly putting people under obligations to him. He cannot feather his nest by plucking his employer. "You cannot serve God and mammon." This states the matter sharply and without equivocation. There are no exceptions, even for difficult or promising cases.

[3]

There would seem to be three residual moral pillars that have, up to the present, survived the earthquakes of controversy about behavior in our Western Christian culture: man, understood in his total nature, is the locus of primary moral value and that which is inhuman is wrong; might does not make right and force must serve the moral law, never subvert it; the end does not justify the means—end and means must partake of the same moral quality. To topple these pillars deliberately or to allow them to crumble might or might not cause the collapse of our culture, but it would cause profound changes in it. There are indications as to what is already taking place with reference to them. We accept the first proposition and, by and large, try to practice it. At least we have fought two wars in this century to prove to ourselves and our enemies that we believe in certain of the primary values of the human spirit. We agree also to the second—that might does not make right; but we have discovered that in validating our faith in the value of man we have been driven to the uses of might that were to be properly validated only by our faith in the rightness of our cause. If we use might to rectify matters now, we persuade ourselves that we do so only when we think it is necessary. The third—that ends and means must be of one moral texture—to this we agree but we don't take it too seriously. "The sons of this world are wiser in their generation than the sons of light."

[4]

What do we mean by ends and means? Does not much of the moral confusion of our times center in this question? There would appear to be four attitudes that we can take, and they represent four answers to our inquiry. The first says that an end is simply the final episode in a series. It is where you are when you stop. Between the origin of a process and its terminus there are intervals, but they have no meaning except in terms of their advance or retardation of the series. Life is aimless; there is therefore no moral quality either to beginning, interim, or end. This is moral nihilism. The second says there are goals toward which something seems to be moving but they are hidden. No amount of cleverness or moral urgency will expose them; therefore their moral quality cannot be known, if indeed they have any moral quality. Man is shut up to the use of such means as come to hand whether they be good or bad, and he will use them in terms of what he knows, not in terms of what is hidden, hoping that everything will finally come out all right. We are told that many scientists employed in the making of the atom bomb did not know the goal of the project. Some suspected it and quit; others assumed their work was important and right; the few knew what was in the making, though the spectacle of Hiroshima was hidden even from their eyes. The third proposition says that there are ends all right enough, and one can see them if one has sufficient historic perspective. He will judge them, however, as good or bad in terms of some transcendent standard or of some common prejudice of his own. If the ends are good enough they will sanctify any means used to reach them; if they are bad they may or may not be salvaged by good means. In the meantime, every man for his own ends and the devil take the equivocators. The fourth proposition is the one set forth in the famous word about God and mammon. There are good ends; they are subsumed in the ultimate experience of God. No evil means can serve them, and no good means can fail to support or advance them.

Our study requires no extended discussion of these propositions, but it is important to indicate that Jesus took his stand in favor of the fourth one and stated his position unambiguously: you cannot serve God and mammon. No, not even the wise sons of this world have wisdom enough to do that. It takes no imagination at all to see what would have happened to him if he had taken the side of any one of the other three. That there are no ends at all would have been as impossible an article of faith for him as it has always been for most people; that there are ends but that they are hidden and moral accountability cannot therefore be expected in one's response to the unknown has the sound of logic but the silence of unfaith. If there was moral conflict in his own experience, it was between the third and fourth propositions. The story of his temptation in the wilderness is the dramatization of this conflict and of the victory of the fourth over the third. What was the essence of the three temptations if not the desirability and the feasibility of using unworthy means to achieve his ends? Such power as he had over nature and over

society was to be displayed in making bread unnaturally for his
hungry body and winning followers fraudulently for his hungry
spirit. A stone turned into bread by a wave of the hand, a crowd
turned into a following by a stunt from the temple's apex—if
these were to serve his plans for redeeming the world, were they
not, by that exalted end, transmuted from trickery into grandeur?
To have worshiped the devil to win the world is clearly a repudiation of God in favor of mammon and is, to the children
of light, unthinkable. That it was proposed simply shows the
rising crescendo of the temptation episode, the fury with which
the effort to baptize evil with holy water was made to appear
to him.

It was his repudiation of the cynic's faith that angered those
who ultimately sought to destroy him. Otherwise, as has been
said, they could have got on with him and shared his program.
They too wanted mankind redeemed—so they thought—but
redemption on any terms and by any means. Against this he set
his face and the anger it incurred did not abate until he was
dead on a cross.

[4]

This introduces a further question: if good ends can only be
served by good means, how could a cross serve the program of
redemption? What is more deliberately and cynically evil than
death imposed by torture (of mind or body) on a human being,
whether guilty or innocent? No sentimentalism can divest the
cross on which Jesus died of its utter and immitigable evil. They
err who, in speaking of the magnitude of the saving grace of
God, seek to heighten it by drawing as black a picture as possible
of the physical torture of the Son of God in death. That makes
redemption turn on pain and ignominy and death. Call it paradox if we will; it is palpably the confusion that lies in the effort
to make evil means serve good ends. This is not to deny the

Cross—and the capital letter is deliberate—saving efficacy. We escape the dilemma of evil serving good only by seeing that the cross had contingent efficacy; it was the great renunciation of the Son of God in order to redeem that is the effective agent in man's salvation.[1] The cross was an incident—one might even say an unimportant incident—in the Cross that is at the heart of the universe. The Lamb has been slain from the foundation of the world (Rev. 13:8) and the manner of his dyings is unimportant. There has always been indefeasible and saving goodness in every act of personal renunciation and it is this that serves redemptive ends, and only thus do we escape the dilemma posed by a hideously evil manner of death seeming superficially to be the means to the redemptive ends of God. Jesus could not serve two masters. What reason do we have for thinking we can?

[5]

That we think so, without good reasons, is the most disquieting fact of modern life. Yet there is an element of nobility in this faith—an element that makes those of us who hold to it, pathetic. There can be no question that men have and do put their trust in great ideals and have sought them heroically by base methods. It has been their fierce faith that the good end could not be forfeited, even by the folly and sin of those who pursue it. It is so close kin to the idea that God can and will overwhelm all man's folly in the final consummation of the Good that it passes for piety. This is essentially the religious mood invoked to support moral error. But how, we ask, in a moral universe, can God convert evil into good? This would be possible only in an amoral universe. He may make the wrath

---

[1] Cf. Rom. 5:10. "If while we were enemies we were reconciled to God by the *death* of his Son, much more, now that we are reconciled, shall we be saved by his *life*." Not every cross has been regarded as a saving symbol. Only one of three on crucifixion day has been so understood. But the Cross is the eternal symbol of redemption.

of men to praise Him but not by turning wrath into gentleness. If God is not limited by the categories that He has created there is no such thing as a universal moral order but one order for man and another for God. And who was it that said: "Be ye therefore perfect as your heavenly Father is perfect"? All the more tragic, therefore, is the frustration and anger of those who are betrayed by the moral error to which they have committed themselves in behalf of the good. If a man is clever—as the dishonest steward in the story—can he be wholly bad?

There is a more practical question however. How sure can we be that the steward really made friends? A relationship that is coerced by blackmail is certainly anything but friendship. The element of mutual confidence is wholly lacking. A man without scruples is always a man without friends. Suppose the factor, after losing his job, had been offered domicile by those he had befriended. How long would he have been welcome? How sure were his hosts to be that their guest who had defrauded his master would not defraud them? The familiar dictum of Immanuel Kant, always treat an individual as an end in himself and never as a means to an end, has ancient sanction. Do men make friends by the use of unrighteous mammon? The answer must be "No," unless the word friend has changed its meaning. Unrighteous mammon may make accomplices or associates, or conspirators, but never friends. It seems that it has rarely occurred to man that he might make a friend of God that way.

"Figs are not gathered from thorns, nor are grapes picked from a bramble bush" (Luke 6:44b), though men have been pricked and bled through all time as their only reward for searching for unnatural fruit in impossible places. "The good man out of the good treasure of his heart produces good, and the evil man out of his evil treasure produces evil" (Luke 6:45a).

The world needs desperately the experience of friendship on a universal scale. So hopeless have appeared its efforts to achieve it that we are now told that in the very nature of things it is impossible within time or on the level of history. It follows that man cannot escape from the folly of seeking good ends by evil means, that he is not free to be anything but a fool. When men persist in seeking peace by risking or making war, and making friends by the promises of pacts that are based on fear, and when we think security is possible by building walls or stock piles, we appear to be working within a pattern or a prison from which there is no escape. If this is so we are the victims of a cruel hoax for we have been led to believe that all good men out of the good treasures of their hearts can produce the total good, only to find out at last that it is not so. This is not only an invitation to pessimism; it is incitement to rebellion. Man's original sin finds itself ranged alongside God's original mistake. What tensions tear at man's soul because of it!

We do not think we are driven to this. The fact is that we are faced with a shattering moral judgment. Again it is not primarily a *post obitum* judgment but one which is written in the moral order within which we live in time. "You cannot serve God and mammon" is no improvised order to meet a partial or particular situation. It is of the very essence of the moral compact. We may argue or we may whimper, we may evade or we may scold, we may plead or we may scream, but the moment we introduce mammon to God as our friend, both condemn us—mammon with a sneer and God with a look of ageless compassion. If this is discouraging to us what must we be to Him? "For what is exalted among men is an abomination in the sight of God."

CHAPTER XII

The Sensualist

W E HAVE BEEN studying the cynic mind. It confronts the tension situations that arise out of the problem of ends and means and concludes that even though the long haul favors the children of light, the considerations of the immediate scene support the children of this generation. As far as this involves moral choices, the cynic decides that for the moment the end justified the means. He therefore adjusts his thinking and acting to this formula. That he is tragically mistaken was the point of the last chapter.

Cynicism is close kin to sensualism. Its relation is both of essence and of sequence. The cynic has abandoned his faith in the value of moral rigorism, and the primary reason for this is that it lays restraints on the exercise of his inclinations that are too grievous to be borne. This is in essential kinship with the sensualist mood. The next step is to give himself over to his appetites. This is the time sequence between cynicism and sensualism.

Let us be clear as to what we mean by sensualism. We use it for its primary rather than for its popular connotations; as it refers to the entire sensorium instead of the simple indulgence of appetite. Ethically, sensualism holds that the pleasures of sense are the highest good; aesthetically its emphasis is on the sensuous elements in, rather than the ideal of, beauty. A sensualist may therefore be a highly perceptive individual, his per-

ceptions coming by means of sensuous experience. He may also
be a highly moral person even though we may think he runs
grave risks and skirts the narrow ledge of overindulgence too
closely for comfort. For all that, however, he may have something important to say about certain aspects of life.

[1]

Eight years ago, Professor Sorokin of Harvard wrote a book
that analyzed the crisis of our age in terms of transition between
a dying sensate culture and a coming ideational culture.[1] The
response to his study was vigorous and varied and ranged from
scholarly approval on one extreme to personal abuse on the
other. The analysis and its merits are not the immediate concern of our reference to the book. We mention it because a
sensate culture as he described it is one that finds its ends and
values to be those that are communicated through the senses.
If this is true, all cultures, however classified, are at least partially sensate since it is impossible for a human being to lack
senses and sensations, and most unlikely that he will not discover through them what to him appears to be value. This does
not necessarily mean debauchery by appetite: eyes bright with
prurience, hands heavy with holding, lips moist with tasting,
and nothing else. If there is a way of stating the matter that fits
our present uses it would run thus: a sensate culture finds ends
and values by means of the senses; a sensualist seeks happiness
by the gratification of normal appetites.

Sensate culture is a real culture as the sensualist is a real person and we all partake inescapably of its qualities and his inclinations. Even those who find ends and values that are supra-
sensate might be legitimately described as seeking to gratify
spiritual appetites. Nor is the sensualist by any means a uniquely
modern or period-bound phenomenon. Epicurus in his bower,

<hr>

[1] Pitirim A. Sorokin, *The Crisis of Our Age* (New York: E. P. Dutton & Co., 1941).

sipping a cool drink, frosted by snow brought by slaves from distant mountains, Nero in his sudorific bath excreting body poisons through his pores, Louis XIV in his boudoir, and the American *nouveau riche* at Miami Beach—these are familiar flowers in the eternal gardens of excess. But they are not the only flowers. There are sybarites who are luxurious without being voluptuous, and there are those to whom sensuous pleasure is an arbiter but not a tyrant.

The parable which now engages us is familiarly known as the story of Dives and Lazarus. Dives is the name given the villain in the piece, partly because, we suspect, he has become in the popular mind such a famous villain that he needed a name. This is a unique distinction. But no such name is attached to him in the record. He is simply a rich man—which is the Latin meaning of Dives. Quite unjustly, we think, Dives has become a symbol for a special kind of hard-hearted and deliberate contempt for poor folk, as if this were true of all rich people. If in this study we employ this generally accepted name it is because it is a convenient rather than an accurate symbol.

"There was a rich man, who was clothed in purple and fine linen and who feasted sumptuously every day. And at his gate lay a poor man named Lazarus, full of sores, who desired to be fed with what fell from the rich man's table; moreover the dogs came and licked his sores. The poor man died and was carried by the angels to Abraham's bosom. The rich man also died and was buried; and in Hades, being in torment, he lifted up his eyes, and saw Abraham far off and Lazarus in his bosom. And he called out, 'Father Abraham, have mercy upon me, and send Lazarus to dip the end of his finger in water and cool my tongue; for I am in anguish in this flame.' But Abraham said, 'Son, remember that you in your lifetime received your good things, and Lazarus in like manner evil things; but now he is comforted here, and you are in anguish. And besides all this, between us and you a great chasm has been fixed, in order that those who would pass from here to you may not be able, and none may cross from there to us.' And he said, 'Then I beg you, father, to send him to my father's house, for I have five brothers, so that he may warn them, lest they also come to this place of torment.' But Abraham said, 'They have Moses and the prophets; let them hear them.' And he said, 'No, father Abraham, but if some one goes to them from the dead, they will repent.' He said to him, 'If they do not hear Moses and the prophets, neither will they be convinced if some one should rise from the dead' " (Luke 16:19-31).

There are, it is apparent, two themes here: one deals with the ultimate justice that will redress after death the inequities of mortal life. It is final and irreversible, for the great chasm fixed makes traffic back and forth, even for so exemplary an end as inducing repentance, impossible. This judgment does not await the end of the world; it runs concurrently for Dives and Lazarus with the five sensualist brothers still living. The second theme deals with the mind of the sensualist. This is not so dramatically spelled out but it is important to a full appreciation of the parable. It is with this second theme that our study for two reasons is concerned: the theme of ultimate justice has been discussed almost exclusively in most considerations of the story. Dives in Hades and Lazarus in the bosom of Abraham is the final act of the drama involving the two men. But the judgment that was concurrent because it was the response of the sensualist to life has not been so generally considered. We assume that some third party arbitrated the case of Dives and Lazarus; it was Dives that arbitrated his own. Similarly the sensualist mind, as the mind of the cynic, is passing judgment on itself in every act and idea that commits it to a sensualist approach to the ends and values of life. Our second reason for concerning ourselves with the sensualist's self-judgment is its relation to the tension situation created by such disparate relationships as those represented by Dives and Lazarus. The sensualist has escaped his tension. It is important to see the way he has done it.

[2]

We encounter this luxurious person, this sensualist, in two scenes in our story. In the first he is one of six brothers in a family of conspicuous wealth. It is an intriguing picture, one that still waits for the artist's brush. Six sybaritic sons, and if we imagine a father for good measure, we have symbolism for the seven deadly sins which the Puritan fathers feared, in which an artist should delight. What a group they would have made in the bright light and heavy shade of a Rembrandt painting. Dives is, we assume, little different from the rest of his family. At least we know that they were all later threatened with Dives' perdition, presumably for Dives' reason. At any rate we see him as a dandy and a gourmet. He loved the feel of fine linen and the elegance of purple, and every day he enjoyed the piquancy of rare foods in sumptuous abundance. We may or may not like him; that is beside the point. He has been made a villain and his name an epithet, but as long as the budget and the digestion of most of us could afford it, we would perhaps go in for his sort of regimen without much annoyance from our consciences.

The second scene in which this hero-villain appears represents the opposite extreme from the first. Here he has passed through the leveling experience of death from which his wealth could not exempt or protect him, and, stripped of his luxury, he is in torment in an anguish of flame. His concern is the most immediate and the most natural—escape from suffering. In his mortal days, raiment and food and their auxiliaries were his bulwark against physical discomforts; in the flame he had no defense. There is no protest against what he might have felt to be an injustice he had suffered; all he wanted was water to assuage his insufferable thirst. Not a deluge but a finger dipped in water and applied to his tongue. Even the untouchable Lazarus would be a welcomed agent of relief.

Lazarus—which means leper—appears also in two scenes. In

the first he is alone except as he is accompanied by the pariah dogs that applied their salivary unguent to his burning sores. The rags that do meager duty as covering for his wretched body do not conceal the leprous lesions that identify his illness and demand his ostracism from his fellows. He subsists on garbage, the rich man's benefaction. In the second scene he appears in unalloyed bliss. He rests in the bosom of Abraham. This is an interesting figure of speech. Hades we know, but what is symbolized by the figure of Father Abraham comforting a son, lately released from the torment of mortality? Was this Paradise? Why was it Father Abraham and not God the Father? There must be some reference here that is lost to us. Suffice it to say that the legendary founder of a culture is set opposite to the disaster that has overcome one of its apparently most fortunate sons. This may represent the finished transition from a sensate to an ideational culture. Even more simply it seems to be the redressing of the injustice that Lazarus had suffered.

[3]

We do well to look at these two men together though their separation is deliberate in the story. In a very real sense, both men were sensate. Each had the same rudimentary desires, physical and spiritual, and each sought to gratify them. The dog licking a sore gave the same qualitative sensation as the savor of an exotic meat, and had Lazarus been given the opportunity of exchanging places with the man within the gate of the great house, the likelihood is that he would have made the change without any hesitation beyond that necessitated by astonishment and momentary confusion. We have good reasons for thinking, however, that they were different at a very important point. Lazarus was sensate as all of us are; Dives was a sensualist as many of us would like to be. He may have been a voluptuary; the suspicion will not down though the evidence is lacking, but that he understood and sought the ends and values of life exclusively in terms of, and by means of, the senses is the fact that identifies him as a sensualist.

The habits of the sensualist are not as important for our present interest as his state of mind; what may be described either as his spiritual condition or his psychological pattern is our intimate concern. Not that this is portrayed explicitly or completely. It is not the property of parables to say everything or to say what they say precisely, and yet the intimations are clear and inescapable. In the second scene Dives in torment cries across the gulf to Abraham afar off, and back across the void the ghostly voice replies: "Son, remember . . ." At first glance it may strike us as odd that he should have been called to the discipline of recollection. Some have argued that Hades is the point or the experience of total recall and that this is its most formidable prospect. To remember the good things that have not saved one the ultimate frustration, and to recall the evil things that have caused it—this is a prescription for Hades excruciating enough for the most sadistic. But it is far more than that. The mind of the sensualist has cultivated—consciously or unconsciously, no matter—the bliss of forgetting. Its preoccupation with immediate pleasures is an effort to insulate one's self from immediate or proximate discomfort, and one way to do so is to put out of mind unpleasant facts, people, ideas. Create oblivion into which all such disturbing things can be discreetly consigned.

Dives does remember, not his lost felicities but his brothers who presumably are clad in purple and fine linen and faring sumptuously every day and shutting out of sight and mind the wretchedness of the scavengers outside the gate. If there is no escape for him, there should be for them if they could be warned in time. So across the abyss the voice of Dives reaches again to the ear of Father Abraham: "Send . . . to my father's house . . . warn them, lest they also come into this place of torment." Once more the ghostly voice replies: "They have Moses and the prophets; let them hear them." No, says Dives, their ears are impervious to those familiar voices; send an emissary from the dead to shock or frighten them into heeding. Again the reply: No, they would no more attend to the preachments of a dead voice than to a living one.

This, we insist is something far more significant than a two-way conversation between discarnate souls, an exchange between Hades and Paradise. It reveals the second quality of the sensualist's mind: his preoccupation with sensation has made him deaf to the law and the prophets. It is not necessarily a studied repudiation of the moral wisdom of the past. There is survival of the fittest in moral principles similar to that in physical organisms. The sensualist does not deny either the truth of that fact or the importance of a moral order. He is simply deaf to them. Having cultivated other faculties of perception, he has allowed the faculty of hearing to atrophy. Even the crepitant voice of a dead man will not excite the insensate ear.

Let us be clear about this. We are all endowed with normal appetites that must be satisfied. The innate desire to improve one's status, the urge toward physical comforts, the sex drive, and the craving for a family or a fellowship within which security can be found—these are the components of our normal psychic equipment. Lazarus had them though they were, we assume, utterly frustrated; Dives had them and, we assume, they were utterly satisfied. In so far as these endowments had been defrauded in the experience of Lazarus, the tensions they create in normal living had been relaxed. In the case of Dives, the tensions had been abated by forgetfulness and deafness. There ought to be a better resolution of the problem than that. The sensate becomes the sensualist when the satisfaction of appetites becomes an end instead of a means to an end, when, that is to say, he can achieve happiness by the elimination of the infelicities of life by the atrophy of the very qualities which—from our perspective—can alone lead to happiness. This is as true of

aesthetic as of physical appetite. This is not to say that the gratification of the sensorium is evil, but that sensuous pleasures must
subserve a higher end if they are not to degrade the soul.

[4]

This is why the sensualist forgets: he has allowed his instinc-
tual processes to dominate the restraints the active mind lays on
him. Our memory is given to guide us. To destroy or deaden it is
to disorient us to the present. This point is made with frightening detail by Orwell in the novel [2] which depicts the methods of
totalitarian government to create a society based on the thesis
that "whoever controls the past controls the present and whoever
controls the present, controls the future." The totalitarian controls the past by rewriting it to suit his present purposes; the
sensualist simply forgets it. This, he thinks, leaves him in control
of his present and his future. If, he would say, we find unpleasant
facts thwarting our sensuous appetites, we will put them out of
mind. An anodyne, a diversion, a curtain of oblivion, a drink—
there are various ways of forgetting. Dives would have been inhumane and cruel by his own moral standards if, seeing Lazarus
at his gate, he had ordered him off the premises. So he simply
didn't "see" him; he "forgot" he was there. This satisfied his
needs and did not interrupt his sumptuous daily regimen.

But these unpleasant things are not forgotten. Just as no
amount of cynical tinkering with the records of history can alter
the facts, so no amount of deliberate blindness or deafness can
alter the situation at our gates. If sights and sounds seem to dis-
appear, it is because they have been pushed down into the subconscious mind in some form or other. There will come a time
—the shock of impending death, the awakening in Hades, the
engulfment of torment—whatever these may mean—and the

---

[2] George Orwell, *Nineteen Eighty-four* (New York: Harcourt, Brace & Company,
1949).

memory is reawakened. It may be the ghostly voice of Father Abraham or another, but the word is always the same: Remember, my son.

Not only so: the sensualist also allows his ears to become insensitive to the moral admonitions of life. This does not mean he is simply irritated by the moralizings of people who cover up their own defections by their vehement exhortations to others to behave themselves. This is common enough, and without much defense. It means rather that life itself is endlessly laying its admonitions upon our consciences. In this story Moses represented the coded law, the certainty of justice with its rewards and penalties—in other words, order. Similarly the prophets in the experience of Israel represented the restless and probing concern of those who saw that law was not enough; that there was a law above law that must be invoked, that justice and mercy and faith were the imponderables that give vitality to the dead letter of the law and activate the conscience.

Now when law as code and law as conscience dispute one's freedom to seek fulfillment by the unqualified exercise of appetite, or when they challenge the values one has accepted because of the standards set by indulgence of the senses alone, they become an impertinence. Let them hear Moses and the prophets, Abraham advised Dives when he sought guidance for his sensualist brothers. But nobody knew better than he that Moses and the prophets had long since been repudiated by his brethren. Had Moses and the prophets lived as they lived, they had laughingly said, they too would have been sensualists! It was the wilderness and the bitter land and hard living that gave the ancient moralists their notions about life. Their authority was as dead as their voices. Other times, other laws. And when Dives, fully aware of this, appealed to Abraham to perform a bizarre bit of magic to shock his brothers—a dead man to come back with a living message—it was Abraham this time who vetoed the suggestion. It was not a question as to what voice would be authoritative; the simple fact was that no voice would be heard.

The heaven of the sensualist, if he were to take time off from his sumptuous living to think about it, is the land where no evil thoughts molest, the land of the glad forgetting, the never-never country, *dolce far niente*, the lotus land, the sweet, sweet opiate of oblivion. Here is no Lazarus with his sores nor any recollection of him. Nor comes hither the impertinent interloper to tell him about his sins and the imperishable moral law under which he stands—or reclines opulently in judgment. He is the typical Bourbon of the days before 1789 in France, of whom it was said that he neither remembered anything nor learned anything. When the mobs in the streets say they have no bread, give them cake. If they cry for jobs, give them rakes and point to the leaves. It is just this distorted perspective on life—this wish to escape it, indeed—that makes him an object of disdain.

The parable daringly gives the opposite of this spurious paradise. From the sybaritic self-indulgences of the sensualist to the searing flame of an awakened memory: first, "Remember, my son," and then the reminder that no portent will stir his like to an acceptance of the moral obligations which are of the very essence of life. "Have mercy on me and send me Lazarus"—was there ever a more ironic cry from the lips of one who had for years been able to dispose of Lazarus by a trick of his insensitive soul?

[5]

This is what happens when a sensate culture, for which there is something good to be said, becomes a sensualist culture, for which there is little to be said. Sensation becomes an end in itself even as it becomes man's only instructor. Dives and his five brothers, bemused with the feel of luxurious garments and the piquancy of rare foods, came to know and seek nothing else. There is a limit to which this pursuit can go. Eventually it ends up in boredom. From one dressmaker to another, from one night club to another, from one bar to another, from one psychiatrist to another, from one wife to another—the effort to escape the intolerable torment of satiation goes on. It does little good to be angry; this is the danger our sensate culture faces and anger is no way to face it. Furthermore we must distrust our anger in such circumstances. Maybe we are unconsciously jealous of Dives. Would not Lazarus himself have liked a fling at linens and table dainties?

It is beyond the purpose of this study to analyze the culture of our times even within the limits of this famous little story. There is no end of such material for those who seek it. It remains to point out that aside from the broad cultural aspects that are implicit in principle in the parable, and which are in a measure responsible for the intercultural tensions of our times, there is here an explanation of individual tensions that grow more and more prevalent. One might cite the increase in hypertension, in neurotic illnesses, in bitterness and frustration that mark our health chart. Return to religion for peace of mind, some say in best sellers, but while sales go up, spirits go down. The reason for this is that we are under judgment for our folly. We have misused our sensations and become sensualists. But we need wait for no awakening in Hades if we can shake ourselves awake here. It is not to dull the sensorium that we are called. He is no man who has lost his sensuous responses to life; he is a clod. But we do not have to be either Dives or Lazarus if we will open our ears to hear and stir our minds to remember. Remember, son—the admonition is as timeless as the delight in lovely things. They have Moses and the prophets; let them hear them—the reminder is as ageless as the moral law.

There is an unidentified Spanish proverb that runs: The pleasures of the senses pass quickly; those of the heart become sorrows; but those of the mind are with us to the end of our journey. One wonders whether the proverb-maker had ever encountered this story by our parable-maker.

CHAPTER XIII

Forgiveness and Duty

THE 17th chapter of Luke contains a brief but important parable and provides the introduction to another. Besides this it has an exhortation about forgiveness, an episode about the grace of gratitude—or the disgrace of the lack of it—and what is called one of the short apocalypses. These are relevant to our study in so far as they help in the understanding of the mounting tension that is increasingly evident from the narrative.

We have been dealing with the cynicism of the "children of this world" and their mistaken faith in practicality for the short haul—which means the accommodation of any means so long as the end is worthy—as opposed to the idealism of the long haul. Also the sensualist's effort to get the ultimate meaning and value from life by the senses alone has engaged us. "There was a rich man" is the sentence that introduces both the cynic and the sensualist and while we have no warrant here for reasoning that cynicism and sensualism are the spiritual deposit that riches leave in a man's soul, there is no little reason for thinking that the man of substance is more prone to such an outlook on life than his less substantial neighbor. It was intimated in our study of the three prodigals that the lost condition of the materialistic-minded father and the frustrated elder brother was unrelieved. We do not need to assign to either of them the roles represented by the cynic and the sensualist, but it is interesting to recall that they—not the more famous prodigal son—were and remained rich men and therefore more easily prey to spiritual defeatism than the penitent wastrel.

That "temptations to sin" were inevitable is the warning word with which chapter 17 opens. It is spoken to the disciples and our assumption is that the author means to indicate another change in the character of those who attended the parable-teller as he and his friends drew nearer to Jerusalem. Multitudes had changed to smaller units or groups, and now, with one exception, the little homilies are addressed to the disciples. This fact in itself provides slight evidence of the rising sense of tension, but matters that concern him do. The inevitability of temptation, the woe pronounced against those who caused "little ones" to sin, and the necessity for unlimited forgiveness, these reflect a growing concern. Even more, they may be taken to indicate something of the growing tautness of his own spirit. How otherwise account for the palpable contradiction involved here?

And he said to his disciples, "Temptations to sin are sure to come; but woe to him by whom they come! It would be better for him if a millstone were hung round his neck and he were cast into the sea, than that he should cause one of these little ones to sin. Take heed to yourselves; if your brother sins, rebuke him, and if he repents, forgive him; and if he sins against you seven times in the day, and turns to you seven times, and says, 'I repent,' you must forgive him" (Luke 17:1-4).

If in the first half of this paragraph he is considering the way of preventing sin—or stumbling, as it is put in earlier translations—we must admit the measure he proposes is a radical one. To intercept the individuals by whom temptations come and to cast them into the sea is assuredly the language of hyperbole. To be protected against sinning by the drowning of its putative human cause, makes havoc of all our ideas about sin and righteousness. One would even assume, in the light of the latter half of the paragraph, that even the one who caused sin was entitled to forgiveness on certain grounds. The sharp juxtaposition of the rigor represented by the millstone and the sea on the one hand and the act of forgiveness offered seven times a day is puzzling. As ideas they are as irreconcilable as they are as methods of dealing with offenders. This is not a paradoxical statement of a moral truth; it is a contradiction in moral ideals. This is made clear in the response that the moral conscience has made to this paragraph. There has never been any consistent and sustained effort to forfend against sin by destroying its agents. Such undertakings as the Inquisition and the massacre of the Huguenots on St. Bartholomew's Day for the purpose of extirpating heresy proved as futile as they were bloody. They were as absurd a confusion of the problem of ends and means as can be imagined. For this reason the idea about millstone drownings has been dismissed as exaggeration. But this is not enough, for if we could reduce the exaggeration to the bare nub of its essence we are still confronted with the problem of using an evil means—destroying the tempter—to secure an exalted end—averting sin. We suggest that this moral tangle is best understood in terms of the crisis through which Jesus and his fellows were passing and the tensions it was creating. How natural for those, caught in a maelstrom of hostility, cynicism, and peril, to wish to escape by dropping their tempters into the sea. How natural, we hasten to add, for Jesus to swing immediately away from this dubious moral innovation by an exhortation to forgiveness that in its own way is quite as radical.

[1]

The inevitability of temptations to sin is one of the facts of our morally contingent human experience. The nature both of personality and society involves this. We pray that we shall not be

led into temptation, but we do not pray that the millstone and
the deep sea shall provide our escape. Woe to him by whom
temptations come. It would conceivably be better for us if he
were cast into the sea, but would it, in all candor, be better for
him? We must preserve the moral perspectives that Jesus has
given us if we are to face this question and answer it correctly.
A human situation that insulates "little ones" against sin is as
amoral as that which by a misconceived idea of "original sin"
makes sin inevitable. In a moral universe the opportunity to be
tempted and to resist or succumb is indefeasible. There are times
enough when we wish this were not so, but these are times when
the strain of coming successfully to terms with the moral universe is like a baptism that must be undergone, and how is one
"constrained until it is accomplished!" (Luke 12:49).

It is this which lifts to heights of moral idealism and puissant
faith the latter half of this paragraph. "Take heed to yourselves."
This is a more practical discipline than seeking out other tempters and millstones and deep places in the sea. Temptation is inevitable and sin is one of two alternative consequences. It is
important therefore that one guard carefully one's own relations to his fellows lest they be accessory before the fact of sin.
If temptation be repelled, well and good, but if not, and one
stumbles and falls, what is one to do? Here the wish for the millstone and the deep is seductive. For that reason it must also be
resisted. The expedient is forgiveness followed by rebuke contingent on repentance.

This is not the place to undertake a discussion of forgiveness
in general. It serves our purpose to indicate simply that as much
as any one single word, forgiveness is a synonym for the Christian
spirit. Vindictiveness, if that be its antonym, is similarly the
antithesis of the Christian spirit. This is the deposit of the Christian testimony that seems least likely to be eroded away by the
cold and heat and flood and blast of modernity even though we
are far from practicing it as thoroughly as this paragraph ad-

monishes. At the time of this admonition, however, there was no a priori validity to forgiveness of this radical sort. It had emerged tentatively in certain prophetic utterances and was to have later formulations as the Christian fellowship grew in extent and in articulateness (cf. I Cor. 13, e.g.). It was therefore a radical demand growing, we think, out of the crisis experience of the times. Tense situations require radical treatment. Offenses against him and the fellowship were sure to multiply. Out of the ready forgiveness Jesus urged was to emerge the creative experience that ultimately was formulated into the identification of forgiveness with love and love with the grace of God.

It is not surprising that the reaction that greeted this radical demand was one of bewildered importunity.

The apostles said to the Lord, "Increase our faith!" And the Lord said, "If you had faith as a grain of mustard seed, you could say to this sycamine tree, 'Be rooted up, and be planted in the sea,' and it would obey you" (Luke 17:5-6).

It was clearly not faith in general for which his friends sought increase; it was faith in forgiveness. Forgiveness is essentially an act of faith whether it be divine or human. It can therefore not find its ultimate validation pragmatically. But this does not say that the primary act of faith cannot be "increased" by experience. It is this latter that has been called the deposit of the Christian experience in our culture. We, culturally speaking, have little to say about faith in forgiveness; if we speak of it at all, we are likely to raise pragmatic questions about its efficacy. But think of what it meant in a situation in which national survival seemed to depend on the inculcation and practice of vengefulness against Rome; when forgiveness was suspected of being treachery or capitulation or faithlessness. The cry "Lord, increase our faith," had poignancy that a prayer for faith in general would not have had. The response to this request showed the utter faith Jesus had in forgiveness. He did not propose a discipline by which such meager faith as they had might be cultivated to invincible proportions. On the contrary he surprised them by saying that after all, a very little faith in forgiveness could perform prodigious wonders. Prejudice, hostility, resentment, vengeance, deep-rooted and sturdily grown could, by faith the size of a mustard seed, be torn from their rootage and tossed into the sea. Here is a use of the depths of the sea as a cure for temptation and the sin of vengeance that is morally more intelligible than that which makes it a place for those persons by whom temptations come.

[2]

Does it need pointing out that while forgiveness is still an apt conventional synonym for the Christian spirit, faith in forgiveness languishes in our tense times? For most of this century faith in other qualities of the spirit has been inculcated and many of them tend to suffocate the impulse to forgive. Here is perhaps the most striking moral failure of our times. Our hostilities must be rooted up and cast into the sea. Do we believe it possible to do this with faith in forgiveness the size of a mustard seed? Even by certain leaders of Christian thought this is regarded as moral naïveté or impractical moralism. The idea that the tensions of our age can be abated by forgiveness is bracketed with other impractical idealisms of the sons of light. And, in accepting this we tumble ingloriously into the morass of evil means for good ends. Crisis and tension, we say, cannot be abated by forgiveness; therefore we will try rough justice or implacability. Or we say that the injunction to radical forgiveness provided an interim expedient for a few who would not, in any event, outlive the doom that vengefulness was sooner or later to incur. It should be something of a scandal to the Christian conscience that the definitive test of the Christian demand for forgiveness in personal, communal and international affairs in our times was given by a Hindu, who falling under the vengeful assault of an assassin made the gesture of forgiveness as he died.

The cynic, the sensualist, the vengeful—these have emerged from our preceding studies. In the short paragraph that follows we have another parable though it is not generally thought of as such. The reference to faith as a grain of mustard seed was a metaphor that has become for us a proverb. Cervantes said a proverb is a short sentence based on long experience, and it was clearly the long experience of Jesus with forgiveness that gave him the authority to make radical claims for it. In what follows we have an emphasis on an aspect of behavior that in a strict sense is not a moral question but which, in a more spacious perspective, gives all behavior a heightened quality. It deals with the relation of duty as an ideal to the practical aspects of character development.

"Will any one of you, who has a servant plowing or keeping sheep, say to him when he has come in from the field, 'Come at once and sit down at table'? Will he not rather say to him, 'Prepare supper for me, and gird yourself and serve me, till I eat and drink; and afterward you shall eat and drink'? Does he thank the servant because he did what was commanded? So you also, when you have done all that is commanded you, say 'We are unworthy servants; we have only done what was our duty' " (Luke 17:7-10).

To do more than one's duty is, like forgiveness, a Christian ideal. Much has been made of this, and correctly so. The second mile, the extra cloak, these were the familiar figures of speech Jesus employed to state it simply. In the above paragraph it is expanded into a general statement and given the form of a maxim. But it is more than that: it is a measure of worth. Worth, we are told, as it applied to performance of the servant was not estimated in terms of having done everything that was expected of him— having done his duty. At this point he was unprofitable (the older translation). Not until he had done *more* than was required did he show a profit. To put it in the language of profit and loss, the dutiful servant only broke even. In language of values, he was unworthy.

This is admittedly a hard saying, hard, that is to say, in that it appears to ask for more than one has a right to. It might even be thought greediness, the effort to get something extra out of someone who has measured up to his contract. The servant who responded to the demand for more might be servile or accommodating, abject or generous; but the master who expected more than duty seems unlikely to be thought of as a big-hearted boss. On the contrary.

This feeling may be accounted for by the mood that prevails today in what we call secular society, a mood that is prevalent in a world supported largely by verbal agreements—treaties we call them between nations, contracts in business, promises in personal affairs. We have an enormous body of law that protects such commitments against unilateral abrogation. It is difficult to imagine what sort of chaos would overwhelm the world if even for a day this orderly pattern were abandoned. One may go further and observe that it is almost as difficult to imagine a world in which everyone and every group lived scrupulously up to the terms of contract by which they are bound. Most of us would settle for that as utopian. It might conceivably be, in our culture, the best of all possible worlds. At what point then does this ideal of duty-plus have relevance to the practicalities of life?

[3]

The four cardinal virtues according to Plato were: courage, wisdom, temperance, and justice. Aristotle added to his master's list two intellectual virtues: caution and intelligence; and Socrates, the spiritual progenitor of both of them, listed modesty, liberality, and amiability as spiritual virtues. The practice of these nine virtues resulted in what was called by the Greeks magnificence or greatness of soul. While we have no reason for thinking that this list was regarded as exhaustive, it is interesting to note that the word "duty" does not appear in it. Neither is the idea implicit. Liberality and amiability might be said to be the state of soul out of which the duty-plus virtue would spring, though it might be argued that the idea of duty as a virtue might emerge from Plato's "justice" and Aristotle's "caution."

Duty, however, is explicitly a Roman ideal. By the time of Jesus the culture that embodied the classic virtues had been taken over by the expanding empire in the Etruscan peninsula. The use of Greek culture by the Romans was designed to aid in the growth and stabilization first of the republic and later of the empire. The result was a mongrelization of the Greek ideals of virtue and the evolving Roman ideals of duty and law. The former became the basis for the imitative art of the Romans; the latter became the basis for their jurisprudence and ethics. The fecundity of Greek culture had declined by the first century to such a point that all that was left of it was the pale imitations and accommodations the Romans made for their own uses. The momentum of empire-building had grown so great that liberality, amiability, modesty, and temperance—the virtues out of which creative art emerges—were conspicuously set aside for the more practical virtues of duty and obedience. It is not implausible to assume then that in Palestine in the first century the Roman ideal of duty as the primary virtue had become as pervasive in the common mind as the emissaries of Rome were in political and administrative affairs. The Pharisees who tithed mint, anise, and cummin and left undone the weightier matters of the law would have insisted that they were virtuous sons of Israel. Their Roman overlords would have quite as reasonably insisted that they were responding to an ancient Jewish law with the regularity of a Roman. It is inevitable that we should identify justice, mercy, and faith, as Jesus used them, as closer kin to the creative virtues of amiability, modesty, liberality, and temperance, than to the conservative virtues of law and duty.

[4]

Let us look again at this parable. The picture is that of a normal master-servant relationship. The servant had been busy all day, plowing or tending sheep. The master may have been doing nothing or occupied industriously with his own chores. Their respective rights and duties were accepted—the master's right to demand immediate service, and the servant's duty to produce it. This having been the accepted code, the deduction that the servant was unprofitable seems odd if not downright perverse. Dutiful he was, and everything was in order; profitable he was not. This is what Jesus was saying.

Is this a fair judgment? What characterizes the duty-bound mind? It does only what others have right or reason to expect of it. Psychologically it can be said to have a low boiling point. It puts a premium on calculation, the minimum, the prudent performance as over against enthusiasm, daring, excitement, creativity. Thus it tends to immobilize or impair the imagination. What others expect is normative, not what a given situation demands. It is therefore the death of the creative impulse; it is bound by contract instead of being set free by creativity. The modern emphasis on having a hobby as an escape from the duty-bound routine into the freedom of self-expression is a tacit recognition of the stultification—or shall we not say the unprofitableness?—of the duty-bound mind. Beyond this it must be said that the duty-bound mind is the essence of regimentation. It cannot endure the experimental, the unorthodox, the inventive. Once the duty is recognized it tends to become regimentive for everybody. The excess to which this can go has been set forth with great imaginative power in Orwell's recent novel.[1] This, it

[1] *Vide supra*, p. 173.

hardly needs to be pointed out is the aim of authoritarian orders whether political, religious, or whatever. The performance of a religious duty for duty's sake is no more edifying than following the party line from a sense of duty.

This is surely not to say that there are no practical values in the exercise of the duty-bound mind. It gets a great deal done without fuss. If everyone in the world did his duty this would be a fabulous place—order, precision, satisfaction, and—we must add—sterility. Furthermore the satisfaction it would provide is not to be discounted, though it is a very low-grade sort of satisfaction. If everyone in the world were satisfied, even on this level, we would be better off, in some respects, than we are now. Yet we cannot disguise the fact that in a very real sense, such a situation would be unprofitable, unworthy. It would be a break-even proposition. It would represent the death of spontaneity—that exciting experience of discovery that arises from the depths of an unpremeditated impulse. It would represent the dead level of mediocrity and standardization—the mechanizing of the mind. For all the prodigies of instantaneous calculation by electronic brains, they only do exactly what is expected of them. This keeps them on the level of the refrigerator or the iron fireman or the alarm clock. Therefore, the duty-bound mind is the negation of progress. It neither knows nor cares for inventiveness. It is content to break even. Little wonder that duty is the dearly loved word of the orthodox, the conservative, and the conformist.

Here is no exhortation to skimp one's duty. The inclination to do that creates another problem on a much more elemental moral level. Jesus was confronting the dominant virtue of the alien culture that had overshadowed his own. He was talking against the unworthy mentality and in favor of the profitable mind. Here was something that could keep alive the flame of imagination in a regimented world; here was something, in fact, that could help restore faith in God and the possibility of a Kingdom of worthy servants. God had not done His duty when

He created a world out of chaos, nor had Abram simply done his daily stint when he left Ur of the Chaldees to become the father of a great people. The Kingdom of God was a towering spiritual invention, higher than the summit of Sinai where man's duties were first thundered forth. It is a concept that still provides for spiritual ingenuity and daring and it will never come about by the performances of the duty-bound who never do more than break even.

[5]

The point has been made that the duty-plus mind is the inspiration of art, of exploration, of play. Too bad that we have no short, pungent word for it and must content ourselves with "greatness of soul" as a synonym. It must now be added that our age is as conspicuously duty-bound as was the time of Jesus. This may be due to the contractual aspect of our political and economic life. The dotted line and the receipt are the symbols of our culture. It may also be partially affected by the progressive militarization of our minds and habits under the impact of almost half a century of war. Inventive we are, and daring almost beyond imagination in the use of the resources and energies of our physical world. Are we similarly so in art? There is an interesting question in this connection, the answer to which must be supplied by the historians of culture. Rome's art was imitative of the genius of the then jejune Hellenic culture that had not regarded duty as a primary virtue. We are told by critics of modern culture that art is decadent. Could it be that our duty-bound ideal of virtue has been the root cause of this decline in great creative art in our times? If the paramountcy of duty and law in Rome caused first an imitative and then a decadent art, is there not found in our devotion to duty qua duty the cause of a similar aesthetic decline today?

There are questions that obviously lie beyond the limits of

this study. What is of more immediate relevance is the relation
of the duty-bound spirit to the growth of the soul. This is what
Jesus was talking about; this is what saves his judgment about
the unworthy servant from being harsh or perverse. We may
easily imagine a way in which the story could have been continued to show the servant in a profitable light. Suppose he had
come in one day and told his master that while tending the sheep
he had been doing some selective breeding on his own and had
developed a long-staple wool that increased the value of his
sheep considerably. Or if, in plowing, he had discovered that
following the land contours and the use of an iron share protected the farm against erosion and held the moisture against dry
spells, he would have shown a profit—or worth—far beyond
the performance of duty. This is, to be sure, a crassly materialis-
tic extension of the meaning of the parable, but it is not, for
that reason, a mistaken one. It can point the way by which the
performance of religious duties—which in their own subtle
way may prove our unworthiness and unprofitability—can be
lifted out of duty-bound constrictions and set in the ways of
creative spiritual living.

There is a final comment: The situation in which Jesus found
himself and his friends was such as was going to call for devotion
beyond the call of duty. Indeed, it is not implausible to assume
that he was confronting, in his own soul, the problem of duty
in its relation to the redemptive enterprise. This takes us toward
hidden areas of his experience into which we cannot go, but
surely one who in his early ministry talked about the second mile
with confidence was entitled to re-examine its validity when the
first mile had already become an ambuscade for indifference and
hostility. If this had increased the tension in his own soul, how
much more evident was it in the faltering friends who still were
with him, largely, perhaps, from a sense of duty. And in our own
times is there not—because of the duty-mindedness of our con-
tractualized culture—a conflict between those spiritual qualities

that make of us duty-bound or duty-plus persons? And if we undertake to resolve that tension are we not most certainly to discover whether we are breaking even, or are really worthy servants of God and our times?

The story of the death of Lord Nelson in the arms of Captain Hardy at the Battle of Trafalgar has it that his last words were: "Now I am satisfied. Thank God I have done my duty." One would not, post mortem, taint his dying self-satisfaction and gratitude to God, but one may ask, what must increasingly be asked in our generation, whether Trafalgar would have been won had the Admiral only done his duty. Such questions are rarely asked and never answered, but somehow they re-echo a timeless judgment about a nameless servant in an ancient age that is important for our consideration today.

CHAPTER XIV

The Widow and the Judge

THERE had been bad blood between Samaria and Galilee ever since the former had been made a garrison by the king of Assyria in 720 B.C. and peopled with aliens. The centuries had not softened the acrimony that divided them. It was still unsafe for travelers to spend their time too leisurely in the margin that divided the territories and afforded thorough-fare north and south. It is to be expected that at this point Jesus' following would have been reduced to a minimum. So it was. The episode (Luke 17:11-19) seems to indicate that he was alone with his disciples when he met the ten lepers and discovered that the grace of gratitude for healing was exhibited only by the Samaritan. It might be observed in passing that this is an instructive item in the way in which group tensions are mitigated. To a Galilean, being a Samaritan was a barrier to fellowship that rested on ethnic and religious grounds. This ancient feud might be taken as the symbol of all such intergroup conflicts. From our perspective it was quite unreasonable and yet for similar or less realistic reasons we preserve our feuds between groups and races. What is of particular interest here is that the Galilean-Samaritan dispute was resolved by the lepers when ten healthy men would have sustained or exaggerated it. The one Samaritan who was a leper was not purged of his anti-Galilean prejudices by his disease nor were his Galilean fellow sufferers softened by their common illness. But the touch of misery that makes the whole world kin had brought them together in their common wretchedness. Who is right in a quarrel between localities is an academic question to a leper. The difference that soured human relations on the level of security were submerged on the level of misery. This datum is as old as human feuding is and has been invoked within the past decade as the basis for settling feuds between nations. If quarreling peoples can be kept miserable they will be kept harmless since their preoccupation with their own misfortunes will desensitize them to their relations with others. This is a cynical disposal of the problem of personal, group, racial (cf. the current strife in South Africa), and national tensions even though it is seriously undertaken. The nine Galilean lepers, sharing a common ostracism, were not concerned to discriminate against the lone Samaritan who had attached his miserable self to their group. And yet an inference we are allowed to draw from the story is that when they were all ten healed, the Galilean-Samaritan difference promptly returned to separate them. Men must be brothers—this seems to be some sort of rudimentary axiom of human life. If they can't be brothers well, they will have to be brothers sick; if men cannot combine by love they will be coalesced by fear; if they are not to find fellowship on the levels of their strength they will be brought together on the level of their common weaknesses.

This could not have been hidden from Jesus and the small group that passed between Samaria and Galilee on their way to Jerusalem. It was a disquieting experience and did nothing to ease the sense of crisis that pressed upon them. When, therefore, a short time afterward, and we assume safely outside the disputed area between Galilee and Samaria, he was confronted with a direct question by certain Pharisees, he replied in a way that revealed the surcharged atmosphere of crisis into which he was moving as they advanced farther south.

[1]

The question introduces what is called one of the little apocalypses. Considerable study has been given to these passages
in the synoptics and we will not concern ourselves with them in
any detail at this point. In this particular case the question was
direct and the answer equally so.

Being asked by the Pharisees when the kingdom of God was coming, he answered them, "The kingdom of God is not coming with
signs to be observed; nor will they say, 'Lo, here it is!' or 'There!'
for behold, the kingdom of God is in the midst of you" (Luke
17:20-21).

We have questioned the propriety of the use of the word
"apocalypse" in describing what followed this direct answer of
Jesus to the question of the Pharisees. In a general manner of
speaking any revelation of present facts, thought for some reason
to be veiled, is an apocalypse. But the word has taken on a special
tincture by its association with such violent and dramatic un-
veilings as the Revelation. What follows in Luke 17:22-37 is
hardly to be classified thus. Indeed as Jesus responded to his
questioners he warned them against "signs to be observed" and
revelations suddenly to be exposed. With a complete absence of
the theatrics with which the coming of the Kingdom had been
mistakenly associated, he said simply that it was already come
and was in their midst. There was nothing apocalyptic in that.
Furthermore in so far as the phrase, "the days of the Son of man,"
is concerned in this passage, Jesus seems to be at special pains
to divest it of mystery or portent. He warns his friends against
following those who promise prodigies in nature. There is to be,
on the contrary, instead of novelty, a continuation of what would
be called the commonplace experiences of average times. The
Flood was certainly no normal fall of rain, nor was the burning
bitumen in Sodom an everyday experience. But the life of the

people before those ancient calamities was unchanged by looking for floods or brimstone fires. Therefore, Jesus says, do not adjust daily routines to bizarre expectations. "Let him who is on the housetop, with his goods in the house, not come down to take them away." "Remember Lot's wife," who, we recall, stubbornly refused to believe the fires of Sodom to be a portent, and that is just as memorable about her as her more celebrated salty meta-morphosis. There is certainly nothing "apocalyptic" in the nub of what he was trying to say, something caught up in one of his most memorable words: "Whoever seeks to gain his life will lose it, but whoever loses his life will preserve it" (Luke 17:33). The truth of that was to be evident to those among whom the Kingdom of God had already come; it was not to be made con-vincing to the obdurate or spiritually blind by handwriting in the sky. "There will be two women grinding together; one will be taken and the other left." This is natural, not supernatural; it happens every day in every community.

That Jesus was trying to discourage mystery and encourage realism with regard to the Kingdom is supported clearly by the final word of this passage. The disciples are reported to have asked bewilderedly: "Where, Lord?" They seem to have forgot-ten his earlier word that the Kingdom was among them. To have remembered that would have been answer enough: all this ex-perience he had been describing was not as remote as the Flood or the plains of Sodom; it was right where they were. But he adds a note that is premonitory in a way that they could hardly have understood. It is indeed more profound than our superficial understanding has allowed it to be. One might indeed claim that it approaches a philosophy of history in its basic reference. Too often the meaning of history has been read in apocalypse or portent or some monstrous or foreboding circumstance. This is to misread it. The vital experiences of history have been the result of the creative spirit of man moving under the inspiration of some great challenge—whether spiritual or physical. Similarly the deaths of history—of groups or cultures—have been the result of inner debilities which destroyed ultimately the heart—spiritual or physical—of a people. Is it not this latter fact that Jesus is referring to in his famous word: "Where the dead body is, there the vultures will be gathered together"? The vulture is a carrion bird; it sails aloft until the wounded quarry it has spied, falls dead. Then it spirals downward to gorge itself on the carcass. This is vivid language and sharp, clear metaphor. Did his hearers understand that he was saying to them that within the commonplaces of human life are both vitalizing and degenerative forces? The culture of his own people was not to be consumed until it had died. No predatory bird would strike it down; it would fall of its own inner feebleness; then the vultures would drift remorselessly down to devour it. This profound and timeless insight has had its authentication in every century since it was uttered and there is nothing in the current scene to encourage us to doubt or discredit it now.

[2]

We must guard against thinking the sequences in the record are exact or even significant. At the same time it is interesting to note that the parable, to which all that we have been saying is preliminary, seems to fit a sequence in ideas even if we are not sure of the sequence in time.

And he told them a parable, to the effect that they ought always to pray and not lose heart. He said, "In a certain city there was a judge who neither feared God nor regarded man; and there was a widow in that city who kept coming to him and saying, 'Vindicate me against my adversary.' For a while he refused; but afterward he said to himself, 'Though I neither fear God nor regard man, yet because this widow bothers me, I will vindicate her, or she will wear me out by her continual coming.' " And the Lord said, "Hear what the unrighteous judge says. And will not God vindicate his elect, who cry to him day and night? Will he delay long over them? I tell you, he will vindicate them speedily. Nevertheless, when the Son of man comes, will he find faith on earth?" (Luke 18:1-9).

It is apparent how aptly this fits the mood of the antecedent paragraphs. What was needed by his followers was not an external portent but inner reinforcement, and he tells a story to say so. This is not a parable about prayer as we use the term conventionally. He was anxious that the point of this lesson should not be lost so he gives the point in advance. Prayer is no doubt a primary necessity for those who, in the face of mounting crisis, feel the need of strength. To say that this is not what is meant by praying in this context does not discountenance that need. But we have here the picture of a petitioner before the court. She, in the language of the law, prays for deliverance from her adversary. The mood and method of such praying may or may not be different from the closeted devotions of the saint, but we have strong reasons for thinking that in this case they were.

The two principal people involved in this story are unevenly described but it is possible to get a clear picture of both of them. The woman was "a widow in that city." It is altogether possible that, having suffered the sudden loss of her spouse, she found herself involved in matters for which she was quite unprepared. Here in embryo are all the tales about hapless widows and ruthless mortgage holders that have regaled our morbid interest in the misfortunes of others or excited our anger against all such spoilers. What resources were hers in her predicament we do not know but we suspect that they had either been unsubstantial or soon exhausted. Those drawn to her in her sorrow were unable to help her in her business affairs, or they were disinclined to share more than their sympathy with her. Nor does it appear that she had an advocate to guide her or present her case before the judge. She was left utterly alone with nothing but a cause which she believed was impregnably right and with a faith that was invincible.

How this jurist got his place on the bench is better left to an examining committee. That he had no moral or legal right to it allows the suspicion at least that he got it by legally devious means. His reputation seemed generally known. He "neither feared God nor regarded man." The former attitude could hardly exclude him on strictly legal grounds from acting as a judge. There have been some jurists whose godlessness has been regarded as a protection rather than a defection. In fact the austere and impartial administrator of the rules of the law might argue that the introduction of religion of any sort into an argument complicates rather than simplifies the doing of justice and that an overly religious man makes a sentimental judge.

That he regarded not man may have a somewhat sinister sound but it can be taken in more than one way. It may mean that he was frivolous regarding human rights before the law or contemptuous of those who could not order their affairs without recourse to the law. Or it may mean that he was scrupulously impartial toward those who came before him. His regard for the integrity of the law was so compelling that he regarded not the personalities involved. A man in court was a case to be adjudicated, not a person to be dealt with.

It would perhaps be more pleasant to make this judge out to be the kind of man that we want all judges to be, than to face up to the man he really was. There are two things that argue against him as a worthy justice. The first is his boastfulness that he feared not God and regarded not man. We have a feeling that he would have been wise if in the dispensation of justice he had kept these personal attitudes out of the picture. The second word against him is supplied by the parable-teller who refers to him as "the unrighteous judge"—more familiarly rendered "the unjust judge." He was a bad man, in short. If this was a correct estimate of him then his attitude toward God and man must be seen in this light. He feared not God, and that meant nothing less than godlessness. He regarded not man, and that meant contempt for his fellows. And if, as is suggested, he was

unjust, he added to his contempt for God and man his contempt
for the law and its just administration.

[3]

Here is a scoundrel if ever there was one. Atheist, misanthrope,
and antinomian; and sitting in spurious splendor on the bench
where justice and mercy and faith should have sat. It was to this
creature that this bereft woman came to claim protection from
one who sought to take advantage of her late misfortune. It is
this that makes us believe that she either had no other help or
had spent it completely. No one not in extremity of need would
have thought to solicit the aid of such a rascal in the adjustment
of her just claims. To what in him did she think she could appeal?
Surely not to his faith in God and in the ultimate justice that
such faith involves; nor in his faith in human kind and in the
rough sort of justice that somehow seems to work itself out in
human affairs. And if not to these two important factors in adjust-
ing grievances, then what of the law which, presumably stands
inviolate apart from divine or human considerations. Here also
she had no reason to hope for help. He didn't believe in law
either!

Everything, we may say, was against the likelihood of her
success. Her adversary was ruthless, her friends were impotent
or uninterested and she could not appeal to the religious, humane, or moral sensibilities of the court. And yet she kept going
back again and again. Did she expect to convert the judge to
belief in God or to soften his sternness toward man or to correct
his flippant attitude toward the law? Obviously not; and yet his
godless and insensitive spirit neither intimidated nor discour-
aged her. Her prayer to the court was the result of desperation
or doggedness or faith—or perhaps of all three. And she won.

It is important to recognize, however, that she won, not by
reversing the base attitudes of which the judge was proud. His

very pride in them would have made him resistant to any assaults on what he regarded elements of strength of character, perverse though they seem to us to be. And yet there was an area in which he was completely disarmed and vulnerable, an area in which he was fatally sensitive. He cared not for God or man or law, but he cared for himself. What else, we may ask, was there left for him to regard as important? He did not want to be bothered; that was the imponderable element in the contest between the two that turned the issue in her favor. "Because this widow bothers me, I will vindicate her, or she will wear me out by her continual coming." This may strike us as a sorry reason for getting justice done and we would much prefer to appear before upright judges than to wear out godless ones, and yet it is within this idea that the point of the parable is set. Indeed Jesus calls particular attention to the judge's disposal of the case! "Hear what the unrighteous judge says"!

We must not allow ourselves to be diverted by certain whimsical aspects of the story from its clear intention: "He told them a parable, to the effect that they ought always to pray and not lose heart." If you believe in the righteousness and justice of your cause, don't give up. Why did he say this? We note that this is an emphasis quite different from what we have hitherto encountered. Spiritual blindness, preoccupation with material concerns, cynicism, sensualism—each of these has been portrayed as creating a tension conflict that is inimical to the success and personal growth of the Kingdom. In the person of the widow we have a positive presentation of something which in its negative aspect takes its place along with these other hazards. It is impatience or faint-heartedness or discouragement. Simpler still, it is lack of faith, faith in the imponderables that are a part of every human situation and which, more often than not turn the tables in favor of the one who will not be put off by weariness or bluff or threat or even by palpable and arrogant evil as it was incarnate in the judge. This situation is always tight with tension and is resolved either by quitting cold or by going on with an ardor that increases the longer one's ends are denied.

Recall at this point the aphorism with which chapter 17 closed. Was it true that evil days were imminent in the life of Israel? Was the body social, political, religious, economic so enervated that to the perceptive eye the ominous sight of carrion birds waiting for death was visible in the upper air? Abundant evidence in the words of Jesus supports the idea that he saw fate approaching remorselessly. Was the temptation to abandon their hopes and their program active within the little fellowship? That Jesus told them this story is proof enough of that. We may go further and ask whether he himself was not straightened by this baptism—to use his own vivid metaphor. And our answer to that question must also be affirmative. Not until Gethsemane was the desirability of escape from the destiny that awaited him completely satisfied by its final repudiation. Was he not indeed telling this story to himself as well as to them?

What was more apparent to him and them than the godlessness, inhumanity and lawlessness with which they were surrounded? Often it masqueraded like the judge, under the guise of respectability, or social form, or so-called practical ,expediency. Was not the situation therefore hopeless? Were it not better to yield to the inevitable and the adversary? The last days of our Lord's life have no meaning at all if they are purged of all such realistic considerations. When everything was against them was there some undisclosed imponderable fact that was to turn their unwearied quest into victory?

[4]

That there was an imponderable—to preserve the idiom—is the testimony of the radiant days that followed debacle. With that we are not here engaged. But point is given by this fact to the questions that Jesus asked after he had wound up the little parable. There are three questions and each is freighted with significance. Two are answered by himself; one is left without a reply.

The first: Will not God vindicate his elect, who cry to him day and night? This is the question of ultimate justice at the hands of God. No doubt it was necessary for him to reassert his faith in it both for his own sake and for the reassurance of his friends. Thus the question is put in such a way as allows only an affirmative reply.

The second deals with an auxiliary aspect of justice—its timing. "Will he [God] delay over them?" Here confidence is not so ready. After all it is not the dubiety of ultimate justice that puzzles us; it is its delay. Even the sons of this world will agree that justice will finally be done; it is its deferment to which they accommodate themselves and with which they tease the sons of light. What does Jesus mean as he asserts that ultimate justice will be speedily done? The readiest answer has been the easiest one: that Jesus thought that *eschaton* was imminent and that vindication was not only to be surely but speedily done. And yet does not such an understanding dilute the point of the parable almost to meaninglessness? So far as the widow knew there was no justice likely at all, taking into consideration all the factors that stood in the way of its performance. Certainly there was even less expectation that she would be vindicated against her adversary speedily. Once again, if this is not to be understood eschatologically it must be understood as a reflection of the tension in the group and in his own soul which tended to equate ultimate justice with speedy justice. This is an error that is involved in the time relations within which history is set. Delay is a time relation and, in the experience of a timeless Judge, would have no meaning at all. It is this that puzzles the elect and shakes their solid faith in ultimate justice. It even goes to the extent of asserting that ultimate justice is not possible within history. This is, we think, a mistake that arises out of the time factor within which the idea of ultimate justice is set by creatures of time. It is outside or beyond time that the ideas of delay and advance have no relevance. The use of the word "delay" fixes therefore his concept within a time dimension and holds it within the frame of history. For this reason we cannot understand it as eschatological. Ultimate justice may be within time, delayed justice within time.

The third question supports the idea that has just been set forth. "Nevertheless"—and the word is important for it carries the idea of speedy vindication over into the question—"when the Son of man comes, will he find faith on earth?" What is meant by faith here? Faith in condign and celeritous justice? If this is the point why, after he has just asserted the fact, does he question ultimate faith in it? Rather is he not asking here whether the faith that had been exhibited in the undiscourageable importunities of the widow would find its exemplars on the earth? We have pointed out that he gave no answer to this very important question. Indeed there are reasons for thinking that from a practical point of view the answer to this is more immediately important than the answer to the other two. And yet he did not answer it. Not however because the answer was hidden from him. Perhaps, indeed, because the answer was so obvious; for if the Son of man finds no faith (like the widow's) on the earth, he will find an earth that has been reduced to ruin by the impatient who, having doubted that godliness, inhumanity and disdain for law could ever be redressed by imponderable factors in the human-divine situation, had taken things finally into their own hasty human hands. Toynbee, surveying the rubble of dead civilizations to which he, as a latter-day son of man has come, seeking for the cause of death, describes it as a loss of nerve on a colossal culture-wide scale. And what is faith, or patience but what we more colloquially call nerve?

To say that there is ageless pertinence in this story is to labor the obvious, yet here was no concern with an ethical problem

but simply with the problem of pertinacity; the argument between quitting when the odds are impossible and going forward
against them no matter how formidable they are. It is a question that has two sides for there is no sure line between wisdom
and folly here, between hardihood and foolhardihood. Had the
widow failed she would have been pitied for a while and then
forgotten forever. The successful revolutionist is a hero; the un-
successful one is a traitor. Who can calculate risks, or who should
defy them?

Our interest here finally is twofold: Were there those in the
little fellowship, in the tense days that brought them nearer to
Jerusalem, who counseled retreat, or withdrawal, or direct aggressive action against the faithless, inhumane, and immoral
rulers who sat in the seat of judgment? If so, was not this story
of Jesus his answer to them, and was it not his invincible faith
in the rightness of his cause and its ultimate vindication that
kept him going even after they forsook him? Again is there not
something more than mildly disturbing about the impatience
of good causes in our times? How easy it is to brand an adversary
as godless, inhumane, lawless and decide to let him alone. He
may be all that and more, but is that reason enough for retreat
or for the abandonment of the cause? One thinks of the Soviet
Union in this connection. How aptly we find the judge to be
the prototype of the men of Politburo! How exhausting has been
the effort to have our cause given just treatment! How impatient
we are with vetoes! How easy it is to counsel violent action, and
to forget that there are imponderables that so often tip the balance in the favor of the undaunted and the tireless.

Remember the widow; and then recall Jesus' last question.
Then it will be necessary to ask ourselves whether modern impatience is not betraying us into the rashness that issues, never
in justice, but always in ruin.

CHAPTER XV

The Snob

WILL he find faith on the earth? With this question the story of the widow and the judge was adjourned. By faith was meant that patience, that pertinacity that will not be put off by adversity or adversary; that morale, that nerve that does not yield or forfeit its cause, but rather with full awareness of the realities of its situation still deeply knows there are always imponderable components that are swung into line only for those who have stood firm in their positions. This is not romantic optimism in a grim world; it is what wins verdicts from the godless, the egoistic and the cynical judge, whoever or whatever that may be.

Now there is a state of mind that is a canker to the fruit of faith. It is self-righteousness. It may even be called a sort of self-reliance if we are careful to define it. Remember the widow won her case not because she relied on herself but on the rightness of her cause and the imponderable factor represented by the judge's annoyance. This was faith. Had she been impressed rather with her own righteousness the contest might have easily turned out inconclusively or to her disadvantage, since the judge was quite as convinced of his unrighteousness and proud of it. Furthermore if the woman's reliance had been self-reliance only, even though we have suggested that it seemed she was shorn of all other support for her cause, she might easily have quit her "continual coming" before the judge yielded to her prayer in order to be quit of her. That would *not* have been faith. What is meant by the self-righteousness or self-reliance here that acts as a barrier to the exercise of faith is set forth in our next parable.

He also told this parable to some who trusted in themselves that they were righteous and despised others. "Two men went up into the temple to pray, one a Pharisee and the other a tax collector. The Pharisee stood and prayed thus with himself, 'God, I thank thee that I am not like other men, extortioners, unjust, adulterers, or even like this tax collector. I fast twice a week, I give tithes of all that I get.' But the tax collector, standing far off, would not even lift up his eyes to heaven, but beat his breast, saying, 'God, be merciful to me a sinner!' I tell you, this man went down to his house justified rather than the other; for every one who exalts himself will be humbled, but he who humbles himself will be exalted" (Luke 18:9-14).

The moral with which the story closes is word for word a repetition of Luke 14:11. There it was uttered as a warning against an inordinate craving for social status at a party—a matter of etiquette or simple amenity. Here it is pronounced as a warning against a presumption of privilege before the face of God. As such it is a graver matter but the law that operates is the same both in the society of one's fellows and in the society of God.

[1]

To those who reflect deeply on human life one of its most engaging qualities is the narrowness and the fragility of the divisions that separate men from each other. Divisions there are because variety is one of the invariables of life. Organisms are dissimilar and often are able to survive because of their disparity. But this does not mean that differences are invariable. On certain levels of life the variability of differences is as fixed a law as their invariability on other levels. Obviously it is on the human level where this is most easily observed, not in the behavior of the human physical organism but in the behavior of the human psyche. This is the essential meaning of the moral referred to above. Man, by his own act or the acts of his fellows, can be raised up or cast down, and in the common judgment of those among whom the process is observed, he is quite a different person when he is up from what he is when he is down. Indeed in his own judgment of himself also he has changed radically.

That Jesus was aware of this is just one indication of the profundity of his penetration into the human situation. With great clarity he apprehended the dialectic of permanence and change. Faith that can cast a mountain into the sea is a dramatization of the fact. That "it was said of old times . . . but I say unto you" is an indication that mores, customs, conventions, laws, change. He saw this, however, not in terms of caprice but of law. A mountain hurtling through space and plummeting into the sea was not the language of miracle but of the commonplace of faith. It is not whimsy that makes rocks out of sand; no more then was the conversion of the granulated fisherman into the rocklike saint an accident. Spiritual laws operated to effect the change. Perhaps we call them psychological laws with great familiarity. However we may phrase it, he who exalts himself *is* humbled in response to a spiritual law of falling bodies. He that humbles himself *is* exalted in response to a spiritual law of convection.

Some needed to have this said to them and as they appeared momentarily before him the parable-teller confronted them. Were there Pharisees and taxgatherers among his listeners? The inference is inescapable. The temple, toward which he and the fellowship were moving, was the scene of the story. In his day it was the center toward which all life ultimately converged. That one man convinced of his righteousness, and another of his sin, should find themselves in the temple together is symbolic of the eternal fact that both sin and righteousness are the temple's business. Thither also went the wise to propound and the simple to ask; there also went the rich man to display his philanthropies and the widow to drop her mite into the treasury; there the moneychanger fleeced the faithful and the poor paid exorbitantly for their faith that two doves would expiate their innocent defections from the law. So, in a sense more complete than we often think, does religion furnish the pivot about which life swings.

An aspect of this—the pivoting of life about religion—is the impulse to pray that brought these men together. One man prayed because it flattered him; the other because it cleansed him. Extrapolation, the psychologists call it, the projection of the self beyond the self. No matter what the reason or the result, men still come into the temple to pray, or pray where they can find no temple.

[2]

It is important to realize that both of these men were telling the truth about themselves; at least in so far as their analysis went they were sincere in what they thought about themselves. When men pray they do not consciously lie to God. Whatever we may think of Pharisees in general, we have no reason for thinking this man not to have been, at least externally, an exemplary citizen. This being so he had good reason for a measure of satisfaction. He was, negatively stated, no extortioner, no defrauder, and no adulterer. Positively he was meticulous about the observance of ritual fasts, and was a strict tither. He was a man of scrupulous and sedate habits; he made his influence for regularity felt in business, home, and temple.

What of the tax collector? There is a subtle hint that but for the odium that attached to his job he might not have been such a bad sort. After the Pharisee has lumped "other men" indiscriminately as extortioners, unjust, adulterers, he adds, as if by making an exception, "or even like this tax collector." One would assume that those who gathered Rome's tribute would be generally regarded as extortioners and unjust. Are we allowed to infer that the Pharisee was conceding the possibility that a man could be a tax collector and still retain some elements of decency? Whatever is to be said about this, we know that the second man did not take advantage of it in his own statement of his credits. He was, by his simple revealing word a sinner. This gave him no sense of gratitude; all he felt was a need for God's mercy. The verdict against the two men is one of the most celebrated of all times: the Pharisee for all his honest righteousness was unjustified; the tax collector, for all his honest sin was justified.

If this is not a perversion of justice it turns our moral order upside down and sin, not expiated or abandoned but merely confessed becomes our credential for justification. Yet this has never been taken as the intention of this story. Somehow men have inevitably seen that beneath the righteous external of one man was corruption and beneath the confession of the sinner there was a purifying element. Let us examine this.

There is nothing wrong in relying on one's righteousness. We must not be either sophisticated or cynical about this. What sort of goodness is any good except that that can be relied on? Is it not, in fact, the pragmatic quality of goodness as a support to life that is its commonest credit? Furthermore, self-reliance, no matter what its moral quality, is a wholesome thing. It is one of the certain evidences of maturity. While all of this is true in our experience we need to be warned against something. These qualities which are good in themselves can, by ever so slight a change—whether a shock or a soporific—become odious. The change in temperature at the point of freezing water is so slight as to be indiscernible except to an instrument, but the difference the change causes is obvious to everybody.

There were two freezing points, let us say, or two changes in temperature that made the righteous man self-righteous, the just man unjustifiable. The first came when he concluded that

he was not like other men. This was true in so far as it is part
of the paradox of the identity and the dissimilarity of all people.
This however is not what he meant. Other men—and the way
he brackets all of them together is significant—are extortioners,
unjust, adulterers. In other words he was better than everyone
else; he stood like a tower of rectitude above the moral rubble
about his feet. Not only so: his sense of superiority—and this is
the second point where the temperature changed his condition—
took the form of despising others. Recall the opening words of
the paragraph: "He also told this parable to some who trusted
in themselves that they were righteous and despised others."
There is not necessarily an identity between self-regard and the
scorn of others in what we have called self-reliance, but the transition from one to the other is very brief; it occurs by an almost
indistinguishable change, and it represents a very great difference
when it has happened. The righteous man has become the self-
righteous man; the sure man has become the cocksure man; the
self-reliant has become the snob, and there is no justification for
snobbishness. Why?

[3]

Because the snob is a fraud, and to most everyone but himself
this is clear. The transition from righteous self-reliance to self-
righteous snobbery is, as we have said both subtle and short,
but it makes a great difference. Indeed it lifts one out of one category and sets him rudely down in another. When one begins to
look down on others, he has already lost his self-reliance though
he will angrily repudiate the charge. He has lost, this is to say,
the solid base upon which he has rested his sense of worth, and
in its stead has been set up the crumbling pedestal of scorn on
which he is now perched. The greater the depth of his scorn,
the more massive he thinks his security is. Snobbishness is a protective device to conceal one's unconscious sense of insecurity

of whatever sort. A snob, therefore, is not self-reliant, and his efforts to appear so simply conceal the spurious quality of his confidence. But he cannot rest comfortably in the simple fool's paradise of snobbery; he ultimately has to regard all other men as "extortioners, unjust, adulterers," or taxgathers or snobs! A part of the ritual of snobbery is the scrupulous maintenance of the disciplines of respectability.[1] The greater the snob the more impeccable his front. He tithes and fasts ceremoniously but with less and less relish because, while he thinks they minister to his superior status, subconsciously they erode it. He stands in the temple for all to see and prays with great ostentation. But while he addresses the deity in somewhat peremptory tones, he is talking to himself, for it is not God that needs placating; it is his own insufferable insufficiency. How deeply the descriptive word of Jesus probed this snob's soul: "The Pharisee stood and prayed thus *with himself*"!

The Pharisee was wracked by inner conflict. He would have disputed this and his refusal to admit it would be evidence of it. Before we ask what is to be done with snobs of this sort—and religious snobbery is perhaps a degree more odious than any other—it is interesting to observe that the tax collector was in a fair way toward settling the problem that had brought him to the temple. It is inaccurate to think of him as the spiritual parallel of the self-righteous snob. Oddly enough there seems to be no such type—the type, we mean, that boasts of his evil and is satisfied in it, looking contemptuously on the righteous. That such persons do not seem to exist is significant either of an innate moral gyroscope that does not allow such extreme imbalance, or of a moral consensus so well established by practice that it is regarded as insanity when it is defied. There literally is no such

---

[1] "There is an interior idolatry in every moment of life. . . . Before God, monstrous crimes, committed by weakness, by passion or by ignorance, are less crimes than are the virtues which a soul full of itself practices in order to relate everything to its own excellence, as though it alone were divine." Fénelon, *Christian Perfection* (New York: Harper & Brothers, 1947), p. 57.

overt amoralism. Such a person, if we follow the Pharisee pattern in reverse, would not stand in the temple, wherever he stood, and he would not address himself to God. He would express his satisfaction that he was not as other men are: deceived slaves of superstition and moral codes imposed by the powerful or the insecure. He would boast that he took what he wanted by extortion or shrewdness, that justice was "the collective egotism of the feeble" [2] and that adultery was a word invented by bourgeois weaklings to protect their women. He would add that such sissy disciplines as fasting and tithing are only for those who suffer from visceral disorders or from sentimentalized regard for undeserving humanity.

Did we say "there is literally no such overt amoralism"? Did we attribute this to an innate moral gyroscope or an explicit moral consensus? We did, and in so speaking deliberately repeated the error of the liberal optimism of the pre-World War days. And this is the formidable fact: that aided and abetted by the self-righteousness of this liberal optimism as it has expressed itself in moral, political, and economic behavior, there has appeared in the world a new type of evil that instead of standing afar off, swaggers to the center of modern life, and instead of asking God for mercy, dares God not to do him honor.

The matter has been put thus because the unjustifiability of self-righteousness has not only been demonstrated in our times but has had pragmatic judgment passed on it. Furthermore, unless somehow something can be done for the Pharisee in our midst—and that means in our individual hearts—the judgment will not be lifted, and that may mean the ultimate doom of the race.

[2] The phrase is Nietzsche's; he was the last-century exponent of this amoralistic attitude, and he died in a madhouse.

[4]

What, we may then ask, was to be done for the snob in this story? Did the verdict in favor of the tax collector shock him into self-examination or did it anger him? We do not know but we strongly suspect the latter. For it is the quality of this hubristic pride that it has no resource within itself to check its excesses. The man in the parable had already got to the point of praying "with himself." This subtle identification of himself with God represented the apex of his self-delusion. He was, he thought, as righteous as God and from that level it was natural to despise others less righteous than he. To have told him that he was a victim of himself would not have evoked a quiet and grateful response. "He that sitteth in the heavens shall laugh," quoth the psalmist; "and so do I," he might have added. We confess therefore that we know nothing that could have saved the snob from himself. It is significant that it was this quality of life that drew from Jesus his most angry and scathing words. It was not that he was angered by their misdeeds so much as that he was baffled by the inability to make them see their condition. They were righteous in their own eyes and from that base they could not be moved. No wonder he demanded of his followers right-eousness superior to that of the scribes and Pharisees; but it was not self-righteousness, it was the righteousness of God. The neo-orthodox have shown us this with great clarity. If we do not agree with them that this adamant self-pride is original sin we do agree that it comes as near as we can get to the unpardonable sin—unpardonable, that is to say, not because of the lack of God's effective grace, but because of its imperviousness to the moral insight that alone leads one to seek His grace in redemption.

[5]

Does it need pointing out that we have here perhaps the most fruitful source of tension in the modern world? And if this is true are we to expect anything less than the abasement that follows self-exaltation? We repeat that the self-righteous man's description of himself was true and entitled him to the status of an exemplary citizen. But we had to add that, without his suspecting it in the least, he tipped off his sense of spiritual inferiority by derogating everybody else. Thus the self-reliant modulated into the snob when his satisfied self-regard became unsatisfied regard of others. This always produces trouble. It is summarized in our story by the reference to his unjustified status before God. That does not specify the ways in which his fellows reacted. What did other eavesdroppers in the temple think when they heard his arrogant prayer? We can only guess. What we do know, however, is that this effort to establish one's superiority by the denigration of others feeds upon itself and grows so prodigiously that, sooner or later, those to whom it has become intolerable will contrive singly or collectively to put the offender in his place. This is the stage of open conflict.

One of the least edifying of spectacles is the operation of this in the field of religion. It is not enough to say that in the past it was the cause of what we call the wars of religion. Nor is it intended here to analyze its full application to our own day. It can be asked, however, how far this sense of self-reliant self-righteousness grown into religious snobbism is responsible first for the great schism that divides the Evangelical bodies from the body of Rome, and second for the divisions within Protestantism. We, both Romanists and Evangelicals, talk unctiously about the sin of schism and in our very words we exhibit our pride—pride that we *see* the sin to be what it is. And yet the proud group—and which of us is not proud?—can no more truly apprehend the nature of its sin than the proud Pharisee. So we prove our righteousness to ourselves by talking about the sin that divides us, unaware that the claim of infallibility that Rome makes and the claim of soul freedom the Evangelical makes may be our ways of saying: we thank God that we are not as other men are. Not until all of us stand afar off—because we fear to drew nigh—and with averted eyes cry "God, be merciful to me a sinner" shall we put ourselves within reach of the justification of God.

This is, to be sure, an old familiar fact, but there is another one that is growing in acerbity and extent. It is the problem of race conflict. We grow weary of it and not a little impatient of the spot announcements on the radio that warn us of its danger to the American way of life and exhort us to do better. Not to discredit the good intentions or the wholesome results of such efforts, but to point out the sinfulness of race pride and its ultimate menace for the life of the human race, we would go deeper than that. The story of the pamphlet prepared for the men and women in the armed services which gave definitive anthropological data on race, and how it was frantically withdrawn because it violated certain service taboos, is well enough known. Does this mean that the dissemination of objective scientific fact is not appropriate if it questions the prideful self-righteousness of the dominant racial group? That is exactly what it means. When an authority on the matter quotes another distinguished colleague, "The idea of a pure race is not even a legitimate abstraction; it is a subterfuge used to cloak one's ignorance of the phenomenon of racial variation," [3] and says himself, "Virtually all human beings are mongrels" and "All snobbism that is supposed to be founded upon biological necessity from one or a few distant ancestors is essentially absurd," how do we react? "Subterfuge to cloak our ignorance," "mongrels," "absurd"— these words are repugnant to those of us who have been thanking

---

[3] Clyde Kluckhohn, *Mirror for Man* (New York: Whittlesey House, 1949), p. 123, 112, 116.

God that we are not like other men, pigmented, mixed, degenerate, or even like that immigrant. So we include in the list of those whom we thank God we are not like, the anthropologists who say that we are!

If pride were amenable to correction by the display of scientific data we could hope that education might provide the solution to this problem. To be sure there is more enlightenment on the subject than ever before and a generation of young folk is being taught and is appropriating the facts. Let us be encouraged by this but let us beware of abandoning the problem to the classroom. Knowledge is a two-edged sword: it can be an inducement to wise action and, at the same time, it can minister to the pride that feels itself superior to action. Perhaps there is another direction from which help can come.

Economic considerations determine to a considerable extent the world's behavior. What shows a profit can't be far wrong; what doesn't can't be good for very long. Slavery proved itself economically unsound in the South as early as 1670 when a petition was presented in the Virginia House of Burgesses for its abolition on those grounds. The present chaos and imminent terror in the Union of South Africa is not unrelated to the discovery that the exploitation of the blacks by the dominant white minority is increasingly costly, and the fear of what will happen when a bankrupt economy turns hundreds of thousands of unemployed natives out of their wretched hovels has led to the excessively repressive measures of the present governmnt. Nowhere has the arrogance of the white man's pride reached such levels of self-righteous snobbery, and at what a cost!

A recent story in *The Christian Century* for July 20, 1949, shows that the economic angle is being given fresh consideration in this country.

Race Bias a Costly National Vice—Damage done by racial discrimination to personalities and to the moral and religious standards of American life has often been described. But it remained for Joseph J. Morrow, personnel director of Pitney-Bowes, Inc., to analyze its cost to our national economy in dollars. Speaking before the notable Race Relations Institute at Fisk University, this Connecticut industrialist said that racial bias is costing the American economy a minimum of $6 billion a year. Buttressing his argument with figures compiled by Elmo Roper, Mr. Morrow said that the 6.5 million wage-earners among the Negroes of this country are now earning and spending at the rate of $10 billion a year. If discriminatory practices were dropped and Negroes were permitted to share equally in the economic process, their earnings would be $16 billion. The difference between these two figures he described as the cost of racism. If these figures may be believed, Mr. Morrow's conclusion is inescapable: "The discriminatory practices in our country are robbing it of a good portion of its production potential and a good portion of the consumer potential which are the heart and soul of a successful free enterprise system."

This is money loss, but not the only loss. When one considers what is spiritually lost by this continued unreasonable and uneconomic pride, there is no computation that can set it forth. In a study of this aspect of our losses Dr. Howard Thurman [4] has described with great discernment but without bitterness the blight of fear, deception and hate that falls on the underprivileged minorities in our culture as the result of their effort to adjust themselves to the privileged snob.

[6]

While our concern with education and economics nudges us slowly in the direction of more rational treatment of the problem, the judgment of God falls inexorably on us. This means the problem is ultimately a moral one to be solved only in terms of correct moral attitudes and actions. This puts it back where

[4] Howard Thurman, *Jesus and the Disinherited* (New York-Nashville: Abingdon-Cokesbury Press, 1949).

it has always been, in the field of religion. The nature of true
righteousness is inseparable from true humility. It is possible
to go beyond that and say that in so far as pride is sin, humility
is goodness. There may have been great sinners who were genu-
inely modest about their exploits but they do not readily come
to mind. The prayer of the tax collector is the authentic—albeit
paradoxical—petition of the good man. "God be merciful to me
a sinner" is the cry of no groveling, abject, morbidly self-accusing
whiner. It is the recognition that all who stand before the in-
effable light of God cast a dark shadow; all who are confronted
with the righteousness of God feel the need of the everlasting
mercy. This is a religious insight, as ageless as it is profound.

All the greater the scandal therefore that the Christian fellowship finds little room for its dark-skinned brethren; that segregation is an established Christian pattern; that we still thank God
that we are not like other races; that we, trusting in ourselves
that we are white, despise others. For the simple point that this
plunging parable makes is that if we want to be proud, we may,
but not without incurring its sure consequences. He that exalteth
himself, exalteth himself. We would settle for that! But that
is not the bargain. He that exalteth himself shall be abased. We
cannot have our pride and swallow it. And so far as we know,
there is no exception to this fair and frightening rule. The
Pharisee *went down* unjustified; the tax collector *went up* in
the divine favor. What of races or groups or classes or churches?
Do they, by the fact that they are not individuals, avert the
operation of this law? There is neither record nor reason to support such hope.

We have written much about tension. At this point in the
record we discover evidences of its tightening toward its ultimate
tautness. Little wonder. His hearers could listen to strictures on
sensualism, cynicism, the godless judge, the foolish farmer. It
actually fed their sense of pride that they were like none of these.
But when he put his finger on their pretentious righteousness

he went too far. One who could pair together the cynic and the snob had lost all sense of ethical distinctions. Now he was a menace to goodness and must be destroyed.

How plausible it all must have sounded to them, when the Pharisees and the rulers took counsel how they might destroy him.

"God be merciful to me, a sinner."

CHAPTER XVI

The Egomaniac

THE continuity between the last parable and the next is important. It is also among the most familiar stretches of narrative in the entire Gospel. Immediately after Jesus has restated the maxim about pride's deflation and humility's elevation he is seen in the midst of a miscellaneous throng among whom were mothers, presumably, bringing children to him for a blessing. This was hardly a ritual act. It apparently was an almost superstitious notion that the mothers had that a touch would confer some magical benefit on their little ones. This is far from uncommon in religion; indeed its vestige if not its essence remains in certain ritual practices in Christendom. That the disciples rebuked this normal maternal concern is clear evidence of the accumulating pressures under which they were living. Deference to motherhood was a Jewish virtue and fondness for children was—as is everywhere—a natural affection. There was surely no menace in a delegation of mothers with babes in arms against which Jesus needed protection. The ill humor of the disciples was more likely touchiness induced by the general atmosphere of uncertainty or portent. The famous response of Jesus to the wish of the mothers is touched with both tenderness and insight that have warmed hearts and engaged minds for centuries.

The rich young ruler—as he is familiarly called—takes his

turn after the children have gone. Had he heard the parable
about the snob? Perhaps. Had he heard about the fool? Possibly
—directly or by gossip. In any case he put a question that reflected what he thought was a serious concern of his: eternal life.
The refusal of Jesus to allow the man to call him "good," insist-
ing that God alone was good, has been variously understood.
More is to be said about this in the next chapter, but can it not
be taken at this point to indicate the inner tension that was
mounting in his own soul? If he was sincerely questioning his
right to the compliment—and we have no right to think him as
merely polite or as consciously flippant—how otherwise is his
remark to be taken if not as evidence of a struggle being con-
tested deeply within him? If he was right in what he was doing,
he was good, if he was wrong or mistaken could he be sure he
was good? There was growing dispute among his immediate
friends, and misgiving and active hostility in wider circles. This
stirring air could not pass over him without bending his mind to
its subtle pressures. When it grew into a wild tempest he recoiled
against its shattering force. "Why do you call me good? No one
is good but God alone." This is deep water but for all that it
does not run smoothly. His understanding of his questioner's
problem was both immediate and profound. The man was
morally Grade A but only because he had refused to do battle
where his moral conflict was really drawn. Being rich and socially secure and officially important there was, we assume, little
temptation to him to be faithless to his wife, to kill, steal, lie, or
be unfilial to his parents. But to deal morally, or, as it might be
put, constructively, with his wealth—here was a problem he had
refused to face. The drastic prescription Jesus gave for facing
the moral issue and overcoming it cannot be normalized as apply-
ing to everybody. If everyone gave away or sold everything he
had it would not be philanthropy; it would be chaos. All the
moral value in social concern would be reduced to absurdity.
But where attachment to one's property becomes a moral issue

—as it very often is—one must deal with it. To take satisfaction from the fact that one has not stolen his neighbor's goods does nothing to resolve the question of his moral use of his own. Little wonder that the point of this was missed by "those who heard it" though it seems clear enough that the young ruler got the point and went off in dismay. "Who then can be saved?" was the sort of despairing question that might be expected from this episode. Who indeed? If this was the tack to be taken from this point on, was not the whole movement destined to end in fiasco? Jesus' reassuring word that all things were possible with God did not register immediately. Peter was quick to claim credit for his abandonment of his home, and Jesus was as quick to point out that all who had done so for the sake of the Kingdom of God would not go unrewarded.

[1]

The clearest evidence of the atmosphere within which Jesus and the disciples were moving is set forth in the four verses that follow.

And taking the twelve aside, he said to them, "Behold, we are going up to Jerusalem, and everything that is written of the Son of man by the prophets will be accomplished. For he will be delivered to the Gentiles, and will be mocked and shamefully treated and spit upon; they will scourge him and kill him, and on the third day he will rise." But they understood none of these things; this saying was hid from them, and they did not grasp what was said (Luke 18:31-34).

This is the first time he explicitly shares with the inner circle his certainty of defeat. It is given them in secret, even in confidence. To us, nothing could be more clear and unequivocal. This was a sentence of death from which there was to be no reprieve. Here the sense of tension approaches its apogee for him; for the others there was to be a delayed reaction due to

some factor that for the moment blinded them to the meaning
of his forecast. One does not face the prospect of violence, of
pain, of contumely, and of ultimate death with equanimity.
There are mitigating factors, to be sure. In the case of Jesus' prediction, he foresaw his rising on the third day. Death itself is
often solidly felt to be a relief from life that has become unbear-
able and as such can be anticipated with calm, but it would have
been insensitiveness bordering on the moribund if Jesus could
have confronted what he described with jauntiness or even with
stoic disdain. At the same time this did not in any way abate his
activity. Indeed the contrary seems to have been the case, for the
multitudes that momentarily had taken leave of him now return.
He has less to say and more to do and it was what he did as he
drew closer to Jerusalem that attracted the crowds. Furthermore
the nearer they got to Jerusalem the greater the number of fellow pilgrims on their way to the holy city. He tells only two more
parables, but he healed a blind man outside Jericho and when
he went into the city electrified it by salvaging Zaccheus and
shaking out of his pockets the wealth he had filched from the
people. These were both spectacular demonstrations of power;
the sort of stories that would fly from lip to lip in excited repeti-
tions and increase the popular interest in the extraordinary man.

[2]

That this newly accreted multitude mistook what was up became the occasion for the next to the last of his stories. Wisely
he falls back to the simple didactic method.

As they heard these things, he proceeded to tell a parable, because
he was near to Jerusalem, and because they supposed that the kingdom of God was to appear immediately.[1] He said therefore, "A

1 How interesting the hurried and unwarranted inference the multitude drew
from his treatment of the blind man and Zaccheus. In the latter particularly, all
that the Kingdom needed to mean to the average mind was that Rome would be

nobleman went into a far country to receive kingly power and then return. Calling ten of his servants, he gave them ten pounds, and said to them, 'Trade with these till I come.' But his citizens hated him and sent an embassy after him saying, 'We do not want this man to reign over us.' When he returned, having received the kingly power, he commanded these servants, to whom he had given the money, to be called to him, that he might know what they had gained by trading. The first came before him, saying, 'Lord, your pound has made ten pounds more.' And he said to him, 'Well done, good servant! Because you have been faithful in a very little, you shall have authority over ten cities.' And the second came, saying, 'Lord, your pound has made five pounds.' And he said to him, 'You are to be over five cities.' Then another came, saying, 'Lord, here is your pound, which I kept laid away in a napkin; for I was afraid of you, because you are a severe man; you take up what you did not lay down, and reap what you did not sow.' He said to him, 'I will condemn you out of your own mouth, you wicked servant! You knew that I was a severe man, taking up what I did not lay down and reaping what I did not sow? Why then did you not put my money into the bank, and at my coming I should have collected it with interest?' And he said to those who stood by, 'Take the pound from him, and give it to him who has the ten pounds.' (And they said to him, 'Lord, he has ten pounds!') 'I tell you, that to every one who has will more be given; but from him who has not, even what he has will be taken away. But as for these enemies of mine, who did not want me to reign over them, bring them here and slay them before me' " (Luke 19:11-27).

We have titled this chapter "The Egomaniac," which seems, at first glance, to be a summary repudiation of a man who has pretty generally been regarded as something of a hero. To have called him simply an egotist would not have been so bad since in our honest moments we all confess to having yielded to the seductions of the ego. Still and all it is possible to see here in this noble-

subverted by tax collectors turning honest. Thus to cut the economic bonds that fastened Palestine to Rome was an exciting and even amusing prospect. If that happened, would not the Kingdom of God come immediately?

man the delineation of a type that is more than mere egotist; he may be seen as the prototype of those who are so addicted to themselves that their love of self is little short of pathological. There are no limits to which they will not go in order to glut this morbid self-lust. All humane considerations and all moral constraints are powerless to restrain them. Presumably there were such monsters in the days of the parable-teller; that there have been such individuals in our times is one of the tragic factors of the moral muddle in which we live, tragic in the meaning that they supply an element to modern life that we do not know how to deal with short of world destruction.

Is this judgment supported by the story? To be sure he is described as a nobleman. This is an accommodation the language has to make to avoid a translator's circumlocution. The Greek word (*eugenes*) simply means one who was well born. We need hardly to be reminded that the circumstance of fortunate birth is far from being a guarantee of genuine nobility. If this man's attitudes and behavior are to be taken as representative of nobility, we will do well to be rid of it. Allow us then to draw up our bill of particulars against this egomaniac, this man who was literally crazy about himself.

Here was a man so affluent that he could practically give away cities. He delivered fifteen cities to two men in the story and unless the balance of the ten to whom money was given for investment all failed as dismally as the one who is indicated as a failure, we may assume that there were other cities distributed or allocations of wealth commensurate with what the first two men got. Indeed this man's wealth is so fabulous as to give this the aspect of a fairy tale, and yet, unsatisfied with his enormous empire he goes abroad to receive a kingdom. Of course it can be argued that he, being of noble lineage was simply ascending to a throne ultimately destined for him. Against this sort of thing there was, once upon a time, no protest. From our perspectives, and indeed from the specific words of the story, he deserved no such elevation. His rule over the cities he owned had not been happy in terms of the ultimate criterion of administrative success—the contentment of the people. He had hardly got out of the borders of his domain before a palace revolt that had been smoldering while he was around burst into flame and an embassy of revolutionists ("His citizens hated him . . . saying 'We do not want this man to reign over us' ") pursued him to announce their independence. Manifestly the revolt was poorly organized and the egomaniac treated their embassage with contempt and sent them cringing back home to report ignominiously their failure to their fellow conspirators.

[3]

In due season he came home with his new royal title and his new territories. His thrifty—or was it parsimonious?—habits had provided that no holiday should attend his return even as his journey abroad had granted no recess. His underlings had been commissioned to trade with funds put into their hands— ten of them, one pound each—and he was no sooner home than these men were summoned to give an account of their stewardship. Conventional interpretations of this parable have made of the two successful traders shining examples for investors, and of the third man, a horrible lesson for the indolent. No matter; we are interested that two men could turn in such an extraordinary account of their enterprise. They had made 1000 per cent and 500 per cent respectively on their investments in the relatively short interval of the lord's absence. This is almost as fabulous a level of performance as the nobleman's record. We have no way of knowing how in days of relatively simple economics such prodigious returns could be won. We claim the right to be suspicious of the probity of their dealings on the simple basis that no one person could earn that much money in so short a time. Our suspicion is confirmed when we discover, later on, the business philosophy of the man who gave them their stake and who was so monstrous pleased with their records. Their rewards were commensurate with their winnings. Why not? Men who could do that were the sort of manipulators the big shot could use in the cities he put under them!

The third man has been the target of endless abuse. The prototype of all the shiftless, the improvident, the meagerly endowed, and the lazy, he has been the favorite whipping boy of the exhorters and the apologists of free enterprise. Here we are told is what happens to the indolent man who tries to make his fear of his master an alibi for his failures. And yet, if this is all that is to be said about him, it is quite possible that we shall miss the whole point of the story. For in a very real sense, this poor little man was the hero of the tale. He may have been a key member of the revolutionary group and for a very good reason. He knew the master to be a spectacular scoundrel and he was going to get rid of him if he could. If he couldn't, he was going to have no part personally in aggrandizing his fortunes.

He was afraid of him, he confessed, but hardly for insufficient reasons. Those who had expressed their hatred of him must have had ample cause for they jeopardized their lives in their revolt when he left and lost them when he got home. Their reasons were perhaps similar to those that inspired fear in the one-pound man. It took conspicuous courage to face his now kingly lord and say what he did, particularly after the award of merit just conferred on his more enterprising—or obsequious—colleagues. Nor did he mince words as he indicted him on three counts: he was a severe man—tough, we would say; he was a thief, for what other meaning can attach to actions that are described as "taking up what [he] did not lay down"? He was, finally an exploiter. What was not his by dint of effort he appropriated; what he had not sown, he reaped.

Now the interesting thing about this daring accusation is that it came from one who confessed that he was scared to death and nevertheless went through with it; and that the accused made no effort to defend himself. On the contrary, he agreed with the indictment in toto. "You knew," he replied to the little man, "that I was a tough, predatory, exploiting scoundrel." Was it that he did not dare to dispute the charge or extenuate his behavior? One even wonders whether the two other servants, secure in their newly won authority over cities, knew it too. There is even a malicious impulse to explain their fantastic success as investors by their having patterned their behavior after the master's. Instead of excusing himself, however, he denounces his accuser as a wicked servant, an old defensive trick. In all conscience one finds it difficult to see wherein lay his wickedness. He had returned the pound, clean and intact. He had spoken honestly as to his reasons for not investing it. It must be that the idea of wickedness to which the master subscribed was failure to make at least five hundred per cent on a trade. This reduces morals to zero: excessive virtue equals 1000 per cent return; commendable goodness equals 500 per cent, and wickedness is just holding your own! This is not so bizarre a moral standard as it may seem; think how closely it approximates the market-place morality of our times.

His proposal that the bankers might have done better by him was weak and evasive particularly in the light of the code current among the Jews that forbade the taking of interest on loans. If they were "heathen" bankers, all the more doubtful does the proposal seem. Of course the nobleman may not have been a Jew —but of this aspect of the story, more presently. What is noteworthy is the palpable injustice that follows with the direction that this infertile pound be put into the fecundating nest of the ten-pound man. The murmur from the crowd, "Lord, he has ten pounds," indicates that a common-sense view of justice had been violated by that odd proposal. But the master's reason for it is at once set forth in the most cynical lines found in the New Testament. Credit the egomaniac with frankness about himself.

He not only did not bother to parry the thrusts of his accuser, he boldly advanced a philosophy of life to support himself. "I tell you, that to everyone who has will more be given; but from him who has not, even what he has will be taken away." No one except a man describable as ruthless, larcenous, and predacious would justify himself with such a monstrous maxim. It is, in the first place, a lie; and if it could be thought the truth, it would hide an intolerable moral error in its heart. That this was not to be thought carelessly tossed out with such bravado as might impress his hearers he adds the ultimate touch to his infamy by his final command: "But as for these enemies of mine, who did not want me to rule over them, bring them here and slay them before me." That's the kind of ruler he was, thoroughly consonant with his general outlook on life. Let all who disagree with me be warned: we have a way of dealing with dissident minorities!

[4]

This is the "nobleman" to whom we have been introduced in this, the longest, and in certain details the most puzzling, of the parables. We have already cautioned against taking all the factors of a parable with equal seriousness and against stretching a parable until it covers everything we want said about a matter. At the same time it is clear that the person depicted here was a thoroughly bad man. All efforts to make him the type of the heavenly Father who endows his children variously and expects diligent use of their talents and liberal returns therefrom have missed the point of the story.

At whom then was it aimed? The point has been made that the other stories have dealt with "good" people whose righteousness was tarnished, or cankered, or canceled by folly, sensualism, greed, cynicism, snobbery, and so on. These good folk were not plain folk; they were the arbiters of taste and the protectors of respectability. They worked hard at being righteous; sometimes they thought themselves tolerant of sincere though misdirected enthusiasm for change. Indeed they would do anything at all to be good. They were, in short, the religious leaders of the day, and every indication points to the fact that when they heard Jesus telling his simple parables, they did not miss the point.

There were, however, some people who made no pretense of being good. They had come from across the great sea to gain kingly possessions. They had boasted their noble lineage and lifted high the imperial eagles that were the insignia of their power. There was no limit to their greed for new lands. There were, among those whom they had forcibly possessed, some who did not like them. It was necessary always to keep a keen eye open and roving to detect incipient rebellion in the rear of marching and conquering armies. To be sure they allowed those who accepted their rule to share in its material advantages. Benefices were farmed out to amenable and industrious subjects and they had profited enormously from them. And yet the rule was ruthless, predacious, and exploitative, first, last, and all the time. Such virtues as it claimed were hard and cynical and selfish, and if anything was believed with honest fervor it was that to everyone (whether empire or individual) who has will more be given; but from him (empire or individual) who has not, even what he has will be taken away. There was, finally, one way by which such a philosophy of life was to be guaranteed: liquidate its enemies. How consistently this principle was lived up to is among the commonest bits of our knowledge of ancient history.

> Now Rome could handle rebels
>   And bring them to their knees;
> There was no ambiguity
>   About her remedies.
> She ruled her subjects,
>   Watched her friends,
>   And smashed her enemies.[2]

[2] From "Sepphóris" in Edwin McNeill Poteat, *Over the Sea, the Sky* (New York: Harper & Brothers, 1945), p. 37.

Now the fact was that the "good" people to whom the parables were for the most part addressed were making common cause with the bad people in order to deal with this dissident Galilean and his friends. He was far too popular with the common folk for he gave voice to their grievances and vigor to their hopes. To be sure he talked about loving one's enemies, but this seemed to do little to abate their hatred of the conqueror. The village of Sepphóris was a reminder of the way Rome dealt with those who rebelled against her rule.

[5]

It is one of the ironies of history that the good people of Palestine and the bad people of Rome found in the parable-teller an object upon which their enmity could agree. In the mind of Jesus it was not enough to rebuke the righteous fictions with which the Pharisees flattered themselves. There was the other side—the open, defiant, hard-fisted amoral civil authority and its horde of underlings who were profiting exorbitantly. It is not without significance that this story was told just after the extraordinary episode in Jericho when Zacchaeus was restored to status as a true son of Abraham by his pragmatic repudiation of Rome. Remember also that the reason for telling this story is clearly stated: "He proceeded to tell a parable, because he was near to Jerusalem, and because they supposed that the kingdom of God was to appear immediately." So long as Rome held Israel as a subject people there was little prospect of the Kingdom coming. The Jericho experience had raised illusory hopes; one Zacchaeus did not make a Kingdom. Until there was righteousness that exceeded that of the scribes and Pharisees there would be no Kingdom; until also there was a withdrawal of the cruel hand of Rome it could not come.

Is it surprising then that he should have directed a parable at those who were already conspiring to destroy him? If so, how more adroitly could it have been done than in this story? Those who heard did not miss, as do we, the ingratiating word "nobleman" or the reference to kingly powers. Were these not used with a gentle irony, touched perhaps with pathos? It was no rallying cry of revolution against Rome. That would have been crushed in an instant with a blow from a giant fist. But those who heard and felt the prick of its subtleties were not to forget. Up to this point he had been, to the authorities of Rome, a nuisance and as such he had value to them. If he was to keep the Pharisees agitated against him they would have less time to worry about Pilate. Now, however, he had become a menace. He had said, couched in the innuendo of a parable, that Rome was a despoiler and that dissenters could expect nothing but death. And if the Kingdom of God could not come except dissenters brought it in, was not his language the words of sedition?

There is about this story, thus understood, the air of menace. Its pertinence for appropriation for modern situations must be deferred to a later point in this discussion. Now, however, we are clear on one point. The tension between him, his friends, and the rulers, both ecclesiastical and civil, rises to new levels of intensity. It is less than a week before tragedy was to shatter like an explosive about them all. It is in the light of this relevant insight that we must study the gala entrance of Jesus and his followers into Jerusalem. In the meantime is there not in the verse that follows the parable just studied, a sense of accelerated tempo?

"And when he had said this, he went on ahead, going up to Jerusalem." The crowd no longer thronged him; he was outpacing them.

CHAPTER XVII

The Crisis

THE last parable of any considerable length is conspicuously different from any of the others told during these last tense days we have been surveying. It is a part of the most dramatic experience of Jesus' career up to the crucifixion and it deals explicitly with himself. It is, in other words, autobiographical in its central focus and it acted catalytically to precipitate the baffled and angry indecision of his enemies into action. Immediately upon its telling, the record reports: "The scribes and the chief priests tried to lay hands on him at that very hour" (Luke 20:19a). It was fully four days, however, before they took him into custody since his popularity was still sufficient, though it was waning, to make them cautious.

This story is different also in its clear and unambiguous point. There was sufficient generalness about his other stories to make it possible for his audience to feel they were directed against absentees. To be sure there were some who got the idea as directed toward themselves. They winced and withdrew to be rankled by recollection. We have undertaken in the previous chapter to point out that the civil rule of Rome was the aim of the tale about the bogus nobleman and that this seditious utterance—for such it would certainly have been—tended, where it was understood, to draw together the civil and ecclesiastical leaders against him. If then there was needed a fillip to incite the scribes and the chief priests, the present parable was it. Up to this point the Pharisees and scribes had been the target of some of his barbed words; now the chief priests—the important religious functionaries—came within range and felt his stinging syllables.

Furthermore this story is told after his entry into the holy city during the festival. It is to be better understood therefore if it is seen within the context of a minor lull before a major storm. Listen to the record: "And he was teaching daily in the temple. The chief priests and the scribes and the principal men of the people sought to destroy him; but they did not find anything they could do, for all the people hung upon his words" (Luke 19:47-48). The coalition against him was tightening its small ranks: chief priests, scribes, principal men. This third category is of interest. They were not, strictly speaking, the elders, who appear later in the story—men in whom vested authority rested as judges and councilors in an extralegal capacity. They were, literally, the first (*protos*) citizens who, we assume, at long last had been convinced that the parable-teller was expendable. That they were facing what was still sizable popular following is clear —the people hung on his words. It is equally clear that all the top-level echelons of authority, the civil, ecclesiastical, and lay, were now ready to make common cause of his elimination.

[1]

Their approach is interesting. Wishing to give a semblance of legality to their attack on him he was asked, in the course of the days that followed his arrival in Jerusalem, three questions. The first dealt with his authority. They had, let us assume, a reserved tolerance for the authority of the prophet and might have conceded limited privileges if he could produce proper credentials to support the prophetic role. This is the sort of question the first citizens and the elders might have asked. He very skillfully parried their thrust. The second question had to do with tribute to Caesar. This was what would interest the civil authorities. Again he disarmed them with his famous answer. The third question dealt with an ecclesiastical problem, something concerning which the two great religious groups—Sadducees and Pharisees—were divided. It turned on what might be called a metaphysical point: the nature of post-mortem existence. Here again his answer was both artless and shrewd. Indeed some of the scribes (20:39) applauded his answer. The consensus at that point seems to have been that to trip him up with a question was not a promising way of taking him.

These exchanges were not calculated to win clemency from those who were already convinced that he could be allowed none. That they rather tended to exacerbate the sense of crisis is what one would expect. Not only between the groups that were contending over him, but within them. We doubt that the alliance between civil rulers and the first citizens was very solid. It was improvised and precariously constructed and didn't last beyond the death of Jesus. We are sure that within the fellowship and the multitudes that still were drawn to him there was uncertainty. It finally broke into panic and flight. What is even more obvious is the mounting tension in the mind of Jesus. Convinced as he was that his cause was—within the perspective of the immediate situation—hopeless, he changed his attitude on certain important points. The "little apocalypse" (21:10-37) is best understood in this light.

Earlier (17:20) when asked by the Pharisees when the Kingdom was coming, he replied that it "is not coming with signs to be observed" since it is an inner experience. Now when asked, "When will this be?" (21:7) he proceeded at considerable length to predict the signs that were to be observed before its coming.[1]

[1] The question that evoked his answer had specifically concerned the destruction of the temple, but in the minds of his hearers the destruction with which they had been threatened for generations was regarded as the preliminary to the resurgence

In the other "little apocalypse" (17:22-37) we have studied he was at great pains to caution against radical action. The experiences they were to face were the normal unfolding of certain cultural processes. "Where the body is, there will the vultures be gathered together." Now he predicts portents in sun and moon and stars and "men fainting with fear and foreboding of what is coming on the world." This will be climaxed by the coming of the Son of man "in a cloud with power and great glory." He concluded with this dramatic exhortation: "Now when these things begin to take place, look up and raise your heads, because your redemption is drawing near" (21:28).

These contradictions have been difficult to resolve. Certainly few things could be more nearly opposite than the sedate history-mindedness of the aphorism about the vultures and the carrion, and the ecstatic supernaturalism of a king ensconced on a cloud, coming in glory. It has been the central concern of these studies to discover the tension situations within which the record of the last fortnight of our Lord's mortal life was spun out. That they gave point and directness to all that he said has been our major emphasis. And in tense times two things are characteristic of the utterances of one who is desperately concerned to fulfill his destiny in a particular situation: he speaks only of those things which he thinks are of pressing importance; he speaks often in terms that are inconsistent. This is due to the inescapable conflict within the psyche in which emotion is pitted against reason or, to speak more moderately, fails to support it. To those who hypothecate a spiritual composite in Jesus that exempted him altogether from the tumult of inner conflict, such an understanding is wholly mistaken or worse. Yet when Jesus himself confessed it, "I have a baptism to be baptized with; and how I am constrained (synecomai: to be hard pressed by the urgency of

of the kingdom. For this reason the matter of the temple's imminent demolition was integral to their expectation of the kingdom.

circumstances) until it is accomplished" (12:49), we have no alternative to it.

[2]

The parable which ends his use of this teaching medium is to be understood within this sort of context. He had passed through the turgid experience of entering into the city. Can we say that the story, directed to the scribes and chief priests with such accuracy that they could not dodge its impact, and dealing quite as clearly with his own sense of impending destiny, represented somehow the level on which his mind had come to rest? Emotionally there was still the Gethsemane struggle to face but from this point on, he knew—however he may have felt—that he was to die, and to die in a succession of other deaths that had had profound significance for the development of the ethical consciousness of his people.

And he began to tell the people this parable: "A man planted a vineyard, and let it out to tenants, and went into another country for a long while. When the time came, he sent a servant to the tenants, that they should give him some of the fruit of the vineyard; but the tenants beat him and sent him away empty-handed. And he sent another servant; him also they beat and treated shamefully, and sent him away empty-handed. And he sent yet a third; this one they wounded and cast out. Then the owner of the vineyard said, 'What shall I do? I will send my beloved son; it may be they will respect him.' But when the tenants saw him they said to themselves, 'This is the heir; let us kill him, that the inheritance may be ours.' And they cast him out of the vineyard and killed him. What then will the owner of the vineyard do to them? He will come and destroy those tenants, and give the vineyard to others" (Luke 20:9-16).

Our primary interest in this lies in its reflection of the sense of crisis, however rewarding it may prove to consideration that approaches it from other angles. At the same time its intention is the same no matter from what viewpoint it is surveyed. It is an elemental presentation of the judgment that always falls on those who usurp the divine prerogative. Here it is set forth in the metaphor of the fruits of the vineyard. The tenants claimed them for their own, refusing even a token to the first emissary. Finally, seeing that their repudiation of the owner's agents seemed to make no very great difference to the owner, they decided to expropriate the vineyard entirely when the heir came to collect. This is an assumption not of the things of God but of the rights of God, in a word, the position of God Himself. It is against this that the doom of their destruction falls and the owner makes a fresh start with new tenants.

That the immediate response was "God forbid" is interesting. Does it piously mean that God should enjoin all such wicked tenantry, or that summary destruction of the embezzlers was a bit drastic? Obviously the latter, for he follows up the story with a look that was so significant that it became a fixed part of the tradition before the synoptist wrote it down. It was certainly anything but a casual glance. Then a question edged with irritation at their moral myopia: "What then is this that is written: 'The very stone which the builders rejected has become the head of the corner'?" And then a warning which, while it contains within it a universal judgment against hubristic pride, also sounds like a threat from Jesus himself. Was he saying that he would break in pieces and crush those who, having rejected him, stumbled, so to speak, against him? If this is the overtone, if not indeed the tone of these words, it is difficult to understand them except as they be seen to reflect the net of tension within which he was already tightly enmeshed.

From this point of view the parable presents another aspect of truth. Prophets are always tense persons. They know the risk they run by challenging the established order; they know, in fact, the issue of the prophet's vehemence. To use the idiom of the story, he is beaten and sent away empty-handed, treated shamefully, wounded, and cast out and not infrequently killed. Prophets, sick of spurious security and tranquillity, deliberately create real crises in order to excite their people to moral seriousness and practical action. Their accomplishments are meager in the short haul but over the centuries they have monuments put up in their honor. No one accepts that role and goes through those experiences without being straitened in countless baptisms of water, flame, frustration, defeat, death. This story could, we think, not well have been told earlier in the ministry of Jesus. It belongs, by the circumstances which evoked it, very near the close of his life.

It is necessary to return to the events of the day (or days) previous if we are to see in clear detail the struggle through which Jesus was passing. It has to do particularly with what has traditionally been referred to as the triumphal entry. Most serious students of the Gospel record have long since abandoned the idea that the entry was in any real sense a triumph. Some go so far as to call it a moral defeat. Certainly Jesus was under no illusions as to what was going on. If he planned the demonstration that accompanied his arrival at the city there is no evidence of it. To secure a beast for his own convenience is one thing; to make his entrance into the city astride a mount instead of afoot is hardly to be regarded as spectacular in itself or likely to excite spectacular consequences. The disciples ("the whole multitude of the disciples") who accompanied broke into shouts of excited praise but this seems to have been on a relatively modest scale since some Pharisees that were in the crowd, and who were annoyed by the outburst, thought it could be quieted by a word from Jesus. "Teacher, rebuke your disciples"; this is far from an effort to suppress a great demonstration by a multitude of partisans. The answer of Jesus is cryptic. He apparently declined the Pharisees' suggestion and there is no evidence that there was need of it after the first salvo of salute. There is a hint in the response of Jesus that he saw beyond the shifting enthusiasms of a crowd the essence of destiny. Stones would shout if human voices were silenced.

It is as he drew near to the city that the mood that was upon him exhibited itself. He wept. This does not evince triumph. On the contrary it was an extension of his own sense of impending personal tragedy to the massive city that loomed before him, crowned with the shining apex of the temple. His prediction of its doom was condign and conclusive. It did not know the things that made for peace; its eyes were blinded; it did not comprehend the portent of its visitation. How, if he was in any way—literally or figuratively—a part of the augury of its doom, could Jerusalem's insensitiveness have been converted into a personal sense of triumph? No; his entry into its purlieus was not an impressive display. The elder gentry asked disdainfully who this was, and the shouting seems to have subsided almost as soon as it was begun.

[3]

If it was not a triumph, what was it? Why did he allow himself to be drawn into even so modest a display, a display so unpretentious in fact as to discredit rather than enhance his prestige? This, we think, cannot be properly understood without seeing the problem in relation to his cleansing of the temple. The fact of tension provides us with two hypotheses if we feel it necessary to abandon the idea of a personally directed triumphal parade. The first hypothesis is that Jesus in the entry and the temple episode was acceding to the pressure of the disciples for decisive, overt action. That there was disaffection within the group is obvious. His idea, shared with them, that he was to die in Jerusalem was to them irresponsible if not foolish. They were not only unready to die; some of them were just getting ready to cash in on their venture. Peter's plaintive, "We have left all to follow thee," and the demand of James and John for preferred positions in the coming Kingdom are typical of what may have been a fairly general state of mind.

Jesus not only knew of this state of mind; he knew what was

likely to happen to his friends and it was not easy for him to contemplate debacle and the personal danger into which he was leading them. That they had other ideas about the way his fortunes and theirs might be better served is indicated all through the parables which rebuked such errors of enthusiasm or blindness. It is easy then to assume, though there is nothing in the record that gives direct support to it, that they might have proposed changes—radical changes—as they drew near to the city to partake of the festival rituals. Was he, as he rode into the city and advanced to the cleansing of the temple, yielding to the disciples' demand for a change of strategy, a sudden and undisguised display of power?

He did not believe in this himself. If the temptations in the wilderness are normative for an understanding of his moral presuppositions, any display of pretentiousness would be repudiated as the leap from the temple was disallowed. But it is not implausible to assume that he could have consented to such a proposal as a final method of proving it to be wrong. For once, he would yield to the frustrated disciples, give them a sense of having their own way at a critical point. It would most certainly fail and then they would perhaps agree with him and stand by when the ultimate test came in Jerusalem. There is something to be said for such an hypothesis but the events prove it to have been impracticable. He went through with it, but nothing significant happened. The disciples, far from being rebuked and recalled to his own way became more and more harassed and frightened and at the last, broke in shameless panic and left him to his own devices before the combined hostility of all the factions that had opposed him. No; this hypothesis, seriously advanced by some scholars, seems to have too slight support to hold it up.

[4]

The second surmise is that because of the "baptism" by which he was "straitened" (tautened) he was consenting, not to the disciples' demand but to the demand of his own ego. We step gingerly here. There is an ancient and powerful tradition of the moral grandeur of Jesus that rests upon a mistaken idea concerning his immunity to *real* temptation. This says that the wilderness experience was either fancied or it was a sort of moral inoculation which immunized him against the real thing, but in so speaking does scant honor to him and his victory over sin. Are we not rather to assume that the ferocity of temptation was in direct ratio to the sensitivity of his spirit, so that he was not less tempted than ordinary mortals, but more? To the completely insensitive soul there is no temptation and no consciousness of sin; to the infinitely sensitive soul, temptation and sin are proportionately heightened. Furthermore this tradition has carried with it the idea that Jesus was equally immune to errors of judgment. This also fails, whatever its intention, to enhance his spiritual stature. Unless he is assumed to have been omniscient —something he specifically denied—the possibility or even the likelihood of errors of judgment must be allowed. What reason do we have for not thinking that there were always alternative choices of action that argued for his preference? Otherwise his every experience of life must be regarded as a regimen through which he moved automatically and without possible deviation. To give him moral grandeur it is not necessary to take from him the vital experiences upon which such grandeur erects itself.

Now the experience of crisis is a profound factor in the choices one makes. If he had the capacity to choose, his choices were not independent of the circumstances within which he moved. Very clearly Jesus had settled the question of the use of force for his own advantage, in the temptations. What else was his refusal to bow down to the evil one in exchange for the world? And yet, by the very word which says that the devil "left him for a season," we have no alternative for thinking that the use of force was always a live option for him.

It would be difficult to overstate the physical and mental strain under which he had been living, strain that was to increase by the hour as he moved forward toward his death. It does him no honor to assume that the outer circumstances of hostility, defection and threat left his inner circumstances untouched and unaffected. Nor do we think it takes from him one cubit of moral stature to assume that in the face of what to him was certain defeat, he changed his mind in order to salvage the possibilities of victory. This is the second hypothesis, one we feel has much to support it in the written record and in its deeper implications. It is that Jesus, when he was within reach of the holy city, yielded to the solicitations of self and to the overwhelming egoistic wish for a significant recognition of his true credentials and his true power. Remember he was come to seek and to save that which was lost. Jerusalem was lost—he said so in memorable words. Could it be shocked into a recognition of the one who alone could save it? If so, was it not important for him to make the effort?

What other practical purpose could the brief adulation of a few festival-bound pilgrims and disciples have served? It could multiply by as many as shouted his acclaim the single testimony of his own purpose. They called him king and for the moment he allowed it. It was a vibrant word. They spoke of peace in heaven and glory in the highest. This lifted him out of the dusty highway to the insubstantial thoroughfares of heaven, and he refused to rebuke them. This, as we have said, is out of character with one who refused by subterfuge to excite the crowded temple court by a leap from the temple dome. Figurative as that leap was, it is no less so than the cries of the accompanying multitudes as he made toward the temple.

We go further to ask what other practical purpose was served by his violent act of cleansing the temple "den" of its "robbers"? The account of this episode is parsimonious in the extreme, limiting itself to seven somewhat inconclusive words, "began to drive out those who sold." One wonders whether the author did not deliberately abbreviate the Markan source from which he got the story. And for reasons. The Fourth Gospel, also for editorial reasons, amplifies the record to heighten, we incline to think, the contrast between his act of aggressiveness and his more characteristic mood of gentleness. Elements in the situation which we can see dimly by hints were monstrous and looming to him. Did they cause him to ask himself whether after all he might have been mistaken in some of the details of the itinerary he had marked out for himself? His success was qualified; the likelihood of failure was apparent. Should he not reappraise the situation? Was the brow of Olivet another wilderness with the sinister, plausible voice of the evil one giving him another chance? "What king, going to encounter another king in war, will not sit down first and take council whether he is able with ten thousand to meet him who comes against him with twenty thousand?" Momentarily he accepted the strident counsel of his ego. He would try a new stratagem; if it worked, well and good; if it failed——? After all, had not God of old, in vexation, shaken the earth?

It appears that momentarily it won him support and threw his enemies back in consternation, but, seeing more deeply than the crowd's acclaim and the temple hucksters' confusion, he knew that it had not worked. This is indicated by the fact that the tactic was abandoned. There is no reason for thinking that the temple courts were never to be cluttered up with illicit commerce again. The chances are that he had hardly got through with his purge before the evicted had reassembled their scattered goods and resumed business as usual. It was the great festival and there was much to be gained. The momentary violence of a Galilean teacher could not interrupt the buying and selling routine very long. Furthermore the parable with which this chapter is concerned was told *after* the abortive cleansing, and it very clearly indicates that he was identifying himself with the prophets who were shamed, and beaten, and killed for their faith in the living God. Is this the sort of story he would have told had he regarded the experience in the temple as normative?

[5]

We do not say that the conflict in his soul was immediately resolved. The parable points in one direction; the extreme tension disclosed in the "little apocalypse" points in a slightly different one; he nips a quarrel about relative greatness in the disciples' group by the famous maxim: "Rather let the greatest among you become as the youngest, and the leader as one who serves. . . . I am among you as one who serves." This does not sound like the person who three days before had caused an uproar in the temple. There is, may we say, a suggestion of equivocation in what was to be his final admonition to his faint-hearted friends. Once he had commissioned them to go forth and "carry no purse, no bag, no sandals; and salute no one on the road. Whatever house you enter, first say, 'Peace be to this house!'" (Luke 10:4-5). Now he admonishes: "Let him who has a purse take it, and likewise a bag. And let him who has no sword sell his mantle and buy one" (22:36). And when he was reminded that their arms equipment consisted of two swords, he said: "It is enough." Enough for what?

The resolution of his inner struggle came, of course, through the agony of the Garden. There has been a tendency to think of Jerusalem as the symbol of triumph and Gethsemane as the symbol of defeat—or more accurately, his capitulation to the certainty of death as part of the infinite will of the Father. Perhaps it should be reversed: Jerusalem may have been the scene of his greatest sorrow and defeat; Gethsemane the scene of final victory and joy. The triumph in the city streets and in the Tem-

ple courts was certainly short-lived. The interval between Jerusalem and the Garden showed the swing of the pendulum of his
fortunes between certainty and uncertainty. Crowds thronged
to him and retreated. The authorities feinted their blows and
recoiled from his answers. He predicted both doom and destruction, triumph and defeat in a range that swept all the way from
individual to cosmic dimensions.

In the Garden, however, we see a situation that is no longer
ambiguous. There is deep poignancy in his first word to the
fellowship as they entered the protective shade of the Garden of
Olives. "When he came to the place he said to them, 'Pray that
you may not enter into temptation' " (22:40). Did not this reflect
the storm through which he had almost passed, the fury of which
was not quite spent and which, if he could, he would spare his
friends? They had repaired to their rendezvous in the Garden
after a celebration of the Passover during which he had spoken
searching and mysterious words. So imminent was the crisis that
he had earnestly desired to eat the Passover before he suffered,
as if he had feared at any moment the interception that would
initiate the final act of the drama. He symbolizes his already
broken body in the broken bread; he announces with irreversible finality the doom of the Son of man but pronounced woe
against the agent of his betrayal. It was with these words tum-
bling about in their befuddled heads that the disciples went with
him into the shadows of the olive trees.

The prayer and the agony of struggle it represented shows us
the ultimate spiritual tension. Now he was not confronting
alternatives between what the multitudes, the rulers, the disciples, and he wanted. Nor was he facing alternatives within his
own soul. Here, stripped of even such solace or harassment—
for it might have been either—that his most intimate friends
afforded, he is alone with God in a final contest. Here he was
either to drink the cup or dash it from his lips. The choice was
starkly and terribly simple. No evasion, no compromise, no de-

lay. Even here the choice was not unrelated to the dramatic use of power. Had he not warned his captors that there were twelve legions of angels in ambuscade waiting his order? Suppose he had called them. Would the fury of angels have served the cause of redemption?

His disappointment with the somnolent disciples is understandable but are not their terrible fatigue and sorrow equally so? The amazing thing about this episode is that Jesus himself did not fall heavily asleep for his weariness was surely as great as theirs. It was only the fury of the conflict within him that kept him awake. Nor was it weakness for them to have fallen asleep; it was, indeed, a sign of physical well-being. The words of their tortured friend were less rebuking than extenuating when he said, as if in self-disclosure: "The spirit is willing but the flesh is weak." His problem was to be settled ultimately in terms of the superior strength of spirit or flesh. It was something far more profound than the issue of whether he should live or die. It was to turn on the question of living either under the direction of the will of God or of his own egoistic will. When he finally rose to his feet, steadied with a great new resolution, he could say, "Rise and pray," with a new timbre in his voice. The ruffians who were out to take him into custody were at hand. His signal to his sleepy friends was the beginning of the ultimate triumph, back to Jerusalem afoot, into the praetorium instead of the temple, to death, but to imperishable victory. As they began their way back to the city he summed it up profoundly: "This is your hour and the power of darkness" (22:53). He would not struggle to take it from them. At another hour and with another portent his power would be manifest.

[6]

The tension was broken at last. What followed in the trial, the scourging and the death, happened to one who had cast his fire on the earth and seen it kindling into flame; he had been baptized with a baptism from which he had recoiled, but the constraint was now gone. In place of tension was a calm that baffled and even angered his accusers and tormentors. And when he died, it was with forgiveness and confidence on his lips—a spectacle so amazing that his executioner was able to account for it by the daring and dangerous announcement that his victim was innocent. What did it mean? Innocent of the crime for which he had been crucified? Perhaps; but one wonders whether he did not speak a truth that was beyond his own comprehension: innocent not only of crime but of the excruciating spiritual torture that wracked the dimming consciousness of the dying.

We do not know what the reference in Luke 23:45 to the rending of the temple veil is designed to convey, whether an historic or spiritual fact. For our purposes, however, it may be used symbolically to suggest a dynamic truth. May it not be taken to depict that awesome experience in every human soul when tautened by tension beyond the point of endurance, the curtain is rent from top to bottom in the violence of strain? It is only when the veil is rent—or to use more congenial language, when the tension is relieved—that the hidden Shekinah light of the soul can shine through again.

CHAPTER XVIII

"Summer Is Already Near"

THIS topical sentence is taken from the last of Jesus'
parables. It is so brief that it seems hardly to justify such
classification. It is little more than a wisp of observation
about the simplest and most obvious of experiences.

And he told them a parable: "Look at the fig tree, and all the
trees; as soon as they come out in leaf, you see for yourselves and
know that the summer is already near. So also, when you see these
things taking place, you know that the kingdom of God is near.
Truly, I say to you, this generation will not pass away till all has
taken place. Heaven and earth will pass away, but my words will
not pass away" (Luke 21:29-33).

It is with this intimation and promise that the little apocalypse
that fills most of the 21st chapter of Luke's record comes to a
close. Except for the equally brief warning about the evil consequences of unreadiness to face the cataclysm, the reported words
of his public ministry are done. Every day he taught in the
temple, we are told, and every night he retreated to the mount
called Olivet, but what he said publicly we do not know. From
then on it was only to the twelve that he spoke words that have
been preserved for our reflection.

It has been our contention that the apocalyptic element, particularly as it was described as imminent and universal represented the inner turmoil of his soul rather than a preview of

"the last days." While this conception is not without its difficulties it would seem to be less puzzling than the other. Illustration of this is seen in the elaborate charting of events and predictions that have resulted from the effort to make it predictive or descriptive of historic events. There are points where the foresight that he exhibited concerning the final destruction of the city of Jerusalem is extraordinary. So much so, indeed, that some scholars still date the Lukan record after the year 70 when Titus put the torch to the holy city. Luke, they insist could not have told the story before it happened.

If Jesus was equating the destruction of the city with the coming of the Son of man and the proximity of the Kingdom of God and if what he envisaged as the judgment of God on the earth was coming within his own living generation, we can only say that events have not supported the predicted denouement. "It will come upon all who dwell upon the face of the whole earth. But watch at all times, praying that you may have strength to escape all these things that will take place and to stand before the Son of man" (Luke 21:35-36). Here the contradiction is explicit. If the cataclysm was to engulf the whole earth, whither was the route of escape? Bits of predictive testimony within this section can be found to have been substantiated here and there. Nations have risen against nation and kingdoms against kingdom; there has been, within our own generation, a fulfillment of the hideous prediction that "parents and brothers and kinsmen and friends" would spy on each other in a farrago of fear and disloyalty, but even the most heroic endurance (cf. verse 19) has not gained the safety that was promised the faithful.

This aspect of *eschaton* has been enormously intriguing and it is not surprising that in certain parts of the modern world the ruin, both physical and spiritual, that has accompanied two world wars should have pointed up with new vividness and plausibility this ancient panoramic picture of cosmic desolation. Yet we cannot believe that within the perspective of nineteen hundred years, this is the proper use to make of it. Not that the

possibility of world destruction is growing more and more remote. The reverse would seem to be true. Nor does it follow
that, abandoning the apocalyptic element here, we are thrown
back upon the liberal optimism of the last century with its facile
gaiety and blindness.

After all, except for those who refuse to allow that Jesus had
the freedom to think that is the very essence of individual self-
hood, the possibility of alternate and alternating opinions must
be conceded. And if alternatives, choices; and if choices, altered
judgments. Such liberty to think and choose would be affected
by all the factors of experience both internal and external. That
these factors were intensified during the climactic days of the
Lord's earthly life has been supported by our efforts to understand them. In so sensitive a spirit as his they were all the more
keenly felt, particularly when the events began to move swiftly
toward climax. In all great souls there is the conflict between
self-assertion and humility, between egoism and selflessness. It
was the same person who said: "He who denies me before men
will be denied before the angels of God" and "Who made me
a judge or divider over you?" He who could ask: "Why do you
call me good? No one is good but God alone," could also accept
without demur the confession of Peter: "You are the Christ, the
Son of the living God". . . . "Blessed are you, Simon Bar-
Jona!" It should not therefore greatly surprise us if when the
pressure was heaviest on his own soul he should have cast the
shadow of its darkness across the world and seen on a vastly extended scale the tug and pull and threat of which he was inwardly aware.

The parables of crisis however reveal tension on the lower
levels of his consciousness where the threat to himself had not
reached its hurricane force. They deal therefore with the peren-
nial and common experiences out of which all tensions grow,
tensions that are more or less drawn depending on the sensitive-
ness of the person caught in them. The rich fool, straitened

because his sudden wealth found him unprepared to take care of it, the democratic-minded citizen, aware of the delicacy of relations between him and his slaves, the vineyard owner, annoyed by the fruitlessness of a fig tree and the urgency of the gardener to give it another chance, the sense of struggle for the achievement of goodness as it confronts the complacency of those who think themselves possessed of inalienable privileges—these are the stuff of which tensions are made. Similarly the amusing antic of the social climber at a formal dinner and his discomfiture, the conflict between one's duty to land and farm and home and the higher desiderata of human fellowship, the uncertainties that beset building and warring and the need for facing them, the torture of loss—whether a sheep, or a coin, or the agony of being lost to fellowship—whether prodigal, elder son, or father—these are facts of life that are to be observed inside any group or found behind any door. The endless conflict between ends and means, the attractiveness of the sensualist outlook on life to those who can afford it, and its fateful nemesis, the balance between the doing of duty and the overeffort that gives life a new dimension and quality, the snob with the futility of his self-elevation, the cynic judge and the desperate widow, each with a tension to ease, the egomaniac with his lust for self and his ferocity toward those who tried to thwart him—these are no strangers to us. If we do not meet them daily in our own souls we see them in the streets among the thronging multitudes.

It was to these that Jesus was giving his mind and heart during his last days. It seems to us that there is a rising crescendo from the fool to the egomaniac which may reflect the rising fury of the outer circumstances of Jesus' life. But if he was aware of his own situation it did not deflect him from a redemptive concern for others who were similarly tautened. Nor did he improvise a solution for them. His penetration into the human problem did not stop short of its ultimate depths and his prescription for it was no interim accommodation. If, as we have said, we encounter these people with their burdens, we discover that they can be lifted today by the same leverage that removed them twenty centuries ago. The diagnosis then was what we discover now and the cure the same: this is universalism both of insight and ethic.

The effort has also been made to educe the sense and meaning of judgment that is a strong factor in the parables. The portent of a world cataclysm by which history was either to be radically changed by extraterrestrial energies or summarily brought to an end is the burden of the tumultuous scenes of the little apocalypse. There is here no vision of a great assize as the First Gospel presents it. There will be a burst of glory in the clouds, an apparition, and the drawing nigh of man's redemption. Of the meaning of this we have already tried to be explicit enough.

And yet the factors both of judgment and redemption are quite as clearly set forth in the parables of crisis. Indeed there is an impressive consistency of witness to these inseparable elements that does not depend on cataclysm or cosmic debacle. What the nature of the last judgment is, "eye hath not seen, ear hath not heard, neither hath it entered into the heart of man." Our moral sense somehow reassures us that *post obitum* there ought to be a reassessment of all human values, achieved and lost, sought and spurned, and an ultimate adjudication. But that such a final rectification does not and should not pre-empt the immediate and immanent judgment that is implicit in every deliberate act is also congenial to our moral sense. At the same time that redemption should finally issue in experiences on a level and in a dimension beyond time, as some would have it. And yet redemption cannot be real if it has to wait always on historic processes or on posthistory development. The basic idea of redemption is that man can, through judgment now, be redeemed of his folly or sin. To postpone redemption is to disqualify it.

Here again it is our contention that the parables of crisis supply the ideas both of immanent judgment and of redemption. Not always, to be sure, in the same degree of depth or explicitness. Some imply more about judgment, some about redemption, but we cannot doubt that in the intention of the parable-teller both elements are there. The rich fool was judged both by the folly of his choice and by the eerie voice in the night that demanded his soul. Of redemption there is no suggestion in the story but there are other rich men in other situations toward whom the redemptive grace was exercised. The democratic householder was judged as righteous by the way he ordered his menage; the tree was judged by its fruitlessness but reprieved for redemptive treatment. How frightening is the judgment on those who scorned the narrow door; how glorious the redemption of the dispossessed who entered in by their tireless striving, to sit down with the patriarchs at the great feast. The man who came to dinner was judged and greatly disconcerted but he left with a formula that was to help him against subsequent *faux pas*. The capitalist, the manufacturer, and the domesticated bridegroom were judged both by their predilections and by the anger of their disappointed host; the contractor and king were counseled as to how they might avoid ridicule and defeat—surely a redemptive gesture. Sheep and coin were lost and found, and the judgment of the three prodigals was condign and definitive though we are left without the redemptive operation that we wish might have saved elder brother and father. The story of the unjust steward who sought by evil means to ingratiate himself is lively with the element of the justice that pursues such error; the sensualist paid for his wealth by a commensurable spiritual loss, and though he was not to be redeemed from his anguish, he had hopes that his brothers might be, a hope, to be sure, that Abraham was quick to discourage. The dutiful servant was unprofitable; that was judgment; the snob was sent down unjustified but the way of his possible redemption was exemplified in

the despised tax collector; the widow was justified and redeemed
of her adversary. Only the egomaniac seems to go free of explicit
judgment and redemption. Is this again to be accounted for by
the fact that he represented Rome, the judge and the monster
for whom, in the tense moment when the story was told, there
was no redemption?

The point of this is that justice was done within the historic
context of these imaginary and yet very real stories. What further treatment awaited them after time had expired we do not
need to ask or to know. Is it enough to believe that just as there
was the element of universalism in the probing insight of Jesus
into the human problem and a similar universalism in his diagnosis and treatment, there is also reason for our believing that
the experience of both judgment and redemption—or justice
and salvation—are to be experienced also within the context of
history? It is to this point that our study has brought us.

We return for a final look at the last parable. Its essence clearly
is that events are predictive, that by even the most casual sort of
observation the shape of things to come and the time of their
coming are discernible. In the way in which the parable put it
this is true. On the contrary any equation which attempts to set
forth the future must provide for many variable factors. This
was part of the intention of the story about the widow and the
judge. There are imponderables that can no more be seen than
weighed, variables that in the nature of things cannot be fixed.
This is the faith of those who believe in the eternal creative
activity of God, in a living universe, as the late Professor L. P.
Jacks once put it in a memorable little book.

But our interest at the moment in the figure Jesus used in his
last parable is incidental to such ponderous and elusive matters.
It rests on the fact that even after he had forecast dire portents
in heaven, famines and pestilences, desolation and vengeance,
distress upon the earth and wrath upon the people, distress of
nations and the roaring of the sea, he could state his ultimate

faith by a figure of speech which predicts the coming of summer. To be sure on its deepest level his idea touches the significance and meaning of observable sequences, but on a level where most of us spiritually live he is expressing what amounts to invincible optimism. It would have been quite as expressive to speak of falling leaves as presaging the coming of winter, but would this not have been a metaphor of pessimism? That he deliberately avoided leaving his puzzled friends in gloom is fortified by the words: "So also, when you see these things taking place, you know that the kingdom of God is near" (21:31). This was his confidence in the final triumph of God's redemptive purposes; to him it was more firmly assured than the perpetuity of heaven and earth.

If this is the ultimate in faith it is also the ultimate in optimism. There is something majestic in the encouragement: lift up your heads, because your redemption is drawing near. Do we, in our times of tumult have that faith? Are the portents of our day the promise of redemption? Can we believe in our day of crisis that the summer is already near?